Semantic Antics

How and Why Words Change Meaning

Sol Steinmetz

RANDOM HOUSE REFERENCE
New York • Toronto • London • Sydney • Auckland

Library of Congress Cataloging-in-Publication Data

Steinmetz, Sol.
   Semantic antics : how and why words change meaning /
by Sol Steinmetz.
      p. cm.
   Includes bibliographical references.
   ISBN-13: 978-0-375-42612-4 (alk. paper)   1. English language—
Semantics.   2. English language—Etymology.   I. Title.
   PE1585.S657 2008
   422—dc22

                                                      2007031265

To my brother Efry
and
my sisters Judy
and Eva

Contents

Words are like bottles.
Their shapes may remain the same,
while their contents vary from
very bitter to very sweet.
—Hugh Rawson

Introduction

If you have ever wondered why words change meanings, just imagine what language would be like if every word had only one meaning. We would have to invent hundreds of thousands of words for all the meanings we'd wish to convey! How would we remember so many words? We'd have to walk around with backpacks stuffed with dictionaries. We would become paralyzed by verbal gridlock. Communication would be so exhausting that many speakers would retreat to the grunts, squeals, and yowls of cavemen.

Changes in meanings make language flexible and malleable. But how do words take on new meanings? The study of meanings and the changes of meaning that words undergo is called *semantics* (from Greek *sēmantikos* "having meaning, signifying"). I've titled this work *Semantic Antics* because many English words have changed meaning in fascinating, unusual, and unexpected ways. Those are the words I focus on in this book.

A new word can develop in a number of ways:

Narrowing of meaning. This happens when a word with a general meaning is by degrees applied to something much more specific. The word *litter*, for example, meant originally (before 1300) "a bed," then gradually narrowed down to "bedding," then to "animals on a bedding of straw," and finally to things scattered about, odds and ends. The technical term for this narrowing process is *specialization*. Other examples of specialization are *deer*, which originally had the general meaning "animal," *girl*, which meant originally "a young person," and *meat*, whose original meaning was "food."

Broadening of meaning. This occurs when a word with a specific or limited meaning is widened. The broadening process is technically called *generalization*. An example of generalization is the word *business*, which originally meant "the state of being busy, careworn, or anxious," and was broadened to encompass all kinds of work or occupations.

Degradation of meaning. This happens when meanings with a positive connotation are replaced with disparaging or unpleasant ones. The word *silly* is a prime example of degradation, also known as *pejoration*. Before 1200, *silly* meant "happy, blessed." People who were considered blessed or happy were also regarded as innocent, simple, and naïve, so after 1200 *silly* took on the meaning of "innocent." From this sense, the word was degraded to "weak," then "weak-minded," and by the 1500s it came to mean "foolish," its current meaning.

Upgrading of meaning. This is also known as *amelioration* or *elevation*, and it occurs when a degraded or derogatory meaning is gradually replaced by a more positive meaning. The word *meticulous* was borrowed in the mid-1500s from Latin with the meaning "fearful, timid." Since a fearful or timid person usually tries to avoid mistakes and is extremely careful about the smallest points, by the 1800s the word took on the upgraded meaning "careful about minute details, thorough, precise."

Transfer or extension of meaning. This is one of the commonest ways in which meanings change or new meanings develop. In the 1400s the word *summit* meant literally "the topmost part, as of a mountain or hill." Later, the meaning was transferred to the figurative sense, "the highest point or degree, the acme," as in *He'd reached the summit of happiness.* The meaning was further extended in the 1950s to "the highest political level," as in *a conference at the summit.* The latter has generated such phrases as *summit meeting, summit conference, summit talks,* referring to meetings between heads of state.

Distortion of meaning. Lack of familiarity with a word leads people to guess at its meaning, which often leads to a distortion of both the word and its meaning. The distortion leads to what is known as *folk etymology.* Hundreds of folk etymologies have found their way into English. Among them are *belfry*, "bell tower," which has nothing to do with a bell but was altered from *berfrey*, meaning "a movable tower."

Changes in meaning are hard to predict. Who could foretell in the year 1200 that the common word *chest*, meaning "box, coffer, casket," would 350 years later take on the meaning "part of the body enclosed by ribs, thorax"? Certainly the thorax resembles a box, but then why don't we call it "the box" instead of "the chest"? Or consider the word *mouse*. For better than 800 years it was the word for the little rodent that cats love to play with and chase into holes. It wasn't hard to imagine that the word *mouse* might be applied to a quiet, timid person, as it was eventually. But in the early 1960s, an American electrical engineer, Douglas Engelbart, gave the name *mouse* to a device for controlling the movement of the pointer on a computer screen.

Changes in meaning occur not just in English. The processes described above operate in all living languages; foreign words, like English ones, not only undergo over time changes in pronunciation and spelling, but also develop new meanings through generalization, specialization, pejoration, amelioration, and so on. Many of the words and meanings discussed in this book came from or are related to foreign languages.

Language scholars give a number of reasons why words develop new meanings. In *Semantics: An Introduction to the Science of Meaning,* published in 1962, the British linguist Stephen Ullmann lists five main causes:

1. **Historical Causes.** Objects, institutions, ideas, and scientific concepts change over the course of time, but the words remain—only their meanings change. The term *humor* referred in the Middle Ages to any liquid or moisture (specifically to any of the four body fluids thought to determine a person's qualities and disposition)—a notion long forgotten—but the word *humor* has stayed in the language with an entirely different meaning.

2. **Social Causes.** When a word passes from one social group or situation to another, its meaning can change into something more specific or more general. A *hospice* once meant a rest house for travelers; the meaning was extended to a home for the needy; finally, it has come to mean "an institution for the care of the terminally ill."

3. **Psychological Causes.** Many changes in meaning come about through figurative or metaphorical uses (*browsing* the Internet, the spicy *tang* of apples), or the use of euphemisms (*undertaker*).

4. **Foreign Influences.** Changes in meaning are often due to the influence of foreign models (e.g., *cartel*, influenced by German *Kartell*).

5. **The Need for a New Name.** When a new name is needed to denote something new, such as a new invention, we can borrow a word from a foreign language, make up a word from existing elements in the language, or simply take an old word and give it a new meaning. Most of the time, the genius or good economical sense of the language will steer us to the latter course. Modern military terms like *torpedo* and *satellite* are examples of old words taking on new meanings.

All the words discussed in this book have undergone changes in meaning that reflect one or more of the aforementioned categories. Wherever possible, I illustrate the usage of different meanings with quotes from varied sources (everything from Shakespeare to the *New York*

Times). You'll also find anecdotes about history, culture, and literature throughout.

A list of names and terms appear in the General Glossary; if you are unfamiliar with a book, name, or other reference cited in an entry, the glossary will help you learn more about it.

The sources I consulted for etymological and other linguistic data are listed in the back pages under *Frequently Consulted Sources*. As a language consultant to the *Oxford English Dictionary,* I was fortunate to have had access to the *OED*'s treasury of historical citations, which I used to trace and illustrate the development of meanings discussed in this book.

I am most thankful to my editor at Random House, Helena Santini, who suggested the idea for this book. Her encouragement and help in bringing it to light made writing it a challenge and a pleasure.

Sol Steinmetz

A, a

A, *a*

B, *b*

C, *c*

D, *d*

E, *e*

F, *f*

G, *g*

H, *h*

I, *i*

J, *j*

K, *k*

L, *l*

M, *m*

N, *n*

O, *o*

P, *p*

Q, *q*

R, *r*

S, *s*

T, *t*

U, *u*

V, *v*

W, *w*

X, *x*

Y, *y*

Z, *z*

A1

When you see the abbreviation *A1* (also spelled *A-one*) in the names of businesses and products such as *A1 pizza*, *A1 locksmith*, *A-one Books*, *A1 Vacation*, *A1 Steak Sauce*, *A-one Travel,* etc., you know it means "first-class, number one, numero uno." This use is first encountered (with an intrusive comma) in Charles Dickens's *Pickwick Papers* (1837): "'He must be a first-rater,' said Sam. 'A, 1,' replied Mr. Roker."

You might think that *A1* got its meaning from the fact that *A* is the first letter in the alphabet . . . and *1* is the first number in the series *1 2 3* . . .—hence "first, prime, first-class." However, this is not the true derivation. Dickens adopted a technical shipping term, *A1*, and used it figuratively. The shipping term was created by Lloyd's Register of Shipping, a British publication founded in 1760 by Edward Lloyd to circulate and exchange shipping news among merchants and underwriters. Lloyd published his first *Register of Ships* in 1764, and in it he devised a system for classifying the condition of every registered ship. In this system, the top classification was *A1*, the letter *A* denoting a first-class condition of a ship's hull, and the number *1*, a top condition of the ship's stores. When shipping merchants would describe a ship's condition as being "A1," it was the highest praise they could assign to it, and so inevitably the term passed into figurative use as a synonym of "first-class, excellent."

ABODE

Abode was one of James Joyce's favorite words, used several times in his novel *Ulysses* (1922) in such sentences as "Their abodes were equipped with every modern home comfort." The term means "dwelling place, residence," and has today a formal sound, even one of affectation.

However, the word's original meaning (circa 1225) was not "home, dwelling," but "the act of staying, a stay," derived from the verb *abide* "to stay." That is how Shakespeare used it in *The*

A, a

B, b
C, c
D, d
E, e
F, f
G, g
H, h
I, i
J, j
K, k
L, l
M, m
N, n
O, o
P, p
Q, q
R, r
S, s
T, t
U, u
V, v
W, w
X, x
Y, y
Z, z

Merchant of Venice: "Sweet friends, your patience for my long abode—not I but my affairs have made you wait." The meaning "act of staying" was extended in the 1500s to "a stay in a place," as in "In hollow caverns vermin make abode" (John Dryden), which in turn was extended to "a place of staying, a dwelling, a residence," the current meaning.

The phrase *Abode of Love* became popular in the 1850s as the name of the headquarters of the Agapemonites, an English religious sect that sought to spiritualize marriage and whose members held all goods in common as they awaited the imminent second coming of Jesus. The phrase *abode of love*, a translation of Greek *agapemone*, was used by Dickens, Shaw, and others, and helped to keep the word *abode* alive. The Agapemonite sect endured until a series of scandals involving charges of immoral practices caused its decline, and it finally dissolved in 1956.

Another phrase, *right of abode*, made headlines after 1997, when Britain handed over Hong Kong to China, and many thousands of Mainland Chinese clamored for the right to establish residences in Hong Kong. The issue of who was granted the right of abode, which meant the right to live and work without restriction in Hong Kong, was heatedly debated until 1999, when a high-court ruling decided the issue. This phrase, too, kept the word *abode* alive in official language.

ABRACADABRA

Abracadabra! is an exclamation used by stage magicians when performing a trick. When the word was first recorded in English in the 1500s, it was as a spell or incantation inscribed on a charm or amulet to ward off illness or some evil. The word was usually written in the form of an inverted cone or triangle on a piece of parchment, thus:

A, *a*

B, *b*

C, *c*

D, *d*

E, *e*

F, *f*

G, *g*

H, *h*

I, *i*

J, *j*

K, *k*

L, *l*

M, *m*

N, *n*

O, *o*

P, *p*

Q, *q*

R, *r*

S, *s*

T, *t*

U, *u*

V, *v*

W, *w*

X, *x*

Y, *y*

Z, *z*

```
ABRACADABRA
 ABRACADABR
  ABRACADAB
   ABRACAD
    ABRAC
     ABRA
      ABR
       AB
        A
```

The spell first appeared in a Latin poem, *De Medicina Praecepta*, by a Roman physician who lived in the 200s c.e. Its exact origin is unknown, though it has been conjectured that it was a Hebrew, Aramaic, or Chaldean phrase and related to the name Abraxas, the chief deity of an ancient sect.

In the 1800s, the word began to be used figuratively in the sense of a word believed to have magical powers, as in *the abracadabra of magicians*. But by the process of degradation it soon came to mean gibberish or meaningless jargon, as in *legal abracadabra*. A typical use of this sense is found in a March, 1940, letter written by the poet Ezra Pound (1885–1972): "Mass ought to be in Latin, unless you could do it in Greek or Chinese. In fact, any abracadabra that no bloody member of the public . . . could think he understood."

A magical word invented by J. K. Rowling in her Harry Potter books seems to have been derived from or influenced by *abracadabra*. The word is *Avada Kadavra*, which is the "killing curse," and appears in such works as *Harry Potter and the Goblet of Fire* (2000) and *Harry Potter and the Half-Blood Prince* (2005). Those who maintain that *abracadabra* derives from an Aramaic phrase, *Avra Kedavra*, meaning "I will create as I speak," surmise that Rowling's coinage is a similar Aramaic (or pseudo-Aramaic) phrase meaning "I will destroy as I speak."

A, *a*

B, *b*

C, *c*

D, *d*

E, *e*

F, *f*

G, *g*

H, *h*

I, *i*

J, *j*

K, *k*

L, *l*

M, *m*

N, *n*

O, *o*

P, *p*

Q, *q*

R, *r*

S, *s*

T, *t*

U, *u*

V, *v*

W, *w*

X, *x*

Y, *y*

Z, *z*

ACCOLADES

Most of us are familiar with the image of an important person being bestowed the honor of knighthood by a royal figure tapping the honoree's shoulders with the flat blade of a sword. This ceremony is known as an *accolade.* The original ceremony, however, involved the neck, which the potential knight stuck out exactly the way those condemned to be beheaded did. That's why the word *accolade*, which came into English from French in the early 1600s, meant originally the bestowal of knighthood by a ceremonial embrace about the neck (the tap with the sword came later). French *accolade* meant, literally, an embrace about the neck, derived from *accoller* "to embrace the neck" (from *a-* "to" + *col* "neck," from Latin *collum* "neck").

Since the accolade represented public recognition of merit or achievement, the word came to be used figuratively in the 1800s for any bestowal of honor or praise, any plaudit or award, as in *The highest accolade a writer can receive is the Nobel Prize.*

ACQUAINT

See QUAINT

ADAMANT

In modern usage, *adamant* means "determined, unyielding, inflexible," as in Agatha Christie's Miss Marple novel *The Moving Finger* (1943): "Both Joanna and I tried to change her mind, but she was quite adamant."

Adamant came into English as a noun—the name of an extremely hard rock or mineral, first recorded about 855 c.e. (in King Alfred's translation of St. Gregory's *Pastoral Care*). It was derived from Latin *adamás, adamant-* and Greek *adámas, adámantos,* meaning the hardest gemstone, the diamond. Variously referring to a magnet, a diamond, or steel, *adamant* has appeared widely in English literature. In the King James Bible, it appears in Ezekiel 3:9 (*"As an adamant harder than flint have I made thy forehead"*) and Zechariah 7:12 (*"Yea, they made their hearts as an adamant stone"*). The 19th-century poet William Wordsworth wrote in his *Ecclesiastical Sonnets*, "But who would force the soul, tilts with a straw / Against a champion cased in adamant."

It is no coincidence that the basic meaning of *adamant* was "diamond." The word *diamond* is a doublet of *adamant*, the two words having come ultimately from the same Greek source, *adámantos*, of uncertain origin.

The present-day adjective, meaning "unyielding, inflexible," usually in the phrase *to be adamant*, is first recorded in the 1930s. It was apparently an extended use of such earlier phrases as *an adamant heart* (1677), meaning "a heart of stone" and *adamant walls* (1878) "stone walls."

ADVENT

Advent is a formal word used for any important or significant arrival. Poems have been written about the *Advent of Spring* and histories about the *Advent of Capitalism* and *The Advent of Islam*. The word appears in such sentences as *Some cultures often mark the advent of adulthood with initiation ceremonies.* But this meaning of *advent* is relatively recent, going back only to the 1800s. The much older and earliest meaning of the word, now usually capitalized as *Advent*, is "the period of four Sundays before Christmas" (first found in the *Anglo-Saxon Chronicle*, 1100s), commemorating the coming of Jesus into the world. This meaning was extended by the 1400s to the anticipated *Second Coming* (as in the *Messianic Advent*). Both the old and new meaning go back to Latin *adventus*, "a coming to, arrival," from *advenīre* "to come to" (*ad-* "to" + *venīre* "to come").

A, *a*

B, *b*

C, *c*

D, *d*

E, *e*

F, *f*

G, *g*

H, *h*

I, *i*

J, *j*

K, *k*

L, *l*

M, *m*

N, *n*

O, *o*

P, *p*

Q, *q*

R, *r*

S, *s*

T, *t*

U, *u*

V, *v*

W, *w*

X, *x*

Y, *y*

Z, *z*

A, a

B, b

C, c

D, d

E, e

F, f

G, g

H, h

I, i

J, j

K, k

L, l

M, m

N, n

O, o

P, p

Q, q

R, r

S, s

T, t

U, u

V, v

W, w

X, x

Y, y

Z, z

ADVENTURE

From the same Latin source as *advent* came the word *adventure*. We think of an adventure as an exciting or remarkable incident that unexpectedly befalls a person, a use found, for example, in Shakespeare's *Pericles, King of Tyre*: "A Gentleman of Tyre looking for adventures in the world." However, the word's earliest meaning (1200s) was "something that comes by chance, a hazard, an accident," still found in *peradventure*, "by chance."

The change in meaning from "a chance happening" to "an exciting incident" came from the fact that adventures never happen naturally or according to a plan, but rather by chance or accident. The adventures of Tarzan, Robin Hood, Sherlock Holmes, Superman, or any other imaginary figure come about through the chance events invented by their fertile creators.

See also VENTURE

AGGRAVATE

If we'd lived in the 1500s, when *aggravate* first came into English, we would use it to mean literally "add weight to, weigh down, overburden," as in *The large suitcase he was carrying aggravated him*. That was the meaning of the word's source, Latin *aggravāre* (past participle *aggravātus*), from *ag-* "to" + *gravāre* "weigh down," from *gravis* "heavy."

The negative connotation of "weigh down" led to the extended meaning "to make worse, exacerbate," as in "Falsehood will only aggravate your guilt" (Henry Fielding, *The History of Tom Jones*). The current meaning, "to irritate, exasperate, annoy," was popularized in the 1700s and 1800s in works like Samuel Richardson's *Clarissa* (" . . . both were to aggravate her parents, as my brother and sister do mine") and William Makepeace Thackeray's *The Virginians* ("Threats only serve to *aggravate* people . . .").

A, a

B, b
C, c
D, d
E, e
F, f
G, g
H, h
I, i
J, j
K, k
L, l
M, m
N, n
O, o
P, p
Q, q
R, r
S, s
T, t
U, u
V, v
W, w
X, x
Y, y
Z, z

ALLUDE
See ELUDE

ANTELOPE
Who hasn't heard the traditional cowboy song (of unknown authorship) *Home on the Range*?

> Oh, give me a home where the buffalo roam,
> Where the deer and the antelope play . . .

Unlike cowboys, city folks usually can't distinguish between antelopes and deer, though the two come from different families (Bovidae and Cervidae, respectively). However, in the early 1400s, an antelope (from Greek *anthólops*) was certainly an animal that would stand out from the pack. *Antelope* referred to a mythical beast (something like a unicorn) appearing on a heraldic coat of arms, with long sawlike horns with which it cut down trees and enemies. It wasn't until 1607 that the modern scientific meaning of an actual hollow-horned animal related to oxen, sheep, and goats was introduced.

See also DEER

ANTHOLOGY
In his great *Dictionary of the English Language* (1755), Samuel Johnson defined *anthology* as "a collection of flowers." It's not clear how he arrived at this definition, since the word's earliest meaning (1640) was "a garland of choice poems by various authors," borrowed from Greek *antholog ía*. Apparently Johnson went back for his definition to the literal meaning of the Greek word, which was "a garland, bouquet, or gathering of flowers" (from *ánthos* "flower" + *-log ía* "collection," from *légein* "to gather"). While Johnson missed the figurative meaning, "a garland or bouquet of poems," both in the Greek and in English, by the 1800s this meaning of *anthology* was well established and

A, a

B, b
C, c
D, d
E, e
F, f
G, g
H, h
I, i
J, j
K, k
L, l
M, m
N, n
O, o
P, p
Q, q
R, r
S, s
T, t
U, u
V, v
W, w
X, x
Y, y
Z, z

extended to any gathering or collection of literary or artistic works. Today almost any such collection can be titled an anthology, such as *An Anthology of Pop Songs, An Anthology of Nursery Rhymes, An Anthology of Abstract Paintings.*

ANTIC ANTICS

A December 2000 review of a musical, "A Child's Garden," included this sentence: "The theater's low ceiling and the stage's lack of depth restrict the staging of the children's antics so they don't seem very antic at all." The reviewer didn't have to explain the word *antics*—they are playful, flighty, or funny gestures, actions, and the like. And their antics not being very *antic* simply meant that they weren't as playful, flighty, or funny as they were expected to be.

The meaning of the word *antic* changed greatly since it came into English from the Italian *antico* in the mid-1500s. The source of the word, Italian *antico,* came from Latin *anticus, antiquus* "old, aged, ancient," since certain grotesque murals unearthed in Rome were ascribed to the ancients. *Antic* was then a technical term in art and architecture, referring to a grotesque or bizarre sculpture or other representation of people, animals, and plants. In the 1600s this meaning of *antic* was extended figuratively to any grotesque or bizarre behavior, as in John Ford's *Love's Sacrifice* (1633): "A pox upon your outlandish feminine antics." From this it was further extended to the meaning "playful, funny, or ludicrous actions," as in *a circus clown's antics,* and the adjective *antic*, "playful, funny, or ludicrous," as in *a comedian making antic faces.*

an **ARCH** *look at archvillains*

Any fan of superheroes, whether those in comic books or in films, knows that every superhero worth his salt has an archvillain to contend with. Think of Batman's archfoe, The Joker, Superman's archenemy Lex Luthor, and Spider-Man's arch-

A, *a*

B, *b*

C, *c*

D, *d*

E, *e*

F, *f*

G, *g*

H, *h*

I, *i*

J, *j*

K, *k*

L, *l*

M, *m*

N, *n*

O, *o*

P, *p*

Q, *q*

R, *r*

S, *s*

T, *t*

U, *u*

V, *v*

W, *w*

X, *x*

Y, *y*

Z, *z*

mad-scientist nemesis, Doctor Octopus. Literary archvillains include Sherlock Holmes's archfoe Professor James Moriarty and Captain Ahab's murderous Moby Dick.

We do not talk of archheroes—only of *archenemies, archfiends, archfoes, archknaves, archrebels, archrogues,* and *archvillains.* This negative use of *arch-,* whose meaning is "chief, principal, leading," represents a degradation of the word's original use, which was positive, and found as a prefix in such honorable words as *archangel, archbishop,* and *archduke.* The first record of *arch* as a separate word rather than as a prefix, in 1547, refers to an *arch prelate*—a positive use. Soon afterwards we find Shakespeare using it negatively in several of his plays, in such sentences as "For I know he is ... A most arch heretic" (*Henry VIII*).

The attachment of *arch* to such words as *rogue, knave,* and *wag* extended its meaning in the 1600s to "roguish, crafty, cunning, sly," as in *an arch lad, an arch look, an arch reply, an arch expression.* In John Bunyan's *Pilgrim's Progress* (1678), Mr. Great-Heart says: "A very arch fellow, a downright hypocrite, one that would be religious, whichever way the world went; but so cunning, that he would be sure never to lose or suffer for it."

the genuine ARTICLE

Ancrene Riwle (Rule for Anchoresses) was a manual written in the 1200s for three anchoresses, or female hermits, setting out the rules and duties of a religious recluse's life. The word *article,* meaning a clause or section of the rules, made its first appearance in English in that document, having been borrowed (through Old French) from Latin *articulus* "small section or joint," from *artus* "joint." It was thought that just as a body's parts are connected by joints, so the parts of any writing are connected and held together by joints. This meaning led in the 1700s to the most common use of the word, a piece of writing forming a part of a newspaper, magazine, or journal.

A, a

B, b

C, c

D, d

E, e

F, f

G, g

H, h

I, i

J, j

K, k

L, l

M, m

N, n

O, o

P, p

Q, q

R, r

S, s

T, t

U, u

V, v

W, w

X, x

Y, y

Z, z

A much more extended use of *article*, "a piece of goods, a commodity," as in *clothing articles, an article of wear, articles of food*, came into use in the 1700s. A hundred years later, this meaning was transferred informally to a person or thing judged to be real and authentic, as in Louisa May Alcott's *Hospital Sketches*, referring to a slave: "Here was a genuine article—no, not the genuine article at all, we must go to Africa for that—but the sort of creatures generations of slavery have made them."

An unusual use of *article* is the grammatical one, denoting either *the* (the definite *article*) or *a, an* (the indefinite *article*), considered by many a distinct part of speech. First recorded in English in 1530, the word came directly from Latin *articulus*, which was a translation of Greek *árthron* "joint," so called because the Greek articles were words joined or linked to nouns.

ASPERSION

The earliest uses of *aspersion*, beginning in the 1500s, were in phrases like *the aspersion of the blood of Jesus Christ*, where the word meant "a sprinkling or spattering (of a liquid)." Shakespeare used the word in *The Tempest* to mean "a sprinkling, a shower, a spray": "No sweet aspersion shall the heavens let fall."

So how did *aspersion* come to mean "a damaging or disparaging remark, a calumny or slander," or "the act of slandering or defaming," as in this quotation from *Cruising Speed* (1971), by William F. Buckley, Jr.: "I mention Robert Kennedy without aspersion of any kind—on the contrary; because his foes and his friends agree that he felt deeply . . ."?

In 1616, the Anglican clergyman Thomas Adams, in his interpretation of Psalm 6:6, used *aspersion* in a negative sense: "Sin is like a stinking candle newly put out, it is soon lighted again. . . . Therefore, whatsoever aspersion the sin of the day has brought upon us, let the tears of the night wash away." The meaning "a sprinkling or spattering" turned by degrees into "a

A, a

B, b

C, c

D, d

E, e

F, f

G, g

H, h

I, i

J, j

K, k

L, l

M, m

N, n

O, o

P, p

Q, q

R, r

S, s

T, t

U, u

V, v

W, w

X, x

Y, y

Z, z

bespatterment, a staining, a soiling," which in turn led to the figurative sense of "something that soils one's character or reputation," as in Henry Fielding's *The History of Tom Jones*: "I defy all the world to cast a just aspersion on my character."

The deterioration in meaning was probably influenced by the verb *asperse*, which originally (late 1400s) meant "to sprinkle," but by the early 1600s it developed into "to spatter or stain (a person's character or reputation)," as in John Speed's *The History of Great Britaine* (1611): "Monkish humours have aspersed other such men with bitter reproaches." While *asperse* is rarely seen or heard nowadays, the phrase *cast aspersions on* has become a commonplace idiom, almost a cliché.

ASTRINGENT
See STRINGENT

ATTACH
Attach came into English in the 1300s from Old French *attachier*, meaning "to arrest or seize by legal authority," as in Shakespeare's *Comedy of Errors*, where a merchant demands that Angelo, a goldsmith, pay back the guilders Angelo owes him: "Therefore make present satisfaction, or I'll attach you by this officer." This legal sense was extended to the figurative meaning "to seize, lay hold of," as in Shakespeare's *The Tempest*: "I'm myself attached with weariness." Since seizing something involves a connecting or fastening to it, *attach* soon acquired the meaning "to tack on, fasten, join," in sentences like "The shoulder blade is attached to the muscles" and "Little belief should be attached to legends"–the current meaning of the word.

toys in the ATTIC
No room in a house is as mysterious as the attic. Typically dark, with exposed rafters and narrow spaces, attics are mainly used to store objects like old toys and games.

A, a

B, b

C, c

D, d

E, e

F, f

G, g

H, h

I, i

J, j

K, k

L, l

M, m

N, n

O, o

P, p

Q, q

R, r

S, s

T, t

U, u

V, v

W, w

X, x

Y, y

Z, z

Lillian Hellman's 1959 play, *Toys in the Attic*, uses the title figuratively, referring to the long-forgotten impressions of childhood stored away in the adult memory.

The attic is the space in a house below the roof. But this was not what an *attic* meant originally. When the word first came into English (from French *attique*) in the 1690s, it meant a decorative structure, consisting of a small column and entablature, above the main facade of a building. French *attique* came from Latin *Atticus*, meaning "of *Attica*," referring to the region in ancient Greece whose architectural style, the Attic order, was represented by this structure. The space enclosed by this structure was called an *attic story*. This phrase was shortened in the early 1800s to *attic*, and the word was applied to the top floor of a house, or the room in it.

ATTITUDE *and* APTITUDE

In current slang an *attitude* means an aggressive, antagonistic manner or outlook, as in *a salesman with an attitude*; *I asked a question and all I got was attitude.* Kids, employees, and bosses are said to have attitude problems. The standard meaning is "a settled manner of behaving, acting, or thinking," as in *maintaining a positive attitude, a respectful attitude toward others.*

Originally, *attitude* was a technical term in the Fine Arts, meaning the posture of the body given to a figure in a statue or painting. The phrase *to strike an attitude* meant "to assume a certain posture deliberately, and not as a spontaneous action." The word was borrowed from French *attitude*, which adopted it from Italian *attitudine* "disposition, fitness," from Late Latin *aptitūdinem*, from *aptus* "fitted, fit, apt."

Late Latin *aptitūdinem* was also the source of English *aptitude*, which came into English in the early 1400s with the meaning "fitness, suitableness," as in *the aptitude of a place for the establishment of a school.* This meaning was extended in the 1600s to "natural tendency, capacity, or skill," as in *She has an aptitude for mathematics.* Having originated from the same Latin word, *attitude* and *aptitude* are doublets.

AUDITION

An *audition* is a trial performance by an actor, dancer, singer, musician, or other performer seeking employment. The audition may be held in an *auditorium* in front of an *audience.* All three words derive ultimately from Latin *audīre* "to hear," since all three have to do with a hearing. The original meaning of *audition*, which was borrowed (through French) from Latin *audītiōnem* in the late 1500s, was "the faculty or power of hearing," as in *His audition was impaired by the accident.* The sense of a trial performance by an actor, and the like, developed from the fact that the applicant for a job receives a "hearing" by a potential employer. This meaning of *audition* was first recorded in 1881, in *Scribner's Monthly*: "The director of the Académie de Musique . . . fixed a day for her *audition* at the theatre."

AVERAGE

We think of the word *average* as a mathematical term meaning an arithmetic mean. Loosely, we use the word to mean typical, regular, or standard, as in *an average student, the average consumer.* In fact, this word came into use in the 1400s as a maritime term, used especially in the Mediterranean trade, and it meant a duty or tax charged in the shipment of goods. It first appeared as a borrowing of Old French *avarie* meaning "a charge on property or goods."

In the late 1500s, the maritime meaning of *average* was extended to "the equal distribution of expenses or losses among various interested parties in proportion to their interests." This meaning was in turn generalized in the 1700s to "the distribution of anything among members of a group based on a median estimate," used especially in the phrases *at an average, on an*

A, *a*

B, *b*

C, *c*

D, *d*

E, *e*

F, *f*

G, *g*

H, *h*

I, *i*

J, *j*

K, *k*

L, *l*

M, *m*

N, *n*

O, *o*

P, *p*

Q, *q*

R, *r*

S, *s*

T, *t*

U, *u*

V, *v*

W, *w*

X, *x*

Y, *y*

Z, *z*

A, a

B, b

C, c

D, d

E, e

F, f

G, g

H, h

I, i

J, j

K, k

L, l

M, m

N, n

O, o

P, p

Q, q

R, r

S, s

T, t

U, u

V, v

W, w

X, x

Y, y

Z, z

average. This use was further extended in the 1700s to the current meaning of "an intermediate value or quantity, the arithmetic mean," in sentences like *The month's average of accidents has been as high as five a day. This restaurant is very much above the average.*

AWKWARD

Before the 1400s there was in English a word, *awk*, meaning "the wrong way, backhanded," that was of Scandinavian origin, probably Old Norse *afug*. Though the word had fallen out of use in English by the 1600s, it survived as part of the compound *awkward*, meaning "turned in the wrong direction, upside down," literally, "toward the wrong way." From the idea of doing things the wrong way, a new meaning, "ungraceful, uncouth," developed, as in Shakespeare's *Troilus and Cressida* (1616), where Ulysses says: "And with ridiculous and awkward action . . . He pageants us." From this sense came the current meaning, "lacking dexterity, clumsy, bungling," applied to persons and things, as in *an awkward gesture, an awkward situation.* "I have not seen a more clumsy, awkward, and unhandy people." (Jonathan Swift, *Gulliver's Travels*)

B, b

A, a

B, b

C, c

D, d

E, e

F, f

G, g

H, h

I, i

J, j

K, k

L, l

M, m

N, n

O, o

P, p

Q, q

R, r

S, s

T, t

U, u

V, v

W, w

X, x

Y, y

Z, z

BALLOON

The balloon has been around since the 1780s in a variety of forms, from small toy balloons to huge hot-air balloons. But the earliest meaning of *balloon* had nothing to do with flying or aircraft.

Balloon came into English in the 1580s from Italian as the name of a ball game (*ballone*) played by striking a large leather ball back and forth with the hand or foot. The names of both the game and the ball were at first spelled *ballone*, as in Italian, where it meant literally "great ball" (from *balla* "ball" + *-one*, a suffix meaning "great, large"). Over the next two hundred years *balloon* was applied to any large ball-like object, such as a bomb or a glass globe used in chemistry. It was in the 1780s, with the invention by two Frenchmen, the brothers Montgolfier, of the hot-air balloon, that *balloon* took on its modern meaning.

In the late 1800s, the word started to be applied to small inflatable balloons for children to play with, as in this passage in H. G. Wells's *War in the Air* (1908): "Small children's air-balloons of the latest model attached to a string became a serious check to the pedestrian in Central Park." The balloon-shaped thought bubble in a comic strip appeared in the mid-1800s, as in Charles Dickens's *Martin Chuzzlewit* (1844): "Diabolical sentiments were represented as issuing from his mouth in fat balloons."

BALONEY

Names of foods have long been applied in English to human types, qualities, and conditions, especially in slang. Some examples are: *chicken* for a coward, *ham* for an amateurish actor, *hash* for a mess or muddle, *goose* for a fool, *turkey* for a failure or flop. *Baloney* belongs in this category. Though literally it's a type of sausage, it has been used in American English since the 1920s to mean "nonsense, humbug," chiefly in phrases like *full of baloney* and *That's a lot of baloney!*

The earliest meaning of *baloney*, however, was "a stupid or clumsy person, an oaf," as in "Kid Roberts . . . won his first professional fight by knocking out a boloney with the *nom du ring* of Young Du Fresne" (*Collier's* magazine, June 5, 1920). The meaning "nonsense, humbug" may have come about through the influence of the similar-sounding *blarney* (1796), meaning "flattery" but also "nonsense." In a speech in 1938, the popular clergyman and author, Fulton J. Sheen, distinguished between the two words: "Baloney is flattery laid so thick it cannot be true, and blarney is flattery so thin we love it."

BAN *and* BANISH

According to the *Oxford English Dictionary*, *ban* in the sense of "to bar, proscribe, prohibit, forbid" is first recorded in 1816, in Lord Byron's *The Prisoner of Chillon*: "And mine has been the fate of those / To whom the goodly earth and air / Are bann'd, and barr'd—forbidden fare." However, the earliest meaning of *ban* was "to curse, anathemize, condemn," which arose in early Middle English from a blend of Old English *bannan* "to summon, proclaim" and Old Norse *banna* "to curse, interdict, prohibit."

How, then, did *ban* get the meaning of "prohibit, forbid"? The answer is that it was influenced by the word *banish* "to drive away, force out," which meant originally (1300s) "to condemn" and came ultimately from a Germanic source related to the source of *ban*. Thus the close historical connection between *ban* and *banish* led to the change in meaning of *ban* from "curse, condemn" to "prohibit, forbid."

My BATTERY *is dead!*

Who among us hasn't uttered this despondent cry? It seems that almost every apparatus that runs on electricity depends on a battery—be it a car, a motorcycle, a cell phone, even a common wristwatch. The first scientist to call a set of connected electric

A, *a*
B, **b**
C, *c*
D, *d*
E, *e*
F, *f*
G, *g*
H, *h*
I, *i*
J, *j*
K, *k*
L, *l*
M, *m*
N, *n*
O, *o*
P, *p*
Q, *q*
R, *r*
S, *s*
T, *t*
U, *u*
V, *v*
W, *w*
X, *x*
Y, *y*
Z, *z*

A, a

B, b

C, c

D, d

E, e

F, f

G, g

H, h

I, i

J, j

K, k

L, l

M, m

N, n

O, o

P, p

Q, q

R, r

S, s

T, t

U, u

V, v

W, w

X, x

Y, y

Z, z

cells a *battery* was Benjamin Franklin, who in 1748 described the apparatus in detail. He derived this use from the earlier military meaning (1555), "a set of mounted guns arranged for combined action and forming a division of artillery," which is still part of the vocabulary of warfare.

As to how this military meaning arose, it came from the idea of the blows inflicted by artillery on the walls of a fortress or other fortification, which developed in the 1500s from the word's earliest meaning (1531), "the action of beating, or assailing with blows." This meaning is still encountered in law, especially in the phrase *assault and battery*, with which one may be charged if he lays a finger on someone in a quarrel instead of just engaging in verbal pugilism.

Battery was borrowed from French *batterie* "a beating or battering, a set of cannons," which was derived from Old French *battre* "to beat, batter." The verb *to batter* came from this Old French word and, ultimately, from Latin *battuere* "to beat," which is thought to be the source of our English *bat* "club, stick," the kind that should be used only to hit a ball and never to commit battery.

prayer BEADS

The small ball of glass or plastic we call a *bead* and use to make necklaces and other jewelry made its debut not as an ornament or decoration but as an aid in saying one's prayers. In fact, the word *bead* meant "prayer" in Old English, where it was spelled *bede*, and was closely related to Old High German *gibet* (modern German *Gebet*) "prayer."

So how did a word meaning "prayer" come to mean a bit of glass decoration? The answer is that many religions, including Christianity, Buddhism, Hinduism, and Islam, customarily used small pieces of glass, amber, or wood to keep count of the prayers they recited every day. For example, Catholics use the string of beads called a rosary to count sequences of "Hail Marys," while Muslims use prayer beads to recite the 114 suras, or chapters, of the Koran.

Sometime in the 1400s, people started to wear these strings of small pieces around their necks or wrists as decorations, at which time speakers began to refer to the perforated globules as *beads*, to distinguish these objects from the *prayers* said while counting them. Today, when we speak of beads we mean the ornaments, and when we wish to refer to the beads used in prayers, we call them by the retronym *prayer beads*.

The last stage in the history of *bead* is its almost inevitable transfer from a droplike ornament to any drop of liquid, molten metal, and the like, as in *beads of sweat*.

going BERSERK

Since 1986, becoming uncontrollably violent at the workplace has been known as *going postal*, a phrase that originated from a series of murderous attacks by post-office employees on managers, fellow workers, and police officers. The phrase caught on, because it was more specific than the older and broader idiom *going berserk*, which has been used since the 1800s in the general sense of "becoming frenzied or madly violent, as in "Party addict . . . went berserk at the London rehab clinic where he is staying this week, punching a nurse, screaming and ramming into walls" (March 2007, *New York Daily News*).

The adjective *berserk* is a modern term derived from the name *Berserkar*, which was introduced and popularized in the early 1800s in the novels of Sir Walter Scott. The Berserkars were wild Norse warriors who fought on the battlefield with frenzied fury. *Berserkar* was borrowed by Scott from Old Icelandic *berserkr*, a compound explained as either "bare shirt" or "bear coat," both apparently referring to the clothing worn by the warriors when they went berserk on the battlefield screaming bloody murder.

A, *a*
B, *b*
C, *c*
D, *d*
E, *e*
F, *f*
G, *g*
H, *h*
I, *i*
J, *j*
K, *k*
L, *l*
M, *m*
N, *n*
O, *o*
P, *p*
Q, *q*
R, *r*
S, *s*
T, *t*
U, *u*
V, *v*
W, *w*
X, *x*
Y, *y*
Z, *z*

A, a

B, b

C, c

D, d

E, e

F, f

G, g

H, h

I, i

J, j

K, k

L, l

M, m

N, n

O, o

P, p

Q, q

R, r

S, s

T, t

U, u

V, v

W, w

X, x

Y, y

Z, z

The name was first used as an adjective by Thomas Carlyle in 1839: "Let no man awaken . . . this same Berserkir-rage!" It was reduced to *Berserk* in 1908 by Rudyard Kipling in *A Diversity of Creatures*: "You went Berserk. . . . you'll probably be liable to fits of it all your life."

BIGOT

"A dogmatist in religion is not a long way off from a bigot," wrote the English theologian Issac Watts in his book *The Improvement of the Mind* (1771). By *bigot* he meant an extremely prejudiced individual, one who clings stubbornly to a particular belief or opinion and is intolerant of other people's beliefs or opinions. This has been the word's meaning since the 1600s.

However, the earliest meaning of *bigot* was not the one we are familiar with.

When the word first appeared in English, in 1598, from Middle French *bigot* (of uncertain origin), it meant a hypocrite, especially a religious hypocrite. Then, in 1661, in his *Discourse concerning . . . Oliver Cromwell,* the poet Abraham Cowley used *bigot* to mean "a person obstinately and unreasonably wedded to a particular religious creed, opinion or ritual" (*Oxford English Dictionary*). "He was rather a well-meaning and deluding Bigot, than a crafty and malicious Impostor," wrote Cowley about Cromwell.

Cowley's use led to the change from "one who professes to be religious, a hypocrite in religious matters" to "one who is obstinately wedded to a particular religious belief."

By 1693, *bigot* was generalized to any individual clinging stubbornly and unreasonably to a belief or opinion.

BLATANT

Blatant is not a kind word. It's commonly used to disparage something as being glaringly or brazenly obvious (*a blatant lie, a blatant error*) or tastelessly conspicuous (*a blatant upstart, a blatant lack of manners*). These uses first appeared in the early 1900s.

Blatant hails from the Latin *blatīre* "to babble" and English *blatter* "to chatter, prate," which is found before 1555 and was borrowed from Latin *blaterāre* "to babble."

In *The Faerie Queene* (1596), Edmund Spenser used the word in the phrase *blatant beast* to describe a thousand-tongued monster, the offspring of Cerberus and Chimæra, by which he symbolized calumny and slander. Since Spenser's *blatant beast* represented slander, it's not far-fetched to assume that he was influenced in coining *blatant* by earlier similar-sounding words meaning "to babble, chatter."

In 1656 the word shifted meaning to "offensively noisy, vulgarly loud," as in *a blatant radical, blatant tongues.* The transition from "offensively noisy, vulgarly loud" to the current meaning of "glaringly obvious" and "tastelessly conspicuous" is an extension of that which is obtrusive or annoying to the ear to that which is obtrusive or annoying to the eye.

BOMBAST

In 1921 the iconoclastic critic H. L. Mencken mounted an attack on the Wilson presidency in the *Smart Set*, by blasting "its ideational hollowness, its ludicrous strutting and bombast, its heavy dependence upon greasy and meaningless words, its frequent descents to mere sound and fury, signifying nothing."

His use of *bombast* in this sentence could just as well be applied to the sentence itself, since the word means "thick, inflated, pompous language." However, the first meaning of *bombast* was

A, a
B, b
C, c
D, d
E, e
F, f
G, g
H, h
I, i
J, j
K, k
L, l
M, m
N, n
O, o
P, p
Q, q
R, r
S, s
T, t
U, u
V, v
W, w
X, x
Y, y
Z, z

A, a

B, b

C, c

D, d

E, e

F, f

G, g

H, h

I, i

J, j

K, k

L, l

M, m

N, n

O, o

P, p

Q, q

R, r

S, s

T, t

U, u

V, v

W, w

X, x

Y, y

Z, z

"cotton wool used as padding or stuffing for clothes, blankets, etc." The word was a variant of the Middle French *bombace* "cotton or cotton wadding," from Medieval Latin *bambac-, bambax* "cotton," from Greek. In the 1500s, *bombast* was used figuratively to mean "thick padding or stuffing" and since 1589, the meaning was extended to a favorite put-down for those who use excessively inflated language.

BOTHER

The word *bother* first appeared in the early 1700s in the writings of various Irishmen, among them Thomas Sheridan, Jonathan Swift, and Laurence Sterne. The meaning of the word was "to deafen with noise" and its earliest recorded use was in a letter that Sheridan wrote to Swift in 1718: "With the din of which tube my head you so bother." Swift and others spelled the word *bodder*, which suggests derivation from Irish *bodar* "deaf," Gaelic *bodhair* "deafen."

By the mid-1700s the meaning was generalized to mean "disturb, irritate, weary," as in a 1762 letter by Sterne: "Civility thus uniform . . . bodders me to death." This use was further generalized to the current meaning, "to give trouble to, annoy," which became widespread in general English in the 1800s, typically in sentences like this: "Races didn't bother the Americans. They were something a lot better than any race. They were a People" (Archibald Macleish, *A Time to Act,* 1943).

BRAND *names*

When you buy a *brand* of soap or coffee, you think of a distinctive word or name (*Ivory, Maxwell House*) that identifies the product. The earliest meaning of *brand* in Old English (about 950) was "a piece of burning wood, and later, a torch, a match," related to Old High German *brant* and Old Norse *brandr* "act or means of burning." As late as 1833, Washington Irving used it in this sense: "The brands of one of their fires were still smoking."

Subsequently, in the Middle Ages, it was the custom to burn a sign or mark on criminals as a stigma of disgrace or infamy. A hot iron was used to press this mark on the criminal's skin, and the mark itself was called a *brand*, since it involved burning. In the 1600s, it became common to *brand* cattle, horses, and the like, i.e., to burn a distinctive mark on them as a sign of ownership.

In the early 1800s, the word's meaning was extended to any trademark, not just one made by burning, applied to wine or liquor casks, timbers, and metals. By the 1850s a *brand* could refer to a particular class of goods as shown by the trademark on them, as in *an ale of superior brand, special brands of textiles.*

military **BRATS**

Brat is a disparaging term for a spoiled, impolite child. The word has been known since the 1500s. In 1712, Sir Richard Steele complained in *The Spectator* about "the noise of those damned nurses and squalling brats."

The word has been traced back to Old English *bratt* "a cloak," spelled in the 1500s as *brat* meaning "an apron, a coarse garment, a rag." Since children in the Middle Ages often wore ragged clothes, it seems likely that the word for a rag was applied contemptuously to the least appealing among them.

The term *army brat*, meaning the son or daughter of a U.S. army officer, arose in the 1930s, and by the 1960s it was expanded to include a child from other service branches, a class known collectively as *military brats*. They were called *brats* presumably because they were cocky, brassy, and generally not likable (though this has never been proven).

A, *a*
B, *b*
C, *c*
D, *d*
E, *e*
F, *f*
G, *g*
H, *h*
I, *i*
J, *j*
K, *k*
L, *l*
M, *m*
N, *n*
O, *o*
P, *p*
Q, *q*
R, *r*
S, *s*
T, *t*
U, *u*
V, *v*
W, *w*
X, *x*
Y, *y*
Z, *z*

A, a

B, b

C, c

D, d

E, e

F, f

G, g

H, h

I, i

J, j

K, k

L, l

M, m

N, n

O, o

P, p

Q, q

R, r

S, s

T, t

U, u

V, v

W, w

X, x

Y, y

Z, z

BRIBE

"It's tough being corrupt," the journalist Richard Morin wrote under the above title in 2004 on the *Washington Post* Web site. "You probably need to bribe lots of people to achieve your ignoble goals."

As anyone who reads crime novels or the daily newspaper knows, to *bribe* someone, say a politician or judge, is to influence him corruptly by means of a gift or reward, and a *bribe* is the gift or reward given to influence him corruptly. This meaning of the word has been around since the early 1500s, as we find it in Shakespeare's *Coriolanus*: "I cannot make my heart consent to take a bribe."

The word's earliest meaning, though, was "to steal, rob, extort" for the verb, and "theft, robbery, extortion" for the noun, both found in Chaucer's *Canterbury Tales* (about 1386) and in other works by writers up to the 1600s. How did a word meaning "to steal" come to mean "influence corruptly by giving a gift"?

The English word was borrowed from Old French *bribe* "piece of bread given to a beggar," *briber* "to go begging, be a beggar." According to the *Oxford English Dictionary* (*OED*) English *briber*, "one who bribes" which is first attested in 1483, had the following successive meanings: "beggar," "vagabond," "scoundrel," "thief," "robber," "extortioner." If we apply this series to *bribe*, the transition from "to steal, extort" to "receive (or give) a bribe" is no less reasonable than to graduate from one type of felony to another.

BROACHING *a subject*

The phrase "broach a subject" always signals that the subject is a sensitive one. *Broach,* meaning "to begin to talk about, introduce in a conversation," is a figurative use, first encountered in 1579, of the earlier literal sense "to pierce (a cask) so as to draw out the liquor, to tap" (about 1440) or the still earlier "to pierce or thrust through" (1377). The word was a verb use of the noun *broach*, meaning "a pointed instrument or tool, like a spear or lance, or a spit for roasting meat" (about 1305), which was borrowed from Old French *broche*, a word corresponding to Spanish *broca* and Italian *brocca*, all derived from Vulgar Latin *brocca* "a sharp-pointed tool, a spike." To *broach a subject*, then, suggests piercing or cutting through it, an action applicable mostly to subjects one has qualms about.

A *brooch*, an ornament fastened to a garment with a safety pin, is pronounced the same way: /brōch/; the different spellings arose in Middle English to differentiate the specialized meaning of an ornamental pin from the general meaning of a pointed instrument.

BROOK *no opposition*

"The dignity of parliament it seems can brook no opposition," wrote Thomas Jefferson in a letter to William Small on May 7, 1775. A century earlier John Milton wrote in *Paradise Lost*, "Heaven brooks not the works of violence and war." This use of the verb *brook* first turned up in 1530 and is still current, found in such phrases as *will not brook a challenge, can't brook dilly-dallying,* and the standard *brook no opposition.* The verb means "to put up with, tolerate, stomach, endure," and is used in constructions that are negative or that preclude something.

Ironically, this word quickly reversed its original meaning. When it originated in Old English (about 725, in the form *brúcan*), it meant "to make use of, enjoy, profit by." Around 950, the word's meaning extended to "make use of (food), digest," as in *to brook meat, to brook rich food.* The current sense "to tolerate" apparently came about as a figurative use of the meaning "to digest," as shown in the writings of a contemporary of Shakespeare, Philip Stubbs, who wrote in his *Anatomy of Abuses* (1583): "They cannot at any hand brook or digest them that would counsel them to that."

A, a

B, b

C, c

D, d

E, e

F, f

G, g

H, h

I, i

J, j

K, k

L, l

M, m

N, n

O, o

P, p

Q, q

R, r

S, s

T, t

U, u

V, v

W, w

X, x

Y, y

Z, z

BROWSE

Thanks to the Internet, you can spend hours *browsing* for just about anything you want. Your computer facilitates your browsing with a *browser*—a program (like Google or Yahoo) that searches for anything you want and displays it for your pleasure or enlightenment. Before there were computers, people did their browsing mostly in or around books. The American essayist James Russell Lowell, in his *Among My Books* (1870), tells us about the English poet John Dryden: "We thus get a glimpse of him browsing—for . . . he was always a random reader—in his father's library." To *browse,* then, is to look at or through anything in a relaxed, casual way.

The original meaning of *browse*, first recorded in 1523, was "(of grazing animals) to crop and eat the leaves, twigs, etc. of plants for food." Thus Charles Darwin writes in his *Origin of Species* (1859): "Little trees . . . have been perpetually browsed down by cattle." *Browse* was borrowed from Middle French *brouster* "to feed on buds and shoots of plants," which derived from the older noun *broust, brost* "bud, sprout, shoot," of Germanic origin. The current meaning, "to look through or at casually," arose in the 1800s as a metaphor comparing a person who sniffs around books to an ox, goat, or deer moving at leisure among bushes and trees and feeding on leaves and shoots.

BUDGET

"A budget takes the fun out of money," wrote the American author Mason Cooley in his *City Aphorisms* (1994). Most everyone would agree that sticking to a budget, which is an itemized estimate of the money to be spent in a certain amount of time, is no fun.

This use of the word *budget* made its debut in 1733, in Great Britain, when the Chancellor of the Exchequer, Sir Robert Walpole, presented his annual estimate of the revenue and expenditure projected for the coming year. He was then said to have "opened the budget." The phrase was a reference to the original meaning of *budget*, which in the 1430s, when the word was borrowed from French, meant a pouch, a bag, a satchel, a wallet, usually made of leather. *Budget* was borrowed from Middle French *bougette* "small bag, wallet," diminutive of *bouge* "leather bag or pouch."

Thanks to Sir Robert Walpole's transfer of the meaning of *budget* from "a wallet" to "an estimate of finances," a *budget* always referred to a government's annual statement of the country's finances until the 1900s. After the turn of the century the word's use expanded and newspapers began writing about "workmen's budgets," and "family budgets."

light BULBS

Q. How many waiters does it take to change a light bulb?

A. None. Even a burned-out light bulb can't catch a waiter's eye.

A *bulb* is any object with a round, swollen end, such as a light bulb or the bulb of a thermometer. This meaning first surfaced in medicine, mainly anatomy, in the 1700s, in reference to certain roundish structures of the body, such as the *olfactory bulb* and the *auditory bulb*. Then, in the early 1800s, people began to call the roundish incandescent electric light lamp a *light bulb*.

But *bulb* entered English in 1568 and was synonymous with "an onion." *Bulb* was borrowed from Latin *bulbus* "onion, bulbous root," from Greek *bolbós*, of the same meaning but of uncertain origin. Later, in the 1600s, *bulb* was also applied to the swollen underground stem of the onion or some other plant. Thereafter, any object that had a shape that resembled or suggested the shape of an onion was called a *bulb*. And so a word meaning "an onion" evolved into a word for a clown's nose and the subject of a thousand electric light jokes.

A, a
B, b
C, c
D, d
E, e
F, f
G, g
H, h
I, i
J, j
K, k
L, l
M, m
N, n
O, o
P, p
Q, q
R, r
S, s
T, t
U, u
V, v
W, w
X, x
Y, y
Z, z

A, a

B, b

C, c

D, d

E, e

F, f

G, g

H, h

I, i

J, j

K, k

L, l

M, m

N, n

O, o

P, p

Q, q

R, r

S, s

T, t

U, u

V, v

W, w

X, x

Y, y

Z, z

BULLDOZE

Bulldoze first appeared in 1876 in an American newspaper as a noun meaning "a severe flogging," and was applied specifically to the whipping of black slaves. The word was a compound of *bull* and *dose*, the whipping being considered "a dose fit for a bull." As a verb, *bulldoze* is recorded since 1880 with the spelling *bulldose*. The use is illustrated in the *Saturday Review* of July 9, 1881: "To 'bull-dose' a negro in the Southern States means to flog him to death, or nearly to death." The word was clearly a vestige of the cruel treatment of slaves before the Civil War. An extended use also appears in the same issue of the *Saturday Review*: "A 'bull-dose' means a large efficient dose of any sort of medicine or punishment." The figurative use of the verb, "to use great force against any obstacle," appeared in the 1890s, as in E. A. Bartlett's *Battlefields of Thessaly* (1897): " . . . English public opinion has been 'bulldozed' and misled."

The derivative *bulldozer*, spelled at first *bull-doser* and meaning one who bulldozes or intimidates by violence, also appeared in 1876. The current sense of a large machine for moving earth, rocks, tree stumps, etc., was derived apparently from the figurative use of the verb, "to use great force against an obstacle," but is not found until the 1930s, after such machines became common, especially the Caterpillar brand.

BULLY

In the mid-1500s, when *bully* first came into use, it was a term of endearment, applied to men as well as to women, and meaning approximately "darling, sweetheart." *Bully* was borrowed into English from Dutch *boel* "lover, brother," related to Middle High German *buole* "friend, relative, lover." It was often found in Shakespeare in this sense, as in *Henry V*, where Pistol says of the king, "I kiss his dirty shoe, and from my heart-strings I love the lovely bully." And in *A Midsummer Night's Dream*, Quince addresses Bottom with "What sayest thou, bully Bottom?"

A, a

B, b

C, c

D, d

E, e

F, f

G, g

H, h

I, i

J, j

K, k

L, l

M, m

N, n

O, o

P, p

Q, q

R, r

S, s

T, t

U, u

V, v

W, w

X, x

Y, y

Z, z

In the 1600s the word's meaning evolved into "a stylish and dashing man, often blustering or swaggering," especially in such phrases as *bully roister* and *bully ruffian*. "Snatch the money like a bully ruffian," wrote John Dryden in his 1668 play *An Evening's Love*. By 1688 this meaning was narrowed down to "a swashbuckling swordsman or adventurer, a hector," which, by influence of the word *bull*, developed into the current meaning, "one who attacks or terrorizes the weak," as in President Lyndon B. Johnson's comment on appeasement: "If you let a bully come in your front yard, he'll be on your porch the next day and the day after that."

BUSINESS *as usual*

There was something prophetic in the original meaning of the word *business*, since it meant "anxiety, distress, uneasiness" when first used in Old English in the form *bisinisse*. The word was derived from Old English *bisig* "anxious, eager, careful," related to Middle Low German *besich* (modern Low German *besig*) and Middle Dutch *bezich* (modern Dutch *bezig*), both meaning "occupied, busy." Curiously, the literal meaning of *business*, "the quality or state of being busy with something," didn't appear until about 1350. This meaning was generalized around 1400 to "anything that keeps one busy," especially serious work as opposed to a pastime or recreation, as in *Business should alternate with pleasure.*

The most common meaning today, "a commercial enterprise," is first found in the 1700s, often attributively in the sense of "dealing with or involving commerce," as in *businessman, business ethics*. While nobody in business will deny that commercial dealings are often accompanied by anxiety, distress, and uneasiness—President Calvin Coolidge proudly said, "The chief business of the American people is business."

A, a

B, b

C, c

D, d

E, e

F, f

G, g

H, h

I, i

J, j

K, k

L, l

M, m

N, n

O, o

P, p

Q, q

R, r

S, s

T, t

U, u

V, v

W, w

X, x

Y, y

Z, z

BUXOM *beauty*

You won't find the word *buxom* applied to men. Since the 1800s, only women have been called *buxom*, that is, "healthily plump and of ample figure."

Surprisingly, the original meaning of *buxom* had nothing to do with women, or beauty, or a full figure. When *buxom* first appeared, in the 1100s, the word meant "obedient, compliant, pliant," in sentences like *Our servants are buxom and meek. The consuls swore to become buxom to the king.* The word's earliest form was *buhsum*, formed from Old English *buh-*, *būgan* "to bow" (the source of modern English *bow* "to bend") and—*sum* "-some" (as in *lonesome, troublesome*). So basically *buxom* meant "bowsome," i.e., given to bowing, compliant, obedient.

This servile meaning shifted in the mid-1300s to the more favorable one of "courteous, obliging, amiable," initiating a pattern of amelioration that led in the 1500s to such meanings as "good-tempered, cheerful," "wholesome and healthy in appearance," and finally the modern meaning, "healthily plump and ample-figured." By the 1800s, the latter was applied mostly to women, as in Sir Walter Scott's novel *Peveril of the Peak* (1823): "She was a buxom dame, about thirty."

C, c

A, a

B, b

C, c

D, d

E, e

F, f

G, g

H, h

I, i

J, j

K, k

L, l

M, m

N, n

O, o

P, p

Q, q

R, r

S, s

T, t

U, u

V, v

W, w

X, x

Y, y

Z, z

CADETS

Before the French Revolution, younger sons of French nobles often joined the army to train for a military career. Since the French word for a younger son was *cadet,* derived from Latin *capitellum* "small head (of a family)," it was in the sense of a younger son or brother that *cadet* first came into English, in 1610. In 1646 Sir Thomas Browne wrote about two Biblical youths: "Joseph was the youngest of twelve, and David the eleventh son, and but the cadet of Jesse," meaning the youngest son. Soon thereafter, in the early 1650s, the word began to be applied to young gentlemen who joined the army without a commission, as did the younger sons of the French nobility. From this came the current meaning of a young trainee in a military or naval academy. In the United States, the term *cadet* is used only for officers in training for the Coast Guard, Air Force, and Army. The U.S. Navy and Marine Corps use the term *midshipman.*

framed CADRES

The term *cadre,* which had been in English since the 1800s, was co-opted by Soviet communists after the Russian Revolution and used to refer to any worker or group of workers trained to promote communism. This meaning came into English in the 1930s and was explained in 1931 in the *Times Literary Supplement:* "The six 'cadres' chosen as typical—Communist, Young Communist, shock worker, cultural worker, collectivized peasant and Red Army man—represent the sum total of the Soviet Government's supporters."

The Communist usage derived from an earlier military meaning, recorded since the 1850s, "the permanent framework of a regiment or squadron." Cadres were used by an army or air force to draw on the reserves in an emergency.

The word's earliest and original meaning was neither military nor Communist.

A *cadre* meant simply "a framework or panel," and was first used by Sir Walter Scott in the Introduction to his poem *The Lay of the Last Minstrel* (1832): "This species of *cadre*, or frame, afterwards afforded the poem its name." Borrowed from the French *cadre* "frame, picture frame, panel," it was this meaning that led to that of the framework of a regiment or squadron.

CAMERA *obscura*

In *On Photography* (1977), the essayist Susan Sontag wrote: "Using a camera appeases the anxiety which the work-driven feel . . . when they are on vacation and supposed to be having fun." The word *camera* in this sentence is so familiar to us that it requires no explanation. Yet before the 1840s, the meaning of *camera* was unrelated to optics or photography.

Camera was first used in the early 1700s as a term in architecture meaning "an arched or vaulted building or upper gallery," borrowed from the Latin meaning "vault, arched chamber." A library building of this type at Oxford University was called *The Camera*. Later on the word was generalized to "chamber, room" and in the early 1700s was "a legislative or council chamber." The turning point in the word's evolution came with the invention of the daguerreotype, an early process for making portrait photographs invented by Louis J. Daguerre, which used a 'chamber' called the *camera*. This word was shortened from the Latin term *camera obscura*, literally, "dark chamber," an optical instrument that admitted light into a darkened chamber.

CANDID CANDIDATES

Despite our familiarity with the word *candid* in the sense of frank, open, sincere, *candid* came late into English (it's first found in print in 1630) and doesn't appear in the Bible, Shakespeare, or other classical sources. Originally the word meant "white" (as in *a candid robe, candid milk, the candid snow*), and was borrowed from Latin *candidus* "white, clear, pure." Various

A, *a*

B, *b*

C, c

D, *d*

E, *e*

F, *f*

G, *g*

H, *h*

I, *i*

J, *j*

K, *k*

L, *l*

M, *m*

N, *n*

O, *o*

P, *p*

Q, *q*

R, *r*

S, *s*

T, *t*

U, *u*

V, *v*

W, *w*

X, *x*

Y, *y*

Z, *z*

figurative meanings developed: "pure, clear, stainless" (before 1667), "fair, impartial" (1643), and finally "frank, open, straight-forward, sincere" (in 1675), as in Oliver Goldsmith's *Retaliation*: "Let us be candid, and speak out our mind." The sense of "un-posed," applied to photographs and photography, as in *candid pictures, candid camera*, is first recorded in 1929.

The sense-development of *candid* shows how a literal meaning ("white") takes on figurative or metaphorical senses ("pure, clear; fair, impartial; frank, sincere").

The connection of *candid* to *candidate* is worth mentioning. *Candidate*, meaning a person seeking an office or position, first appeared in English in 1609 as a borrowing from Latin *candida-tus*, literally, "clothed in white" (from *candidus* "white"), a term applied in ancient Rome to aspirants to political office because they wore a white toga.

CANT, CHANT

The secret language or jargon used by professional beggars, thieves, hustlers, etc., is called *cant*. The word in this sense is first recorded in 1706, in an edition of Edward Phillips's *New World of Words*. An earlier meaning (1640) was "the speech of beggars, etc., especially a whining manner of speaking used by beggars." This meaning was extended in 1709 to mean "insin-cere or affected language, pretending to be a sign of goodness or piety." In 1716, Joseph Addison lumped *cant* and *hypocrisy* together as synonyms.

The original meaning of *cant*, recorded about 1501, was "singing, musical sound," as in "Cant and Vision are to the Ear and Eye, the same as Tickling is to the Touch" (1704, Jonathan Swift, *A Tale of a Tub*). This meaning represents Old North French *cant*, corre-sponding to Old French *chant* (the source of English *chant*), both from Latin *cantus* "singing, song, chant," derived from the verb *canere* "to sing," the source of English *cantor*.

English *cant* thus developed in meaning from a "song or chant" to the "singsong of whining beggars" to "insincere language" to "the language or jargon of beggars, thieves, etc." The word is an example of pejoration, a gradual worsening of meaning that has never affected its doublet, *chant*.

CANVASSING *for votes*

What does canvassing for votes have to do with *canvas*, the cloth used for sails and tents? The two words are clearly the same, despite their slightly different spellings. (As a matter of fact, *canvas*, the cloth, was spelled with two *s*'s for some 300 years before it dropped the second *s* in the 1800s.)

The standard meaning of *canvass*, "to solicit votes or support," has been traced to the 1600s, but the first recorded meaning of this verb, occurring in 1508, was "to toss someone into the air in a canvas sheet or garment as a sport or punishment." Shakespeare used it in this sense before 1616 in *Henry VI, Part 1*: "I'll canvas thee in thy broad Cardinal's hat, if thou proceed in this thy insolence."

This meaning is followed in 1530 by the figurative sense "to shake up (a subject or matter) so as to investigate thoroughly its parts; to discuss or scrutinize fully," as in Disraeli's novel *Sybil* (1845): "It was canvassed and criticized sentence by sentence." The next definition was most likely "to try to obtain information by questioning or scrutinizing" and finally "to solicit votes, support, contributions, orders for goods, etc." Samuel Johnson, author of the great *Dictionary of the English Language,* explained the connection between the two meanings as the result of "a mixing up of the notions of soliciting and of discussing or investigating."

A, *a*

B, *b*

C, *c*

D, *d*

E, *e*

F, *f*

G, *g*

H, *h*

I, *i*

J, *j*

K, *k*

L, *l*

M, *m*

N, *n*

O, *o*

P, *p*

Q, *q*

R, *r*

S, *s*

T, *t*

U, *u*

V, *v*

W, *w*

X, *x*

Y, *y*

Z, *z*

A, a

B, b

C, c

D, d

E, e

F, f

G, g

H, h

I, i

J, j

K, k

L, l

M, m

N, n

O, o

P, p

Q, q

R, r

S, s

T, t

U, u

V, v

W, w

X, x

Y, y

Z, z

CAPTION

The word *caption* means a heading or title, as of a chapter or a page. This meaning is first found in 1789 in the writings of James Madison. *Caption* can also mean the title or text below an illustration, or what is also called a subtitle. This meaning appeared in the 1920s to describe the text under a photograph or under a picture on a movie screen.

The earliest meaning of *caption*, though, was not a heading or subtitle. In 1382, when the word first appeared, it meant "a taking or catching; seizure, capture," as in "The caption of some of the most violent appeased the riot" (1837, *New Month Magazine*). So how did *caption* become "a heading or title"?

The change occurred partly through the influence of the similar-sounding Latin word *caput* "head," and partly through an earlier legal use (1670), *certificate or note of caption*, referring to a part of a document showing where it was to be executed. The phrase "certificate of caption" was sometimes interpreted as "the beginning or heading of a warrant, indictment, etc."

Students of word history take note: *caption* was borrowed from Latin *captiōnem* "a taking," from *capit-*, stem of *capere* "to take," the source of English *captive* and *capture*. That is why the earliest meaning of *caption* was "a taking or catching; capture" and not the mistaken—but alas, fully established—meaning of "heading or title."

CARTEL

A *cartel* is an association of rival business groups created to fix prices, regulate output, and curb competition. A cartel is also called a syndicate, a trust, and an oligopoly.

When *cartel* first appeared in English, in 1560, its meaning was "a written challenge; a letter of defiance" borrowed from French *cartel*, literally, "little card," which borrowed it from Italian *cartello*, a diminutive of *carta* "paper letter, bill," from Latin *carta, charta* "paper, card." In 1693, the word appeared with the general meaning of a written or printed paper or card, as in "He ordered a cartel with some Greek verses . . . to be affixed to the frame [of a painting]." (1762, Sir Horace Walpole, *Anecdotes of Painting*). And in 1696 it was used to mean "a written agreement for the exchange or ransom of prisoners between armies or countries."

So how did the current meaning of *cartel* arise? In 1887, two German parties, the Conservatives and the National Liberals, agreed in writing to form a coalition to advance Chancellor Bismarck's imperial policies. Their agreement was called in German *Kartell,* translated to English as *cartel* in 1889. Then, in 1902, the term was extended to not just a written agreement, but any agreement between two or more business firms to combine into a syndicate in order to control prices and regulate output.

CATASTROPHE

A *catastrophe* is a sudden major disaster, such as a devastating hurricane or flood. In a looser application to misfortunes, some consider a computer malfunction or an overcooked dinner a catastrophe; somewhere between these extremes is the use of the word by D. H. Lawrence: "Oh, what a catastrophe for man when he cut himself off from the rhythm of the year, from his unison with the sun and the earth."

In the mid-1500s, when the word passed from Greek into English, *catastrophe* was a literary and dramatic term meaning "the concluding event of a story or drama; the outcome or upshot of a plot." This was how Spenser, in *The Shepheardes Calendar* (1579) used it: "This tale is much like that in Aesop's fables, but the catastrophe and end is far different." In the 1600s, the original meaning was generalized to "a concluding event, upshot, conclusion," as in "This miserable catastrophe to a miserable career" (1850, Washington Irving, *Mahomet and His Successors*).

A, a

B, b

C, c

D, d

E, e

F, f

G, g

H, h

I, i

J, j

K, k

L, l

M, m

N, n

O, o

P, p

Q, q

R, r

S, s

T, t

U, u

V, v

W, w

X, x

Y, y

Z, z

The current meaning of *catastrophe*, used since 1748, came about by associating final events with calamitous endings. This notion was probably influenced by the meaning of the Greek word *katastrophe* "an overturning, reversal, (literally) a downturn," which was the source of the English word and which implied an unexpected, disastrous reversal. The Greek word derived from *kata-* "down" + *strephein* "to turn," the source of English *strophe*.

CATTLE, CHATTEL, CAPITAL

These words are triplets, deriving ultimately from the same source, Medieval Latin *capitale*, meaning "principal money, property, wealth, capital," from Latin *capitalis* "of the head, chief, principal," from *caput* "head." Even though these triplets carried the same or similar meanings, they were not identical in form because they came into English by way of various intermediate dialects of French. *Cattle* came from Old North French *catel*; *chattel* came from Parisian Old French *chatel*; and *capital* came from a direct Old French borrowing of Medieval Latin *capitale*. For a while the three forms coexisted as synonyms; but eventually they began to clash with each other. There were only two choices for them: either they give up the fight and disappear from the scene or they survive by developing specialized meanings.

Naturally they chose the latter, since words, like everything else, prefer survival over extinction. And so, because in the Middle Ages personal property and wealth were measured by the number of cows, bulls, and other livestock in one's possession, by the 1500s the word *cattle* came to mean farm animals or livestock, which is the word's meaning today. Meanwhile, *chattel* retained its legal sense of "property that is not real estate, movable property," while *capital* went on to mean "chief, principal" (as in *capital city*), "involving loss of the head" (as in *capital punishment*, since beheading was the common method of execution), and "upper-case" (as in *capital letters*, since such letters appear at the head of sentences).

A, a

B, b

C, c

D, d

E, e

F, f

G, g

H, h

I, i

J, j

K, k

L, l

M, m

N, n

O, o

P, p

Q, q

R, r

S, s

T, t

U, u

V, v

W, w

X, x

Y, y

Z, z

CAVALIER

A *cavalier* attitude, tone, etc., is one that is casual, offhand, light-hearted. The American humorist Jack Handey used the word in 1991 in an oft-repeated one-liner: "If trees could scream, would we be so cavalier about cutting them down?" He added: "We might, if they screamed all the time for no good reason."

In 1589, when the word came into English, a *cavalier* was a noun synonymous with a dashing military man, a knight on horseback, and later a courtly gentleman or gallant. The word was borrowed from French *cavalier* (literally) "horseman," from Italian *cavalliere*, from Late Latin *caballārius,* from Latin *caballus* "horse." It is a doublet of *chevalier*, a word meaning "knight" that was spared the pejorative fate of *cavalier.*

In the 1640s, swashbuckling royalists who fought on the side of Charles I against the Parliament started to be called disparagingly Cavaliers. They were criticized for their swaggering ways, long curls, and carefree, offhand style, what today would be called "laid back." So began the downgrading of *cavalier*, which resulted in the adjective changing from "brave, gallant" to "careless in manner, free and easy, offhand."

The adjective *cavalier* first showed up in the sense of "haughty, arrogant" in Tobias Smollett's 1751 novel *The Adventures of Peregrine Pickle* ("This cavalier declaration of the young man . . ."). The development shows a gradual depreciation of meaning, from "brave" to "offhand" to "haughty."

CHAFING *at the bit*

In an essay about Mark Twain and his fictional character Huckleberry Finn, the poet and novelist Robert Penn Warren wrote in 1981: "Huck's real story does not even begin until he . . . in the well-meaning clutches of the Widow and Miss Watson, begins to chafe under the ministrations." To *chafe* under some restraint or obstacle means "to display irritation, ruffle in temper, fume or

A, a

B, b

C, c

D, d

E, e

F, f

G, g

H, h

I, i

J, j

K, k

L, l

M, m

N, n

O, o

P, p

Q, q

R, r

S, s

T, t

U, u

V, v

W, w

X, x

Y, y

Z, z

fret." This meaning, first recorded in 1526, developed over a period of two hundred years from the word's earliest meaning, which was "to warm or heat," recorded since the 1300s and taken directly with the borrowed word from Old French *chaufer* "to make warm, heat."

The word developed next into "to inflame the feelings, excite" (about 1325), then "to rub (a person's limbs, etc.) so as to restore warmth" (about 1440). The third was the common meaning, "to make sore by rubbing, to abrade" (1425), as in "How easily the tender skin gets chafed" (1861, Florence Nightingale, *Nursing*). From there, the word easily made the jump from literal to figurative "irritated."

The expression *chafe at the bit*, meaning "to wait impatiently or restlessly to start," refers figuratively to a horse's habit of biting on the bit in its mouth in its eagerness to take off, and is a variant of the older phrase *champ at the bit*.

CHEERS!

A *cheer*, as any cheerleader will tell you, is a shout of approbation or encouragement, as in this salute written (not shouted) by the British novelist E. M. Forster in *What I Believe* (1939): "So, two cheers for Democracy: one because it admits variety and two because it permits criticism."

The earliest meaning of the word *cheer* (before 1225) was "the face," borrowed in Middle English from Old French *chere* "face," from Late Latin *cara* "face, countenance" as in Spenser's *Faerie Queene* (1596): "The devilish hag by changes of my cheer / Perceived my thought." Next came "disposition, mood, frame of mind, as shown by one's demeanor or expression," a sense qualified by adjectives like *good, glad, sad, dreary,* etc., as in Shakespeare's *Sonnets* (1609): "If they sing, 'tis with so dull a cheer." Because the word was frequently used with *good, glad, merry,* and the like, its meaning evolved into "gladness, joy, mirth." The current use of *cheer,* "shout of approbation or encouragement," that every sports fan or spectator is familiar with was first recorded in 1720, in Daniel Defoe's *Captain Singleton*: "We gave them a Chear [sic], as the Seamen call it."

CLERK *or cleric?*

In its earliest incarnation (about 1050), *clerk* meant exactly what *cleric* means today: "an ordained minister of the Christian church, a churchman, a clergyman." A clerk was a highly respected person in the hierarchy of professionals in medieval England and performed all the writing and secretarial work. The word *clerk* became synonymous with "scholar" and "scribe." Gradually *clerk* was applied to high-level notaries, secretaries, accountants, and writers, especially to officers of a court or legislature who were entrusted with keeping the records and performing routine business, as in *town clerk.*

After the 1500s, *clerk* dropped a notch on the employment scale, becoming the designation of anyone employed in any office to keep accounts, maintain records, and the like. In his *Autobiography* (before 1790), Benjamin Franklin wrote: "He propos'd to take me over as his Clerk, to keep his Books (in which he would instruct me), copy his Letters, and attend the Store." By the 1800s the word was applied mostly to someone employed to attend to customers, such as a salesperson at a store (*a store clerk*).

It's interesting to note that the adjective *clerical* can refer to both clerks and clerics. A clerk is said to have a *clerical job* and be on the *clerical staff* of an office; but only a cleric can wear a *clerical collar* or belong to a *clerical order.*

CLINIC

When it first came into English, a *clinic* meant "one who is confined to a sickbed; a bedridden person; a hospital patient." The word was borrowed in 1626 from Latin *clīnicus* "of or

A, a
B, b
C, c
D, d
E, e
F, f
G, g
H, h
I, i
J, j
K, k
L, l
M, m
N, n
O, o
P, p
Q, q
R, r
S, s
T, t
U, u
V, v
W, w
X, x
Y, y
Z, z

pertaining to a bed," from Greek *klīnikós*, derived from *klīnē* "bed," from *klīnein* "to incline, lean."

No major change occurred in the word's development until the 1840s, when the original meaning of "a bedridden patient" was extended to "medical instruction at the bedside of a hospital patient." This might have remained the word's final sense had not the influence of French *clinique* and German *Klinik* entered the picture. The French and German terms, borrowed from the Latin and Greek, had extended the meaning of "medical instruction at a hospital" to "a part of a hospital where patients receive specialized treatment." This meaning passed into English in 1889, in such uses as *a diabetic clinic, a dental clinic, a children's clinic.*

The medical use was transferred in the 1920s to a generalized use meaning "any group that meets for instruction in or study of a particular subject; a seminar," as in *a writing clinic, a reading clinic, a football-coaching clinic.*

CLONE

In *The Boys from Brazil*, a 1978 movie based on an earlier novel of the same title by Ira Levin, the Nazi "Angel of Death," Dr. Josef Mengele, creates 94 *clones* of Adolf Hitler in order to create a new breed of Nazis to take over the world. That film preceded by some twenty years the actual cloning of a mammal, Dolly the sheep, which made *clone* a household word internationally.

Let's backtrack a hundred years. It was in 1903 that *clone* came into the language as a technical term in botany meaning "a group of plants propagated from transplanted parts of an original stock (by using grafts, bulbs, etc.)." The word was borrowed from Greek *klón* "twig," related to *kládos* "sprout, branch." In the 1920s, the word was expanded to encompass any group of cells or organisms produced asexually from a sexually produced ancestor.

The current biological meaning, "a person, animal, or any organism developed asexually from a single somatic, or body, cell of its parent and therefore genetically identical to the parent," represents a huge leap from the 1920s meaning, since the donor cell is no longer a specialized sex cell but a cell from the parent body.

In the 1980s the word became widely applied informally to any person or thing that is a close imitation or replica of another, such as impersonators of Elvis Presley being dubbed *Elvis clones*, and duplicates of well-known computer systems being called *PC clones, IBM clones, Unix clones*, and so on. This use has become mainly pejorative, implying a cheap, tawdry imitation of the genuine article.

So we have in *clone* a two-faced word: one is a facetious synonym of crass imitation and duplication, the other a serious term for the scientific replication of humans.

Such a word, having one favorable and one unfavorable meaning, is often popularly called a "Janus word," after Janus, the Roman god of doorways who faces two ways.

CONCOCT

To *concoct* a story, a scheme, a fraud, etc., means to fabricate it. "In modern America," writes the humorist Calvin Trillin in *Uncivil Liberties* (1982), "anyone who attempts to write satirically . . . finds it difficult to concoct a situation so bizarre that it may not actually come to pass while his article is still on the presses."

Concoct came from Latin into English in 1533 with the meaning "to digest (food) in the stomach," as in Charles Lamb's *Popular Fallacies* (1833): "We cannot concoct our food with interruptions." *Concoct* was borrowed from Latin *concoct-*, the stem of *concoquere* "boil together, digest," from *com-* "together" +

A, a
B, b
C, c
D, d
E, e
F, f
G, g
H, h
I, i
J, j
K, k
L, l
M, m
N, n
O, o
P, p
Q, q
R, r
S, s
T, t
U, u
V, v
W, w
X, x
Y, y
Z, z

A, a
B, b
C, c
D, d
E, e
F, f
G, g
H, h
I, i
J, j
K, k
L, l
M, m
N, n
O, o
P, p
Q, q
R, r
S, s
T, t
U, u
V, v
W, w
X, x
Y, y
Z, z

coquere "to cook." Another meaning was "to prepare (a drink, soup, etc.) by mixing various ingredients," as in John Evelyn's *A Philosophical Discourse of Earth*: "Compost should be thoroughly concocted, aired, of a scent agreeable."

Today's use of the word is a figurative extension of this earlier meaning. It was first recorded in 1792, in Mary Wollstonecraft's *Vindication of the Rights of Woman*: "They maintain [opinions] with a degree of obstinacy that would surprise even the person who concocted them."

grand CONCOURSE

A *concourse* is an open space through which many people regularly pass. This use of the word was originally an Americanism, first recorded in 1862 in reference to the wide-open Sheep Meadow of New York's Central Park. It was later applied to the main hall of the Grand Central Terminal in midtown Manhattan, still called the *main concourse.*

The word's earliest meaning, found in 1382 in the Wycliffe Bible, was "a confluence or flocking together of people; a crowd," as in Edward Gibbon's *The Decline and Fall of the Roman Empire* (1781): "The main body is . . . increased by the accidental concourse of idle or dependent plebeians."

How did "a confluence or assemblage of people or things" lead to the modern meaning of "an open space or central hall"? Because crowds would congregate in large, open spaces, people began to identify such spaces with the crowds that flocked to them. The notion of a *concourse* of people thus became that of the *concourse* they filled. A linguistic explanation may be that the current use of *concourse* was strongly influenced by the word *course*, as in *a ship's course, a race course* (a meaning attested since 1380). The word came into English from Old French *concours*, a borrowing of Latin *concursus* "a running together, confluence," from *concurrere* "to run or come together."

CONTACT
See TACT

COUTH
See UNCOUTH

CRAFTY *and* CUNNING

These two words are examples of the process of pejoration—a degradation of meaning. *Crafty* means "skillfully using deceitful or underhand schemes," as used by James Madison in this sentence, written in 1822, and inscribed in the Madison Memorial Hall of the Library of Congress: "Learned institutions . . . throw that light over the public mind which is the best security against crafty & dangerous encroachments on the public liberty." *Cunning* means "skilled in devising or carrying out evil schemes," as used in the poet William Blake's *A Cradle Song* (1789):

> "O the cunning wiles that creep
> In thy little heart asleep!
> When thy little heart doth wake
> Then the dreadful night shall break."

Both *crafty* and *cunning* were originally words of praise and commendation. *Crafty* developed from Old English `cræftig` "strong, powerful, mighty," a word found in other Germanic languages, such as Old High German *chreftig* (Modern German *kräftig*). In its earliest use, in Old English, *crafty* meant "skillful, clever, showing skill or cleverness," as in *crafty hands, a crafty dog*. However, by the 1380s, it appeared in such phrases as *a crafty knave, crafty schemes*.

Cunning derived from Old English *cunnan* "to know, be able, can," the source of modern English *couth* and *uncouth*. *Cunning* first appeared in Middle English about 1325 with the meaning "possessing knowledge, learned," followed in 1382 by "possess-

A, a

B, b

C, c

D, d

E, e

F, f

G, g

H, h

I, i

J, j

K, k

L, l

M, m

N, n

O, o

P, p

Q, q

R, r

S, s

T, t

U, u

V, v

W, w

X, x

Y, y

Z, z

ing or showing skill; able, skillful, clever," as in *cunning crafts-men, cunning workmanship*. But by 1590, the meaning shifted to "skillful in devising underhanded or evil schemes," as in *cunning wiles, cunning thieves, cunning craftiness*.

CRAZY

After the poet Ezra Pound was declared insane in 1946 and confined in a hospital in Washington, D.C., Ernest Hemingway remarked, "Pound's crazy. All poets are ... They have to be. You don't put a poet like Pound in a loony bin." Pound's own comment was, "America is a lunatic asylum."

The association of the word *crazy* with mental illness or insanity is relatively recent, first appearing in a 1617 letter in Thomas Birch's *The Court and Times of James I* (1848): "He was noted to be crazy and distempered before." This meaning developed from the earlier ones of "broken down, diseased, sickly" (1576), which was a figurative use of "cracked or flawed, damaged, impaired" (1583), as in "The house is crazy ... and will not stand very long" (1776, Adam Smith, *The Wealth of Nations*).

Crazy was derived from the verb *craze*, whose earliest meaning, about 1369, was "to break in pieces, to shatter." The verb shifted to a noun use in the 1500s, with such meanings as "a flaw, defect" (1534) and "a crack, breach" (1587). The meaning "an insane or irrational fancy, a mania" didn't appear until 1813, chiefly in the weakened sense of a whimsical, usually temporary enthusiasm, as in *a craze for antiques, the latest craze in sports*.

Craze came into English from a Scandinavian source, such as Swedish *krasa* "to crack, crackle." Ultimately, *crazy* and *craze* carry the idea of a crack or break in an object, a body, or the mind. It's no coincidence that the slang terms for going or becoming crazy include *to crack up* or *be cracked*, and that a crazy person is called a *crackpot*.

CROTCHET

A *crotchet*, as anyone who has a crotchety relative knows, is defined as "an odd, whimsical, or peculiar notion; a fancy or whim," as exemplified in Robert Burton's *Anatomy of Melancholy* (1638): "That castle in the air, that crotchet, that whimsey."

This meaning is first recorded in 1573, and, according to the *Oxford English Dictionary* (*OED*), it may have been based on the notion of "a mental twist or crook," derived from the original meaning of *crotchet*, "an architectural ornament in the form of curled leaves or branches" (about 1394).

Alternatively, the current meaning might be a figurative use of an earlier one (about 1430), "a hook or hooked instrument, especially a small hook for fastening things." So when Matthew Arnold wrote in 1861, "Opinions which have no ground in reason . . . mere crotchets, or mere prejudices," he may have had in mind the image of a hook on which to hang one's opinions.

Crotchet was borrowed from Old French *crochet* "small hook," diminutive of *croche, croc* "hook," of Germanic origin (compare Old Norse *krokr* "hook," Old High German *krācho* "hooked tool").

A, a
B, b
C, c
D, d
E, e
F, f
G, g
H, h
I, i
J, j
K, k
L, l
M, m
N, n
O, o
P, p
Q, q
R, r
S, s
T, t
U, u
V, v
W, w
X, x
Y, y
Z, z

D, d

A, *a*

B, *b*

C, *c*

D, *d*

E, *e*

F, *f*

G, *g*

H, *h*

I, *i*

J, *j*

K, *k*

L, *l*

M, *m*

N, *n*

O, *o*

P, *p*

Q, *q*

R, *r*

S, *s*

T, *t*

U, *u*

V, *v*

W, *w*

X, *x*

Y, *y*

Z, *z*

DEBACLE

Headline writers love *debacle* (*Spying Debacle at HP, AOL Privacy Debacle, The Enron Debacle*), probably because it takes up a little less space than *disaster* and a lot less than *catastrophe*. Literary writers have also a fondness for this word. The Swiss dramatist Friedrich Dürrenmatt has this line in his play *Portrait of a Planet* (1970): "A major power can afford a military debacle only when it looks like a political victory."

The word's source, French *débâcle*, was formed from the verb *débâcler* "to remove a bar, unbar, free." In 1802, however, the word came into English as "a breaking up of ice in a river." It was a term adopted from geology, where it stood for a sudden, violent rush of water that broke down barriers, like blocks of ice or stone, carrying them away in its destructive path.

The transferred, figurative meaning, "a sudden breakdown of order; a stampede or disaster," appeared first in Thackeray's novel *Vanity Fair* (1847): "The Brunswickers were routed and had fled—their Duke was killed. It was a general *debacle*." This use caught on and was perpetuated by countless writers of fiction.

DEER

The original meaning of *deer* (in Old English *dēor* and early Middle English *der*) was "a beast or any four-legged animal, as distinguished from birds and fishes." Camels, sheep, and other wild or undomesticated animals were all called *deer*. The Old English word came from the same Germanic source as Old Saxon, Old Frisian and Low German *dier*, Middle High German *tier* (modern German *Tier*), Old Norse *dýr*, and Gothic *diuz-, dius*—all meaning a beast or four-legged animal.

The change in the word's meaning, from the general to the specific, occurred in the 1200s, when *deer* began to be rivaled by the word *beast*, which had come into English from Old French as

A, a
B, b
C, c
D, d
E, e
F, f
G, g
H, h
I, i
J, j
K, k
L, l
M, m
N, n
O, o
P, p
Q, q
R, r
S, s
T, t
U, u
V, v
W, w
X, x
Y, y
Z, z

a translation of the Latin *animal*. Since quadrupeds of the family *Cervidae* were much prized by hunters, the word *deer* began to be applied specifically to them, thus allowing *beast* to become the general term for any quadruped, until it too became threatened and eventually practically replaced by the Latin-origin *animal*.

DELUDE
See ELUDE

DEMISE

The search engine Google records over 1,200 instances of a famous quotation attributed to Mark Twain: "Rumors of my demise have been greatly exaggerated." What Mark Twain actually wrote to the *New York Journal* in 1897 was, "The report of my death was an exaggeration."

Yet *demise* has become a fashionable synonym for "death," even though the original meaning of *demise* was not "death" or "termination." In the 1400s, *demise* was a legal term meaning "transfer of an estate by a will," borrowed from Middle French *demise*, literally, "a sending away, a dismissal." Middle French *demise* was derived from Old French *demettre, desmettre* "to send away, put away, dismiss" (from Latin *mittere* "send"). In the 1500s, the term was also used to mean "transfer of sovereignty, as by the death of a sovereign," especially in the phrase *demise of the crown*. Since the cause of the transfer of an estate was the death of the testator, *demise* was popularly extended during the 1700s from "the transfer of the estate of Mr. Smith" to "the death of Mr. Smith." Hence *demise* became synonymous with "death."

DEPRECATE

"Those who profess to favor freedom and yet deprecate agitation," wrote the African-American abolitionist and reformer

A, a
B, b
C, c
D, d
E, e
F, f
G, g
H, h
I, i
J, j
K, k
L, l
M, m
N, n
O, o
P, p
Q, q
R, r
S, s
T, t
U, u
V, v
W, w
X, x
Y, y
Z, z

Frederick Douglass (1818–1895), "are men who . . . want rain without thunder and lightning." In this sentence Douglass used the word *deprecate* in its most current sense, "to show strong disapproval of, to protest against."

The original meaning of *deprecate* was "to pray, supplicate," first recorded in 1624 and used in a 1626 sermon by John Donne: "He falls upon his face . . . and deprecates on their behalf." The word was borrowed from Latin *dēprecāt-, dēprecāri* "to pray against, avert by prayer" (from *dē-* "off, away" + *precāri* "beg earnestly, pray"). The negative Latin meaning "to pray against" came into English in 1629, and before 1649 took on the more general meaning of "to express or show strong disapproval of (a course, plan, action, etc.), as in "No body should deprecate what I had done" (1742, Henry Fielding, *Joseph Andrews*). This became the current meaning.

DIE
See I'm STARVING!

DISINTERESTED, UNINTERESTED
Here's a short lesson on the vagaries of usage.

Usage books are always telling readers to avoid using *disinterested* to mean "not interested, uninterested." The word, they insist, means "impartial, neutral" (as in *a disinterested judge*) and shouldn't be used in a sentence like *Some parents are disinterested in their children's schooling.* Ironically, the oldest meaning of the word (before 1631) was "not interested, unconcerned, uninterested" and so, despite being often criticized, it continues to be used, as in "These walks . . . smack of herding disinterested people around things they don't want to see" (2007, BBC, "A Wolverhampton Wander").

The reverse situation occurred with *uninterested*. This word's oldest meaning, recorded before 1646, was "unbiased, impartial," as in a 1767 letter by the English poet William Cowper: "You know me to be an uninterested person." But by 1771, the word was used in the *Annual Register* in the sense of "unconcerned, indifferent": "He is no cold, uninterested, and uninteresting advocate for the cause he espouses."

DIVAN

Divan is a word found widely in English literature since the mid-1800s, as the name of a kind of a sofa or couch. It's found in Dickens's *The Old Curiosity Shop* (1841): " . . . the bed being soft and comfortable, Mr. Quilp determined to use it . . . as a kind of Divan by day," and in Margaret Forster's *The Bogeyman* (1965): "The cover over her divan was red and white striped cotton."

The original meaning of *divan*, first found in English in 1586, was "an Oriental council of state." The term, a borrowing of Turkish *divān* (from Persian), was applied especially to the privy council in Turkey, presided over by the sultan or his grand vizier. In the 1600s, *divan* came to mean "the hall or council chamber where the Turkish council was held." The long cushioned seats that furnished the hall came in turn to be called *divans*. In the 1800s, *divan* was applied in European countries to any type of couch or sofa without a back or arms.

Divan invites comparison with *ottoman,* a low cushioned seat without a back or arms. The word came into English in 1806 from French *ottomane* "Turkish, of the Turkish or Ottoman empire," apparently so named because the seat was of a style used in the Orient.

A, a

B, b

C, c

D, *d*

E, e

F, f

G, g

H, h

I, i

J, j

K, k

L, l

M, m

N, n

O, o

P, p

Q, q

R, r

S, s

T, t

U, u

V, v

W, w

X, x

Y, y

Z, z

DIVEST

To divest meant in 1583 "to strip of clothing or other covering, unclothe," as in "Divesting herself of her out-of-door attire" (1848, Charles Dickens, *The Haunted Man*).

Divest was an alteration of earlier *devest*, from Old French *devestir* "to unclothe, undress," formed from *de-*"down, off" + *vestir* "to dress," from Latin *vestīre* "to clothe, dress." This extended to a figurative meaning in 1604, "to strip or rid oneself of, throw off," which is found in Shakespeare's *King Lear:* "Now we will divest us both of rule, Interest of Territory, Cares of State."

The financial sense of "to sell off or dispose of a company, property, investment, etc." (the opposite of *invest*) is first recorded in 1961 but widely used ever since, as in "She advises American people to divest their investments in South Africa" (1986, *The Christian Science Monitor*).

See also INVEST

I feel DIZZY

A memorable song in the musical *West Side Story* is the one sung by Maria as she prances before a mirror:

> I feel dizzy,
> I feel sunny,
> I feel fizzy and funny and fine,
> And so pretty,
> Miss America can just resign!

Dizzy, meaning "affected with vertigo, with proneness to fall, giddy," is first found in the language about 1340. The original meaning, occurring in Old English as early as 825, meant "foolish, stupid," and was related to Old Frisian *dusig* "foolish, stupid" and Old High German *tusig* "foolish, weak."

A, a
B, b
C, c
D, d
E, e
F, f
G, g
H, h
I, i
J, j
K, k
L, l
M, m
N, n
O, o
P, p
Q, q
R, r
S, s
T, t
U, u
V, v
W, w
X, x
Y, y
Z, z

The development of meaning from "foolish, stupid" to "affected with vertigo, giddy" can be explained by a perceived absence of mental stability in someone foolish as well as in someone light-headed and unsteady. A foolish person can strike one as giddily confused. The sexist phrase *dizzy blonde*, recorded since 1888 in dialectal American English, seems to equate foolishness and giddiness.

See also GIDDY

DOCILE, DOCTOR

A person who is submissive, easily managed or controlled, is said to be *docile*. The word is frequently used to describe a domesticated animal, such as a horse, a dog, or a cat. As a human characteristic, to be docile is not a much-admired quality in a society that favors and encourages drive and assertiveness.

For some two hundred years before the current meaning of *docile* took root, the word meant something quite positive and admirable. In 1483, in William Caxton's *The Golden Legend,* the word meant "easily or readily taught; willing to learn; teachable," as in *a docile mind, docile readers.* Samuel Johnson, writing in 1751 in *The Rambler,* used it in this sense: "Flattering comparisons of my own proficiency with that of others . . . less docile by nature." In this way the positive meaning slid into a negative one.

Docile was borrowed, through French or Italian, from Latin *docilis* "easily taught," from *docēre* "to teach," the source of *doctor* "teacher." When the word *doctor* came into English in 1303 from Medieval Latin, it was not as a physician but as an early teacher in the Church, and later (1387) as a schoolteacher. Even as late as 1841, Ralph Waldo Emerson used it in this sense: "The wisest doctor is gravelled by the inquisitiveness of a child." It was not until Shakespeare's time that the word was commonly applied to doctors of medicine, as in "Shall I lose my doctor? No, he gives me the...potions" (1602, *The Merry Wives of Windsor*).

DOMINO *theories*

The game of *domino* (or *dominoes*) was not known in English-speaking countries until the turn of the 19th century. Its first mention in English was in 1801: "Domino...a very childish sport, imported from France a few years back."

The word *domino*, however, had been in English since at least 1719, with the meaning "a loose cloak, with a small mask covering the upper part of the face, worn by Venetian noblemen, chiefly at masquerades." The word had been borrowed from French *domino*, originally "a kind of hood worn by canons or priests." The name of this cloak has been traced to a form of Latin *dominus* "master, lord," presumably because the priestly cloak was associated with certain standard Latin phrases, such as *benedicamus Domino* "let us bless the Lord." Most sources agree that the name of the game was coined from the resemblance of the black spots on the rectangular domino tiles to the half-masks with eyeholes worn at masquerades.

Similar to a row of dominoes getting knocked over, the phrase *domino theory* has since been often used as a metaphor for any event that inevitably leads to another. It was popularized in 1954 by President Dwight D. Eisenhower to mean that if one country falls to the enemy (Communism), others will be sure to fall.

A, *a*
B, *b*
C, *c*
D, *d*
E, *e*
F, *f*
G, *g*
H, *h*
I, *i*
J, *j*
K, *k*
L, *l*
M, *m*
N, *n*
O, *o*
P, *p*
Q, *q*
R, *r*
S, *s*
T, *t*
U, *u*
V, *v*
W, *w*
X, *x*
Y, *y*
Z, *z*

A, a

B, b

C, c

D, d

E, e

F, f

G, g

H, h

I, i

J, j

K, k

L, l

· M, m

N, n

O, o

P, p

Q, q

R, r

S, s

T, t

U, u

V, v

W, w

X, x

Y, y

Z, z

DOOM, DOOMSDAY

In his "Ode on a Distant Prospect of Eton College" (1742), the English poet Thomas Gray wrote about his fellow pupils on the playing fields of Eton:

> Alas! Regardless of their doom,
> The little victims play!
> No sense have they of ills to come
> Nor care beyond today.

By *doom* Gray meant "final fate, extinction, death," the word's current meaning.

Doom developed from Old English (about 825) *dōm* "statute, law, decree, ordinance." This was the word's basic sense in Germanic, found in Old High German *tuom,* Old Norse *dómr,* and Gothic *dōms*—all meaning "statute, law." Already in Old English, the word developed the meaning "a judgment or decision, especially one formally pronounced." A *day of doom,* therefore, meant a day of judgment or *doomsday* (recorded before 1200), which was when one's fate or lot was decided or decreed. From this use, the meaning "fate, lot, irrevocable destiny" followed, usually in an adverse sense, leading in 1609 to the meaning "final fate, extinction, death" in Shakespeare's *Sonnet xiv*: "Thy end is Truth's and Beauty's doom."

The verb *to doom* shows a similar development. When it appeared in 1503, it meant "to pronounce judgment on or against," as in "Tribunes with their tongues doom men to death" (1594, Shakespeare, *Titus Andronicus*). By 1603 it had developed the meaning "to destine or consign to some fate or lot," as in Shakespeare's *Hamlet* (1603): "I am thy father's spirit, doomed for a time to walk the night."

pure DRIVEL

Commenting on James Joyce's masterpiece, *Ulysses* (1922), the novelist Edith Wharton wrote in 1923 to the art critic Bernard Berenson: "It's a turgid welter of pornography (the rudest schoolboy kind) and unformed and unimportant drivel." *Drivel,* meaning "silly nonsense," has been a favorite snub or put-down of critics since the 1850s.

The source of *drivel* was the verb *to drivel,* defined in the *OED* as "to let saliva flow from the mouth or nose, as young children and idiots do; to slaver; dribble," found in Middle English before 1325. The Middle English verb *drivelen* developed from Old English *dreflian* (about 1000) "to slaver, dribble," related to Middle English *draf* "dregs."

Not long after that (in 1362) came the transferred sense defined in the *OED* as "to talk childishly or idiotically; to let silly nonsense drop from the lips; to rave." The transferred sense thus existed in English for hundreds of years, but only as a verb; its late appearance as a noun in 1852 may have been due to either an imperfect record of its use or the reluctance of excessively proper writers to print or publish a word felt to be disparaging or derogatory.

A, *a*

B, *b*

C, *c*

D, *d*

E, *e*

F, *f*

G, *g*

H, *h*

I, *i*

J, *j*

K, *k*

L, *l*

M, *m*

N, *n*

O, *o*

P, *p*

Q, *q*

R, *r*

S, *s*

T, *t*

U, *u*

V, *v*

W, *w*

X, *x*

Y, *y*

Z, *z*

E, e

ECCENTRIC

In 1859 the British philosopher John Stuart Mill, in his essay *On Liberty*, gave the highest praise to eccentrics: "That so few now dare to be eccentric, marks the chief danger of the time."

Eccentric first came into English in 1551 as a technical term in astronomy, meaning "a circle in which the earth, sun, etc. deviates from its center." The adjective, meaning "(of a circle or orbit) not having the earth, sun, etc., precisely in its center," followed in 1556. Both uses were borrowed, apparently simultaneously, from Medieval Latin *eccentricus*, derived from Greek *ékkentros* "out of the center," from *ek-, ex-* "out of" + *kéntron* "center."

In 1685, the definition slid from the literal to the figurative. *Eccentric* was defined as "deviating from the usual character or practice; unconventional; whimsical; odd," as in *an eccentric genius, an eccentric millionaire*. The noun, which didn't show up until 1832, is defined as "a person whose conduct is irregular, unconventional, whimsical, or odd." The astronomical meaning of *eccentric* has only historical relevance today, while the figurative meaning is the commonly recognized one, as in this comment in a *Wall Street Journal* editorial: "Proper eccentrics are more likely to shrink from the limelight than to slaver at its prospect."

EGREGIOUS

Egregious is a word whose meaning has turned upside down. Originally (about 1534) it meant "remarkable, distinguished, eminent, excellent," as in "Egregious viceroys of these eastern parts" (1590, Christopher Marlowe, *Tambourlaine*), a meaning found as late as the 1800s, as in "When he wanted to draw . . . someone splendid and egregious, it was Clive he took for a model" (1854, Thackeray, *The Newcomes*). The word was borrowed from Latin *ēgregius* "outstanding, remarkable," (literally) "standing out from the flock."

A, *a*
B, *b*
C, *c*
D, *d*
E, *e*
F, *f*
G, *g*
H, *h*
I, *i*
J, *j*
K, *k*
L, *l*
M, *m*
N, *n*
O, *o*
P, *p*
Q, *q*
R, *r*
S, *s*
T, *t*
U, *u*
V, *v*
W, *w*
X, *x*
Y, *y*
Z, *z*

A, a

B, b

C, c

D, d

E, e

F, f

G, g

H, h

I, i

J, j

K, k

L, l

M, m

N, n

O, o

P, p

Q, q

R, r

S, s

T, t

U, u

V, v

W, w

X, x

Y, y

Z, z

But, still in the 1500s, the word suddenly acquired a negative connotation, perhaps from an ironical use of the original sense, or from "remarkable" being interpreted as "remarkably bad." And so, in 1573, *egregious* came to mean "outrageous, flagrant, gross," as the Elizabethan writer Thomas Nashe pointed out in *Strange News* (1593): "Egregious is never used in english but in the extreme ill part."

This is an example of pejoration, or a bad use driving out a good one. We find it in Shakespeare's *Cymbeline* (before 1616): "Italian Fiend ... egregious murderer," in Milton's *Observations Upon the Articles of Peace* (1649): "Egregious liars and impostors," and in Fielding's *Universal Gallant* (1735): "He would be an egregious Ass who would venture to lay out his Money in them [jewels]."

ELUDE

To elude made its appearance in 1594, with the meaning "to fool, deceive," in William West's *Symbolaeography*: "A witch or hag is she which [is] eluded by a league made with the devil ..." Since one who fools or deceives others often does so by slipping away from their grasp or pursuit, by 1612 *elude* came to mean "to slip away from, evade," as in "Providence has thought fit to elude our curiosity" (1772, Oliver Goldsmith, *The Vicar of Wakefield*). A contemporary writer used the word in a similar vein: "If you want something, it will elude you. If you do not want something, you will get ten of it in the mail" (Anna Quindlen, *Living Out Loud*, 1994).

It's interesting to note that *elude* is part of a set of quadruplets: *elude, allude, delude,* and *illude,* all of which descended from the Latin word *lūdere* "to play." All four words came into English with the basic meaning of "to play with, make sport of, fool, mock," and blossomed in the rarified air of Elizabethan England.

EMOLLIENT

See LENIENT

ENGROSS

To engross meant originally (before 1400) "to buy up wholesale, buy up the whole stock of (a commodity)," as in *to engross corn, to engross great tracts of land.*

This meaning was broadened in the late 1500s into "to gain exclusive possession of, (property, trade, privileges, etc.), monopolize." In the 1600s the word developed the figurative meaning "to occupy exclusively, absorb (the mind, attention, time, etc.)," which evolved in 1709 into the current one of "to absorb or engage the whole attention of (a person)," as in *to be engrossed in a story, a game,* or *a show.*

Engross was formed from the Old French phrase *en gros* "in the lump, by wholesale," from *en* "in" and *gros* "lump, whole amount." The Old French noun *gros* developed from the adjective *gros* "thick, bulky, coarse," from Late Latin *grossus.*

the ENORMITY *of it all*

Webster's Dictionary of English Usage (1989) devotes almost five long columns to defending the use of *enormity* to denote a large or great size, as in *The enormity of the task before us is daunting.* The reason for *Webster's* defense is the insistence of many critics over the last hundred years that this word doesn't mean "enormousness" but "extreme wickedness." *Enormity* was borrowed from Middle French *énormité*, a learned borrowing from Latin *ēnormitātem* "divergence from norm, irregularity," from *ēnormis* "irregular, extraordinary, enormous."

The first use of this word, in 1475, was in the sense of "a breach of law or morality, a transgression or crime," as in "We shall

A, *a*
B, *b*
C, *c*
D, *d*
E, *e*
F, *f*
G, *g*
H, *h*
I, *i*
J, *j*
K, *k*
L, *l*
M, *m*
N, *n*
O, *o*
P, *p*
Q, *q*
R, *r*
S, *s*
T, *t*
U, *u*
V, *v*
W, *w*
X, *x*
Y, *y*
Z, *z*

A, *a*

B, *b*

C, *c*

D, *d*

E, *e*

F, *f*

G, *g*

H, *h*

I, *i*

J, *j*

K, *k*

L, *l*

M, *m*

N, *n*

O, *o*

P, *p*

Q, *q*

R, *r*

S, *s*

T, *t*

U, *u*

V, *v*

W, *w*

X, *x*

Y, *y*

Z, *z*

speak of the particular abuses and enormities of the government" (1755, Samuel Johnson, quoting Edmund Spenser).

Ironically, the meaning of "excess in size, hugeness, vastness," shows up for the first time in a source noted for its enormous exaggerations. The source was *The Surprising Adventures of Baron Munchausen* (1792), by Rudolf Erich Raspe, a book of tall tales. Everything in the story is enormous. For example, in describing a house, he writes:

> It was a prodigious dimension, large enough to contain more stowage than the tun of Heidelberg, and globular like a hazel-nut: in fact, it seemed to be really a hazel-nut grown to a most extravagant dimension, and that a great worm of proportionable enormity had bored a hole in the shell. Through this same entrance I was ushered ...

In the end, this meaning won the day, resulting in the common usage of such phrases as *the enormity of the explosion, the enormity of his good fortune, the enormity of her popularity.*

EPIPHANY

In *Stephen Hero*, an early version of the masterpiece *Portrait of the Artist as a Young Man* (1916), James Joyce gave the word *epiphany* a new literary meaning: "a flash of insight brought on by a trivial incident." After overhearing a trivial fragment of conversation between a young woman and young man, Stephen Daedalus (James Joyce's alter ego), has an epiphany, which leads him to believe "that it was for the man of letters to record these epiphanies with extreme care, seeing that they themselves are the most delicate and evanescent of moments." It was through Joyce's use of the word and his application of the concept in his stories and plays that *epiphany* became a well-known literary term.

The earliest meaning of *epiphany*, recorded before 1310, meant "the manifestation or revelation of the infant Jesus to the Magi, or three Wise Men, in Bethlehem." This came from the Greek *epipháneia* "manifestation." The meaning extended to "a manifestation of some divine or superhuman being," used since before 1667, as in "The Grecians in commemoration of these epiphanies or apparitions of their gods instituted certain Festival-days" (1677, Thomas Gale, *Court Gentiles*).

A figurative extension was first used in the 1800s: "There had been two manifestations or bright epiphanies of the Greek intellect" (1859, Thomas De Quincey, *Style*). It was from this figurative meaning that Joyce adopted the term.

EXCORIATE

"Counterparts Excoriate Red Cross Katrina Effort," blared the headline in the *Washington Post* of April 5, 2006. What this meant was that those in charge of recovery efforts after the devastating Katrina hurricane were scathingly censured. This common and current meaning of *excoriate*, recorded since 1882, has been popular with writers for almost as long. A 1957 book review in the *Times Literary Supplement* observes that "*The Groves of Academe,* an investigation of life on the faculty of an American college . . . excoriates almost every member of the faculty."

The verb *to excoriate* has been in English since 1497 as a technical term meaning "to remove parts of the skin from, to strip, peel, or rub off the skin or hide, to flay," as in "They compliment [their victims] upon . . . the delicacy of their limbs prior to excoriating them" (1826, Benjamin Disraeli, *Vivian Grey*). *Excoriate* was borrowed from Latin *excoriāt-, excoriāre* "to strip off the hide," from *ex-* "off" + *corium* "hide."

Since the 1700s the word has been used in reference to the action of corrosives or of abrasion, as in "My lips were . . . excori-

A, a

B, b

C, c

D, d

E, e

F, f

G, g

H, h

I, i

J, j

K, k

L, l

M, m

N, n

O, o

P, p

Q, q

R, r

S, s

T, t

U, u

V, v

W, w

X, x

Y, y

Z, z

ated as with vinegar and gall" (1855, Charlotte Brontë, *The Professor*). The current meaning of "to censure or upbraid harshly" is a figurative extension of this last use and carries with it a suggestion of the scathing pain involved in stripping off someone's skin.

EXPLODE, EXPLOSION

When *explode* came into English, before 1552, it meant "to reject, discard," as in "But the court *una voce* exploded this reason . . ." (1609, Francis Bacon, *Works*). Similarly, the first evidence of *explosion* is found in 1656, in Thomas Blount's *Glossographia*, where he defines the word: "*Explosion*, a casting off or rejecting, a hissing a thing out."

By "hissing out" Blount was harking back to the Latin meaning of the word. In Latin, *explōdere* was a theatrical word meaning "to clap, hoot, or hiss (an actor, play, etc.) off the stage," and *explōsiōnem* meant "the act of rejecting or driving away by hissing, hooting, etc."

The modern meanings of these words are first found in the 1700s. *Explosion,* meaning "the action of bursting or going off with a loud noise," appeared in 1744, followed in 1790 by *explode* "(of gas, gunpowder, etc.) to burst or go off with a loud noise." The figurative meanings of an outburst or outbreak followed in the early 1800s in such phrases as *to explode with fury, an explosion of laughter*. A more recent figurative meaning of *explosion*, "a sudden and rapid increase or development," came into use in 1953 with *population explosion*. A corresponding verb appeared in 1959 in the *New York Times*: "The population in the Bandung area has exploded from 167,000 . . . to 1,200,000 this year."

EXULT

See INSULT

F, f

A, a
B, b
C, c
D, d
E, e
F, f
G, g
H, h
I, i
J, j
K, k
L, l
M, m
N, n
O, o
P, p
Q, q
R, r
S, s
T, t
U, u
V, v
W, w
X, x
Y, y
Z, z

a **FACT** *of life*

Some of the commonest phrases in English include the word *fact*. We often begin sentences with *The fact is that....* When we require exact information about something, we demand *facts and figures*. To emphasize or assert that we're telling the truth, we say *in fact*, and to clinch the matter (and permit no rejoinder) we say *and that's a fact!*

Dictionaries define the chief meaning of *fact* as "something that actually exists or is the case, as opposed to what is inferred or made up." This meaning is first recorded in 1632, as in "The very great advantage of being a fact and not fiction" (1875, Benjamin Jowett, translation of Plato's *Dialogues*).

The original meaning of *fact*, in the 1500s and 1600s, was "an evil deed, a crime," used mainly in law, in phrases like *to confess the fact*. The word appeared first in 1539, in *Acts of Henry VIII*: "Every such [person] shall be adjudged a traitor, and his fact high treason." This sense is still found in legal use in the phrases *accessory before the fact*, "guilty of aiding and abetting a felony, though not present at its commission," and *accessory after the fact*, "guilty of assisting or concealing one who has committed a felony."

The change from "an evil deed" to "any deed or action" occurred through the influence of the word's Latin source, *factum*, meaning "a thing done, an occurrence, an event," derived from *facere* "to do."

from **FANATIC** *to* **FAN**

"A fanatic," wrote the humorist Finley Peter Dunne in 1890, "is a man that does what he thinks the Lord would do if He knew the facts." His reference to what we might call today a religious fanatic is interesting, since the word *fanatic* had originally a religious connotation.

When first borrowed from Latin *fānāticus*, *fanatic* meant a madman, one thought to be possessed by a deity or demon. Latin *fānāticus*, meaning "mad, frenzied, possessed by a deity," and earlier, "pertaining to a temple," was derived from *fānum* "temple." As late as 1806, a British medical journal informed its readers that "Dr. G gave . . . hints how to treat fanatics, by using topical remedies and poultices."

By the 1600s, the meaning of madman or religious maniac had given way to the more general sense of a person possessed by an extreme and uncritical enthusiasm or zeal for some cause, which is the current meaning.

The de-escalation from a maniacal religious *fanatic* to a garden-variety U.S. *fan* was completed by 1909, when the American opera singer Lulu Glaser was quoted in *Baseball Magazine*: "Anyone with any real blood in his or her . . . veins cannot help being a fan . . . Being a true American and being a fan are synonymous."

FANG

Readers of the American writer Jack London might be familiar with his novel *White Fang* (1906), dealing with the taming of a wild dog in the Klondike. Here's a key sentence, spoken by a native: " . . . his father was a wolf. Wherefore is there in him little dog and much wolf. His fangs be white, and White Fang be his name."

A *fang* is a canine tooth, and the word is generally applied to the sharp, pointed teeth of dogs and wolves. This meaning of the word appeared in 1555, but is not its first meaning.

When *fang* first appeared in early Middle English (1016, *Anglo-Saxon Chronicle*), its meaning was "something caught or captured, such as game; booty, plunder, spoils." A somewhat later meaning (before 1400) was "a catch, capture, a tight grip."

A, *a*
B, *b*
C, *c*
D, *d*
E, *e*
F, *f*
G, *g*
H, *h*
I, *i*
J, *j*
K, *k*
L, *l*
M, *m*
N, *n*
O, *o*
P, *p*
Q, *q*
R, *r*
S, *s*
T, *t*
U, *u*
V, *v*
W, *w*
X, *x*
Y, *y*
Z, *z*

A, a

B, b

C, c

D, d

E, e

F, f

G, g

H, h

I, i

J, j

K, k

L, l

M, m

N, n

O, o

P, p

Q, q

R, r

S, s

T, t

U, u

V, v

W, w

X, x

Y, y

Z, z

The word derived from Old English *fang* and *feng* "a seizing, catching, or grasping," related to Old High German *fang* (Modern German *fangen* "to catch") and Old Norse *fang*.

After that, it was widely applied to many figurative and transferred uses, especially in the plural, among them to human teeth (dentists were slangily called "fang-wrenchers," "fang farriers," and "fang-fakers" in the 1800s), to the mandibles of insects, to claws or talons, and to anchors, prongs, valves, and the like, until it arrived at its current use.

To lease a FARM

To the poet and philosopher Ralph Waldo Emerson, writing in 1836, the thought of a farm inspired this lyrical paean: "What is a farm but a mute gospel? The chaff and the wheat, weeds and plants, blight, rain, insects, sun—it is a sacred emblem from the first furrow of spring to the last stack which the snow of winter overtakes in the fields." The dictionary definition of a farm is "a tract of land on which crops and often livestock are raised." This familiar meaning is first recorded in 1523.

The word is much older. It's been traced back to 1297, when *farm* meant "a fixed yearly rent, tax, or other charge, as opposed to a variable amount." That meaning came (through Old French *ferme*) from the Medieval Latin *firma* "fixed payment," derived from Latin *firmāre* "to fix, settle, make firm," from *firmus* "firm." Thus Sir William Blackstone, in his *Commentaries on the Laws of England* (1767), writes: "The most usual and customary farm or rent . . . must be reserved yearly on such lease." Before the 1300s, this meaning was extended to "the condition of being let at a fixed rent," then to "a lease," and in the 1500s to "a tract of land held on lease for the purpose of cultivation."

FASTIDIOUS

To be *fastidious* is to be overly meticulous or particular about matters of taste or propriety. In describing his masterpiece, *Moby-Dick,* in an 1851 letter to a Mrs. Morewood, Herman Melville wrote: "It is not a piece of fine feminine . . . silk—but it is of the horrible texture of a fabric that should be woven of ships' cables & hausers. . . . Warn all gentle fastidious people from so much as peeping into the book—on risk of a lumbago & sciatics."

Though *fastidious* is usually used in a favorable sense, as in *She is fastidious about her appearance*, it wasn't always. First occurring around 1440, *fastidious* meant "full of pride, disdainful of others, haughty," and by 1531 it had come to mean "disgusting, disagreeable, distasteful or unpleasant," as in *fastidious and irksome companions, a fastidious ulcer. Fastidious* was borrowed from Latin *fastīdiōsus* "disdainful, disgusted," from *fastīdium* "loathing."

The more positive current meaning first surfaced in 1848, in Thomas Macaulay's *History of England*: "People whom the habit of seeing magnificent buildings . . . had made fastidious." The word is thus an example of amelioration, or improved meaning.

FLAGRANT *uses and abuses*

In a unanimous opinion by the U.S. Supreme Court that a disorderly defendant may forfeit his constitutional right to be present in court, Associate Justice Hugo L. Black wrote in 1970: "The flagrant disregard in the courtroom of elementary standards of proper conduct should not and cannot be tolerated." By *flagrant* he meant "glaringly offensive, scandalous," which is the current use of the word, and also the latest.

When *flagrant* came into English from the Latin *flagrant-, flagrāns* "burning," derived from *flagrāre* "to burn," in 1513, it had the literal meaning of "burning, blazing, flaming," as in "His

A, *a*

B, *b*

C, *c*

D, *d*

E, *e*

F, *f*

G, *g*

H, *h*

I, *i*

J, *j*

K, *k*

L, *l*

M, *m*

N, *n*

O, *o*

P, *p*

Q, *q*

R, *r*

S, *s*

T, *t*

U, *u*

V, *v*

W, *w*

X, *x*

Y, *y*

Z, *z*

A, a

B, b

C, c

D, d

E, e

F, f

G, g

H, h

I, i

J, j

K, k

L, l

M, m

N, n

O, o

P, p

Q, q

R, r

S, s

T, t

U, u

V, v

W, w

X, x

Y, y

Z, z

mother snatched it . . . Out of the fire, and quenched the flagrant brand" (1626, George Sandys, translation of Ovid's *Metamorphosis*).

The original literal meaning of "burning, flaming" was transferred in 1706 to an offense, crime, etc., in a negative sense of "glaring, notorious, scandalous," as in *flagrant abuses, a flagrant violation of the law.*

The legal Latin term *in flagrante delicto*, literally, "while the crime is burning," has passed into English in the phrase *caught in flagrante delicto* "caught in the very act (of committing a crime)," often used euphemistically for a couple discovered having illicit sexual relations.

FLAMBOYANT

Stage and screen performers known for their extravagantly dashing and showy style are often described as *flamboyant.* It was an apt description for the pianist entertainer Liberace, the sexually daring blond bombshell Mae West, and certain dramatic screen divas like Bette Davis. But it wasn't until the 20th century that the word was applied to personalities.

The earliest meaning of the word, first recorded in 1832, referred to a style of architecture prevalent in France in the 15th and part of the 16th centuries. The style, used in tracery and window decorations, was characterized by wavy lines in the form of flames. Wavy hair or flame-shaped swords were described as *flamboyant,* as well as objects gorgeously colored, such as flowers and paintings. The word was borrowed from French *flamboyant* "flaming, wavy," from *flamboyer* "to flame," from *flambe* "flame," the source of English *flame.*

The current sense of "strikingly or extravagantly bold or showy" appeared in 1879, in Edward Dowden's *Southey*: "That flamboyant penmanship admired by our ancestors." In a House of Commons debate in 1959, the Opposition leader Aneurin Bevan scathingly declared: "The Prime Minister [Harold Macmillan] has an absolute genius for putting flamboyant labels on empty luggage."

fatal FLAW

Great tragic heroes are known for their fatal flaws, defects in character that lead to their doom. Some of Shakespeare's classic examples are: Hamlet's irresoluteness, Othello's jealousy, Julius Caesar's ambition. Since a *flaw* is a defect, blemish, or imperfection, a diamond can have a flaw; as can a reputation or an argument.

This is the familiar meaning of *flaw*, first recorded in 1586 and used by Shakespeare in *Love's Labour's Lost* (1598): "My love to thee is sound, sans crack or flaw." From 1626 on, *flaw* was also used to mean a broken or faulty place in an object, a breach, crack, or fissure, as in "Or some frail China Jar receive a Flaw" (1714, Alexander Pope, *The Rape of the Lock*).

Flaw was of Scandinavian origin, related to Swedish *flaga* "flake." In its first use, before 1400, a *flaw* meant a flake, as of snow, or a spark of fire; its basic meaning was "something broken off or detached, a fragment of something." Since a fragment or detached part often indicated a break or defect in an object, a *flaw* came to mean the latter. A *flaw* in someone's character or reputation was thus a figurative extension of some defect in material things.

FLIRT

Flirt belongs to the cluster of onomatopoeic or imitative words that begin with *fl-* and indicate quick motion, such as *flick, flip, flit, flop, flutter, flurry,* and *fly.* An early meaning of *flirt,* recorded in 1570, was "to flit from one object to another," followed by the noun *flirt,* meaning "a sudden movement, a darting motion," before 1592.

A, a
B, b
C, c
D, d
E, e
F, f
G, g
H, h
I, i
J, j
K, k
L, l
M, m
N, n
O, o
P, p
Q, q
R, r
S, s
T, t
U, u
V, v
W, w
X, x
Y, y
Z, z

A, a

B, b

C, c

D, d

E, e

F, f

G, g

H, h

I, i

J, j

K, k

L, l

M, m

N, n

O, o

P, p

Q, q

R, r

S, s

T, t

U, u

V, v

W, w

X, x

Y, y

Z, z

According to the *OED*, the current meaning of *flirt*, "a woman of giddy or flighty character" (1621) developed from the onomatopoeic sense of "a sudden movement, a darting motion." This was followed by "a woman of loose character," as in *the town flirt*, and by "a woman who plays at courtship or practices coquetry," in 1747, in Samuel Richardson's novel *Clarissa*: "She was not one of those flirts . . . who would give pain to a person that deserved to be well-treated." The corresponding verb, "to play at courtship, practice coquetry," is first found in 1781, in David Garrick's *Prologue* to Sheridan's *School for Scandal*: "If Mrs. B. will still continue flirting, We hope she'll DRAW the curtain."

FULSOME *praise*

Fulsome came into the language about 1250 with the meaning "abundant, plentiful, lavish, full" which made sense, since the word was composed of *full* + the suffix –*some* "quite, considerably." In the 1340s, the word went on to mean "plump, fat, well-grown," as in *a fulsome body*. And in the early 1400s, *fulsome* was frequently applied to food in the sense of "filling, satiating," as in *a fulsome meal*.

Then, in the 1500s, the word took a negative turn to "wearisome from excess, cloying, gross," as in "As too little action is cold, so too much is fulsome" (1709, Sir Richard Steele, in *The Tatler*). Soon the word was used exclusively in an offensive sense, including "disgusting, loathsome" (*a fulsome disease*), "repugnant, repulsive" (*a foul and fulsome insect*), and, when applied to language, style, or behavior, "offending from excess, overdone, in poor taste," as in *fulsome flattery, fulsome adulation, fulsome endearment*.

Sometime in the 1900s, the word's history came full circle when its original meaning of "abundant, lavish" was revived, especially with the phrase *fulsome praise* (as in "I thank our M.C. for his fulsome praise of my contributions"). The problem with this usage was that it clashed with the still existing negative meaning of "offensively excessive, tastelessly overdone," so that many took *fulsome praise* to be an insult rather than a compliment. Today one of the meanings of *fulsome* is "insincerely lavish."

FUSTIAN

"Don't squander the court's patience puffing your cheeks up on stately bombast and lofty fustian. Speak plainly!" This passage, from Richard Dooling's 1998 novel *Brain Storm*, places side by side two synonyms, *bombast* and *fustian*, to make its point. The pair shares a parallel history; just as the literal meaning of *bombast* was "a thick padding or stuffing made of cotton wool," so *fustian* denoted originally "a coarse, thick cloth made of cotton and flax."

The rough, thick cloth called *fustian* came into the language from Old French around 1200. The figurative meaning "inflated, high-sounding, bombastic speech or writing; (also) gibberish, claptrap" is found about 1590, in Marlowe's play *Faustus*: "God forgive me, he speaks Dutch fustian." In 1681 John Dryden had this to say in *The Spanish Fryar* about the nature of fustian: "I am much deceiv'd if this be not abominable fustian, that is, thoughts and words ill sorted, and without the least relation to each other."

The adjective meaning, "high-flown, inflated, bombastic, pompous," followed shortly after, and was used in such phrases as *fustian language, fustian eulogiums, fustian words.*

The Middle English word, spelled *fustane, fustyan,* was borrowed from Old French *fustaigne, fustaine,* representing Medieval Latin *fustānea,* of uncertain origin.

A, *a*
B, *b*
C, *c*
D, *d*
E, *e*
F, *f*
G, *g*
H, *h*
I, *i*
J, *j*
K, *k*
L, *l*
M, *m*
N, *n*
O, *o*
P, *p*
Q, *q*
R, *r*
S, *s*
T, *t*
U, *u*
V, *v*
W, *w*
X, *x*
Y, *y*
Z, *z*

G, g

running the GAMUT

The American writer and wit Dorothy Parker, reviewing a theater performance by Katharine Hepburn in *The Lake* (1933), famously quipped: "She runs the gamut of emotions from A to B." The joke is an allusion to the original meaning of *gamut* (before 1529), "the series of all recognized musical notes in medieval music." *Gamut* was a contraction of Medieval Latin *gamma ut*, from *gamma*, name of the Greek letter used as a symbol for the lowest note on the stave, and *ut*, the first note in any scale.

The current meaning of *gamut*, "the entire scale, range, or compass of anything," as in *a gamut of colors, the gamut of stock prices,* appeared in 1626 as a figurative extension of the musical term. This meaning is found most often in the phrase *run the gamut,* as in "The outdoor furniture runs the gamut from prim poolside pieces to the frankly zany" (1980, *New York Times*).

While *run the gamut* has become a cliché, the word *gamut* itself is an acceptable one-word synonym of "wide range" or "wide spectrum," as in *Time* magazine (April 7, 1961) quoting the art photographer Edward Steichen: "Photography records the gamut of feelings written on the human face," and in the film director George Stevens's criterion for movies: "A motion picture should be respected as being more than a tool for selling soap, toothpaste, deodorant, used cars, beer, and the whole gamut of products advertised on television."

GANG *of One*

Except when used informally for a group of close friends or associates (as in "The gang's here!"), *gang* refers chiefly to a group of people associated for some criminal or antisocial purpose, as in *a gang of thieves, a gang of juvenile delinquents.* In 1976, the phrase *Gang of Four* became notorious as the nickname of four Chinese Communist leaders who were discredited and humiliated after the death of Mao Tse-tung. The epithet even generated a

A, *a*

B, *b*

C, *c*

D, *d*

E, *e*

F, *f*

G, *g*

H, *h*

I, *i*

J, *j*

K, *k*

L, *l*

M, *m*

N, *n*

O, *o*

P, *p*

Q, *q*

R, *r*

S, *s*

T, *t*

U, *u*

V, *v*

W, *w*

X, *x*

Y, *y*

Z, *z*

A, *a*

B, *b*

C, *c*

D, *d*

E, *e*

F, *f*

G, *g*

H, *h*

I, *i*

J, *j*

K, *k*

L, *l*

M, *m*

N, *n*

O, *o*

P, *p*

Q, *q*

R, *r*

S, *s*

T, *t*

U, *u*

V, *v*

W, *w*

X, *x*

Y, *y*

Z, *z*

facetious self-contradictory name, *Gang of One*, which was used as the title of two books about China.

In Middle English, about 1340, *gang* is found in the sense "a set of things that usually go together," as in *a gang of horseshoes, a gang of teeth. Gang* goes back to Old English *gong* "a going, a journey, a way," corresponding to Old High German *gang,* Old Norse *gangr.* The Middle English sense of "a set of things going together" was apparently influenced by Old Norse *gangr,* which also meant "a group of things."

The extension of the meaning "set of things" to that of "set of persons" is first recorded in 1627, in nautical use, when the crew of a boat was referred to as a *gang of men.* The negative sense associated with delinquent or criminal activity appeared in 1701, with the *London Gazette* expressing concern over "a Gang of House-breakers," followed in 1782 by *a gang of thieves,* and in 1849 by *a gang of crazy heretics.*

GARBAGE

Computer aficionados are familiar with the acronym GIGO for "garbage in, garbage out," meaning that if the input is garbage, the output will be garbage too.

The computer use of *garbage* is a transferred use of the figurative meaning "worthless matter," a meaning recorded since 1592 and much used colloquially today, as in this use by the politician and author Patrick Buchanan: " . . . there is garbage polluting our culture. We need an Environmental Protection Agency to clean it up."

The *garbage* we are most familiar with is the household refuse in our garbage cans that is collected periodically or that we dispose of in our garbage disposal units. This meaning of *garbage* came into use in 1582. It was not, however, the word's original meaning. The original meaning, which appeared about 1430, was "the viscera of an animal used for food, especially the entrails." This meaning was in use until the late 1800s, in such phrases as *the garbage of fish, the garbage of fowls*, and in such contexts as Samuel Butler's *Hudibras* (1664): "Augury, that out of garbages of cattle, Presag'd the events of truce, or battle."

How the meaning of "animal viscera or entrails" came to mean "refuse, trash" is not exactly known, but it seems likely that as people became more prosperous and selective in their diet, they discarded the intestines and other digestive organs of animals, considering them gross or indelicate. Hence *garbage* took on the meaning "discarded food, refuse."

According to the *Middle English Dictionary* (*MED*), the word is related to Middle English *garbelage* "removal of waste from spices," traceable to Old French. According to the *OED,* it's probably from Anglo-Norman, since the earliest example of its use comes from a cookbook, and many other words for food are found in early Anglo-Norman books on cookery.

See also A PILE OF JUNK.

GARBLE

To *garble* means to mix up, mangle, or mutilate a word, sentence, statement, etc., unintentionally. Garbled words are endless wellsprings of humor. Spoonerisms (named after the Reverend William Spooner, 1844–1930, famous for his garbled sentences) are still popular. They include the Reverend's "The Lord is a shoving leopard" and his loving reference to Queen Victoria as "our queer old dean." In the 1940s, the humorist F. Chase Taylor, under the pen name Colonel Stoopnagle, wrote mangled fairy tales filled with spoonerisms, such as "Prinderella and the Cince," which begins with "Here, indeed, is a story that'll make your cresh fleep. It will give you poose gimples."

A, a
B, b
C, c
D, d
E, e
F, f
G, g
H, h
I, i
J, j
K, k
L, l
M, m
N, n
O, o
P, p
Q, q
R, r
S, s
T, t
U, u
V, v
W, w
X, x
Y, y
Z, z

A, a

B, b

C, c

D, d

E, e

F, f

G, g

H, h

I, i

J, j

K, k

L, l

M, m

N, n

O, o

P, p

Q, q

R, r

S, s

T, t

U, u

V, v

W, w

X, x

Y, y

Z, z

According to *The Barnhart Dictionary of Etymology*, the verb *garble* is first found in 1419–1420, in Middle English *garbelen*, meaning "to inspect and remove refuse from, to sift or cleanse (spice, pepper, etc.)." This was borrowed from Middle French *garbeler* or Italian *garbellare* from a widely used term in Mediterranean commerce adopted from Arabic *gharbala* or *karbala* "to sift, select."

In 1630, the word's meaning was extended to "select, sort out, or take the pick of (wools, plants, etc.)." The idea of sifting or selecting among things so as to exclude unfit or objectionable material led to the notion of selecting or sifting from writing or speech in order to confuse or misrepresent. This meaning of *garble* appeared in 1689–1692, in the writings of John Locke, chiefly in the sense of deliberately distorting in order to misrepresent or confuse, as in "By garbling me he indulges in uncandid suppression of the truth" (1885, Fitzedward Hall, *Two Trifles*).

a **GAY** *time*

When *gay* originated in the 1300s, its chief meaning was "joyous, lighthearted, cheerful, merry," as in Chaucer's *The Miller's Tale* (circa 1386): "This Absolon, that jolly was and gay, Goeth with a censer on the holiday."

In the early 1400s there developed the extended meaning, "habitually given to social pleasures, addicted to reveling and self-indulgence," as in Nicolas Rowe's *The Fair Penitent* (1703): "Is this that Haughty, Gallant, Gay Lothario?" This led in the early 1800s to the word's application to an immoral woman, especially one given to prostitution, as in J. E. Ritchie's *Night Side of London* (1867): "The gay women, as they were termed, are worse off than American slaves."

The current meaning, "homosexual," is traced by the *Random House Historical Dictionary of American Slang* (*HDAS*) to 1933, while the *OED* cites its first sources from 1941, among them G. Legman's *The Language of Homosexuality,* which includes this definition: "*Gay,* an adjective used almost exclusively by homosexuals to denote homosexuality, sexual attractiveness, promiscuity ... Often given the French spelling, *gai* or *gaie,* by cultured homosexuals of both sexes." *Gay boy,* a disparaging term, appeared in 1945, followed by *gay bar,* for a bar frequented by homosexuals, in 1947. By 1970 the adjective *gay* had become widespread, generating such terms as *Gay Day, gay ghetto, gay village, Gay Liberation Front,* and *Gay Lib.*

The noun *gay* for a homosexual is first recorded in the *HDAS* in 1953, and illustrated among others by a 1993 quotation from *Newsweek*: "If gays and lesbians have one term even more than the crudest epithet hurled at them, it's got to be 'lifestyle choice'."

As a Middle English word, *gay* was borrowed from Old French *gai* "joyous, merry," found also in Provencal *gai,* Old Spanish *gayo,* Portuguese *gaio,* and Italian *gajo.* Scholars trace the word to Frankish, the West Germanic language of northern Gaul; some compare it to Old High German *gāhi* "swift, impetuous," while others connect it with Old High German *wāhi* "pretty."

GENEROUS

This word was introduced into English by Shakespeare, who used it the first time in *Love's Labour's Lost* (1598). The nobleman Don Adriano de Armado is referred to as "most generous sir." Here, *generous* means "of noble birth, high-born," borrowed from French *généreux* or from the Latin *generōsus* "of noble stock," from *gener-, genus* "stock, race."

In the 1600s *generous* was also applied to animals of good breed or stock, as in "The plains ... bred a generous race of horses" (1781, Edward Gibbon, *The Decline and Fall of the Roman Empire*).

A, a
B, b
C, c
D, d
E, e
F, f
G, g
H, h
I, i
J, j
K, k
L, l
M, m
N, n
O, o
P, p
Q, q
R, r
S, s
T, t
U, u
V, v
W, w
X, x
Y, y
Z, z

A, a
B, b
C, c
D, d
E, e
F, f
G, g
H, h
I, i
J, j
K, k
L, l
M, m
N, n
O, o
P, p
Q, q
R, r
S, s
T, t
U, u
V, v
W, w
X, x
Y, y
Z, z

The current meaning, "free in giving, liberal, munificent," is first recorded in 1696, and exemplified in Laurence Sterne's *Sentimental Journey* (1768): "The king . . . was the most generous of princes, but his generosity could neither relieve or reward every one." The meaning "free in giving" was extended from that of "high-born, noble" through the idea that only a nobleman or aristocrat would have the freedom, ability, and means to support the needy with donations. This notion has long ago disappeared. As Thomas J. Watson (1874–1956), the head of IBM, put it, "Really big people are . . . courteous, considerate and generous—not just to some people in some circumstances, but to everyone all the time."

GENIAL

The poet Edmund Spenser wrote in 1595 about "the bridal bower and genial bed." By *genial* he meant "of marriage, nuptial, generative," which was the word's original meaning, recorded since 1566. The word was borrowed from Latin *geniālis* "pertaining to marriage rites, festive, pleasant," from *genius* "one's guiding spirit from birth, guardian deity, inclination," the source of English *genius*.

In the 1600s the word was frequently applied to climate, sunshine, air, etc., in the sense of "conducive to generation or growth; temperate, warm, mild," as in *the genial month of May,* and "A genial heat warms thee within" (1647, Abraham Cowley, *Mistress*).

The current meaning, "pleasantly cheerful, cordial, jovial," developed from the above in the 1700s, as in "Let every polish'd dame, and genial lord Employ the social chair and venal board (1746, Tobias Smollett, *Reproof*). A more recent use is by the British philanthropist John Paul Getty (1932–2003): "I was the most genial and jovial of babies, a child with a consistently sanguine outlook."

GENIUS

The word *genius* evokes for most of us the image of an individual endowed with extraordinary mental, artistic, musical, or other gifts—Einstein, Da Vinci, Shakespeare, Mozart. However, in the 1390s, in the pagan belief prevalent in ancient Rome, a *genius* was a guardian or protective spirit or god assigned to every person at birth. The word's source, Latin *genius* "guardian spirit or deity, characteristic inclination or disposition," was derived from the root of *gignere* "to beget, produce," related to *genus* "race, stock, kind." The *genius* was thought to govern the person's fortune and determine his or her character in life.

A natural extension of the original meaning was "a person's characteristic inclination, disposition, or turn of mind," which appeared in 1581 in Sir Philip Sidney's *An Apology for Poetry*, where he writes: "A Poet no industry can make, if his own genius be not carried unto it."

From the sense of "characteristic inclination" there developed in the mid-1600s the meaning "natural ability, aptitude, or talent" in phrases like *a genius for mathematics, a genius for science*. In the mid-1700s this meaning was extended to "a native intellectual or mental power possessed by the greatest thinkers, artists, scientists, etc." According to Thomas Carlyle, "Genius . . . means transcendent capacity for taking trouble, first of all" (1858), often misquoted as "Genius is an infinite capacity for taking pains." A perhaps more famous statement is Thomas Edison's: "Genius is one per cent inspiration, ninety-nine per cent perspiration."

The common meaning, "a person endowed with genius (however one defines it)" also came into use in the 1700s, and in 1711, Joseph Addison poked fun at its overuse by writing in *The Spectator*: "There is no character more frequently given to a Writer, than that of being a Genius. I have heard many a little Sonneteer called a *fine Genius*."

A, a
B, b
C, c
D, d
E, e
F, f
G, g
H, h
I, i
J, j
K, k
L, l
M, m
N, n
O, o
P, p
Q, q
R, r
S, s
T, t
U, u
V, v
W, w
X, x
Y, y
Z, z

A, a

B, b

C, c

D, d

E, e

F, f

G, g

H, h

I, i

J, j

K, k

L, l

M, m

N, n

O, o

P, p

Q, q

R, r

S, s

T, t

U, u

V, v

W, w

X, x

Y, y

Z, z

GIDDY

Today the words *dizzy* and *giddy* are synonyms for "affected with vertigo" and are often used interchangeably. What's surprising about this pair of words is that, originally, in Old English, they were also synonyms, but with entirely different meanings than they have today. In Old English, *dizzy* meant "foolish, stupid," and *giddy* meant "mad, crazy, foolish, stupid."

Middle English *giddy* (about 1200) developed from Old English *gidi* (about 1000), variant of *gydig* "mad, insane," (literally) "god-possessed," from a prehistoric word parallel to Old English *ylfig* "insane," (literally) "elf-possessed." By the early 1500s *giddy* commonly meant "mentally unstable, mad, flighty," as in Shakespeare's *Henry VI* (1590): [They] do pelt so fast at one another's pate, That many have their giddy brains knocked out." This meaning passed in the 1700s to "easily excited, lightheaded, frivolous," as in "A mere playful, giddy, romping child" (1779, Franny Burney's *Diary*).

The meaning "affected with vertigo, dizzy" appeared in 1570, and developed from the notion that the sensation of swimming or whirling in the head was characteristic of mental confusion or instability. In dialectal English, some of the sense of the original Old English is retained in the use of *giddy* to mean "mad with anger, furious" and "wild and untamed," as in *a giddy horse*.

GIRL

It may be hard to believe, but when the word *girl* came into the language around 1290, it simply meant a young person, a child of either sex, with the plural *girls* meaning "children." Some scholars believe that the word may represent Old English *gyrele*, an unrecorded form from a Germanic source found in Low German *göre* "child" and dialectal Swedish *garre* "little child." So Chaucer, in the Prologue to *The Canterbury Tales* (about 1386), describes the Summoner as

A, a
B, b
C, c
D, d
E, e
F, f
G, g
H, h
I, i
J, j
K, k
L, l
M, m
N, n
O, o
P, p
Q, q
R, r
S, s
T, t
U, u
V, v
W, w
X, x
Y, y
Z, z

> In daunger hadde he at his own gyse
> The yonge *girles* of the diocise,
> And knew hir counseil, and was all hir reed.
> (In his power had he in his own way
> The young *children* of the diocese,
> And knew their secrets, and advised them all.)

A boy was already called a boy in those days, but what did they call a girl? They called her a *wench* or a *maid* or *maiden*, and sometimes a *lass* (when contrasted with a *lad*). It wasn't until about 1530 that *girl* was applied to a female child, and commonly to a young unmarried woman, as in John Heywood's *Proverbs* (1546): "The boy thy husband, and thou the girl, his wife."

the magic of GLAMOUR

The elusive quality of *glamour* is captured by this comment attributed to the fashion designer Lilly Daché: "Glamour is what makes a man ask for your telephone number. But it also is what makes a woman ask for the name of your dressmaker."

This popular use of *glamour*, meaning "physical allure or attractiveness," has been in use since the 1930s. But the word's original meaning, encountered in 1720, was "magic, enchantment, spell," used especially in the phrase *cast a glamour over one*. The word is an alteration of the earlier form *gramarye*, attested since about 1320 in the sense "grammar, learning in general," and since about 1470, in the transferred meaning "occult learning, magic, necromancy." *Gramarye*, "grammar," was borrowed from Old French *grammaire* "learning, philology."

The word was commonly used by Scottish poets in the 1700s, as in a poem by Robert Burns in 1793: "Ye gipsy-gang that deal in glamor, and you, deep-read in . . . Warlocks and witches." In 1830, Sir Walter Scott introduced the word in *Letters on Demonology and Witchcraft*: "This species of Witchcraft is well known in Scotland as the glamour, . . . and was supposed to be a special attribute of the race of Gipsies." Then in 1840, the meaning broadened to "a magical or fictitious beauty, a delusive charm." From there, it developed into the meaning we know today.

GLANCE

The verb *to glance*, meaning "to look quickly," was a favorite of the playwright Eugene O'Neill, frequently used in his stage directions, as in his masterpiece, *Long Day's Journey into Night* (1956): "As she talks, she glances everywhere except at any of their faces." "He glances away, ignoring his question." "He glances up at the chandelier disapprovingly." "She glances around vaguely." This useful and versatile meaning was a latecomer in English, first recorded in 1582, well over a hundred years after the word's entry into the language with a different meaning.

To glance was borrowed from Old French *glacer, glacier* "to glide, slip," from *glace* "ice," the source of English *glacier*. It appeared before 1450 with the meaning "(of an ax, spear, arrow, or other weapon) to glide off an object at a slant, without delivering a full blow," as in Sir Walter Scott's *Fair Maid of Perth* (1828): "The blow only glanced on the bone, and scarce drew blood." A figurative meaning, "(of light) to dart, flash, gleam," turned up in 1568. It was used in Harriet Beecher Stowe's *Uncle Tom's Cabin*: "An insane light glanced in her heavy black eyes."

The current meaning, "(of the eye) to move quickly, to cast a momentary look, to look quickly," developed from both the notion of a weapon moving or striking rapidly and from that of a light flashing or darting.

GLIMPSE

To glimpse or *to catch a glimpse* is to catch a momentary view or passing glance of something. "Visitors rush to glimpse vanishing glaciers," ran the headline in the August 22, 2005 issue of *The Guardian,* referring to the rapidly receding (and aptly named) Exit Glacier in Alaska. "Space probe to glimpse infancy of the universe," headlined an article in the *Princeton Bulletin* of June 18, 2001, about a NASA satellite designed to measure an echo of the Big Bang. Who wouldn't want to glimpse such natural wonders?

The meaning of *glimpse*, "a momentary view or passing glance," first showed up in 1580, while the verb *to glimpse*, "to catch a glimpse of," appeared in 1779. But neither of these uses was the original meaning of the word.

The verb first appeared in Middle English (about 1400) in the form *glimsen* (thought to be related to Old English *glæm* "brightness," the source of English *gleam*), with the meaning "to shine faintly, to glimmer or glitter." In 1592, the word was changed to *glimpse*, with the *p-* sound introduced, probably to ease the pronunciation. The noun also appeared originally with the spelling *glimse* before 1547, and in 1600 Shakespeare used it in *Hamlet*, when Hamlet says to his father's ghost, "What may this mean, That thou . . . revisit'st thus the glimses of the moon," meaning that the father makes a faint, momentary shining appearance on earth by night.

The original meaning passed into that of "a momentary view or passing glance" in 1580, in John Lyly's *Euphues*: "The Basiliske, whose eyes procure delight to the looker at the first glimse, and death at the second glance." The verb meaning appeared later, in 1779, and quickly passed into common use both in the sense of "to catch a glimpse of" (as in "I glimpsed some figures in the distance") and "to cast a passing glance (at, upon, etc.)," as in John Greenleaf Whittier's *New England Legends* (1833):

> No more the unquiet churchyard dead
> Glimpse upward from their turfy bed.

A, a
B, b
C, c
D, d
E, e
F, f
G, g
H, h
I, i
J, j
K, k
L, l
M, m
N, n
O, o
P, p
Q, q
R, r
S, s
T, t
U, u
V, v
W, w
X, x
Y, y
Z, z

GLOOM

Gloom in the sense of darkness or obscurity, as in *the twilight gloom, the winter gloom,* was apparently an innovation by the poet Milton, in whose poems it occurs (according to the *OED*) nine times, starting with *On the Morning of Christ's Nativity* (1629). A figurative use of this meaning, "a state of depression or melancholy," as in *a fit of gloom,* appeared in 1744 in James Harris's *Three Treatises*: "The Face of Nature . . . will perhaps dispel these Glooms."

Before 1400, the meaning of the verb *to gloom,* was "to look dark or threatening," as in *the sky is glooming, the clouds gloomed over us.* This was a figurative use of the verb's original meaning (around 1300), "to look sullen or displeased, to frown or scowl." The origin of the verb *gloom* can be traced back to Low German *glūm* "muddiness," and Middle Dutch *gloom, glomich* "foggy."

blood and GORE

Perhaps no author-artist was blessed with a more felicitous name than Edward Gorey (1925–2000), whose darkly humorous, often gruesome illustrated books with their eerie Victorian settings have long enjoyed a cult following. Gorey was very conscious of the resemblance of his name to the words *gore* and *gory,* and made a point of publishing a number of his books under pseudonyms that were ominous reminders of this resemblance, notably the name Eduard Blutig; *blutig* means "bloody" in German.

The word *gore* means "blood in the thickened form after its shedding, clotted blood." This meaning of *gore* is first found in 1563, occasionally in the phrase *blood and gore.* The original meaning of *gore* in Middle English (about 1300) was "dung, feces," also "filth of any kind, dirt, slime," a meaning still found in some dialects of England. Middle English *gore* developed from Old English (about 725) *gor* "dung, dirt," corresponding to

Middle Dutch and Dutch *goor* "mud, filth," Old High German *gor* "dung," and Old Norse *gor* "cud, slimy matter." The transferred meaning, from "dung, feces" to "clotted blood," is accounted for by a perceived similarity between the texture or color of the two substances.

GOSSIP

No one can resist some good *gossip* from time to time. However, in 1325, the meaning of *gossip* bore no resemblance to the "tattler" meaning it has today.

In 1325, Middle English *gossib* (as it was then spelled) meant "a child's godparent," and developed from Old English (1014) *god-sibb* "a person acting as a sponsor at a baptism; a godfather or godmother." *Godsibb* was formed from *god* "God" and *sibb* "akin, related; kinship, relationship," the source of English *sibling*. Since such a person was regarded as a close friend, the word had acquired the meaning of "good friend, familiar acquaintance" as early as 1362.

In the late 1500s, the word was applied especially to a woman's female friends invited to be present at a birth, as recorded in Nathan Bailey's *Universal Etymological English Dictionary* (1721–1800): "*A Gossiping,* a merry Meeting of Gossips, at a Woman's Lying in." This sort of gathering, in which a great deal of idle talk was exchanged, led to the derogatory meaning, recorded since 1580, of "a person, mainly a woman, who engages in idle talk, a newsmonger or tattler."

The most current meaning, "the talk of a gossip; idle talk, trifling rumor; chatter," turned up in 1811, and was used in 1820 in Washington Irving's *Sketch Book*: "A kind of travelling gazette, carrying the whole budget of local gossip from house to house."

A, *a*
B, *b*
C, *c*
D, *d*
E, *e*
F, *f*
G, *g*
H, *h*
I, *i*
J, *j*
K, *k*
L, *l*
M, *m*
N, *n*
O, *o*
P, *p*
Q, *q*
R, *r*
S, *s*
T, *t*
U, *u*
V, *v*
W, *w*
X, *x*
Y, *y*
Z, *z*

A, *a*

B, *b*

C, *c*

D, *d*

E, *e*

F, *f*

G, *g*

H, *h*

I, *i*

J, *j*

K, *k*

L, *l*

M, *m*

N, *n*

O, *o*

P, *p*

Q, *q*

R, *r*

S, *s*

T, *t*

U, *u*

V, *v*

W, *w*

X, *x*

Y, *y*

Z, *z*

GROOM *and* BRIDEGROOM

When we hear the word *groom*, we immediately associate it with *bride* and picture a man in a tux about to be married. This meaning of *groom* is first encountered in Shakespeare's *Othello* (1604), where Iago compares fellowship between friends to marriage: " . . . friends all but now, even now, In quarter, and in terms like bride and groom Divesting them for bed." As in this passage, the word was rarely used except in context with *bride*, and for a good reason. *Groom* was a shortening of the much older term *bridegroom*, which was an alteration of Middle English *bridegome,* from Old English *brýdguma* "man about to take a bride," (literally) "bride-man." The Middle English form *-gome* was altered to *-groom* by influence of the word *groom*, because one of the meanings of *groom* in Middle English (about 1330) was "male person, man."

This meaning grew out of the earliest one, "a male child, a boy," first recorded before 1225 in the *Ancrene Riwle*, a manual of monastic rules, and used in this sense until the 1600s by poets like Charles Cotton, who, in *Burlesque upon Burlesque* (1675), writes: "To bring him Plums and Mackaroons, Which welcome are to such small Grooms."

The origin of *groom* is uncertain. In light of the word's earliest known meaning, "a male child, a boy," it might possibly represent an unrecorded Old English *grōm*, from the root of *grōwan* "to grow."

GROSS

Gross is a word having both a favorable and an unfavorable meaning. The favorable, or positive, meaning, "entire, total, whole," is found chiefly in commerce, as in *gross income, gross receipts, gross national product*. This meaning first occurred in 1523, and contrasted sharply with the earlier negative meaning of "coarse, uncultivated, common," recorded since 1474 in phrases like *gross language, gross behavior, gross morals*.

Both meanings are figurative and stem from the original literal meaning, although the definitions went down separate paths. Originally (before 1400) *gross* meant "thick, stout, big," and was borrowed from Old French *gros, grosse* "thick, bulky, coarse," from Late Latin *grossus* "thick, stout, coarse," of uncertain origin, but also the source of Spanish *grueso* and Portuguese and Italian *grosso* "thick, stout, coarse."

See also ENGROSS

GUTS
See PLUCK

A, a
B, b
C, c
D, d
E, e
F, f
G, g
H, h
I, i
J, j
K, k
L, l
M, m
N, n
O, o
P, p
Q, q
R, r
S, s
T, t
U, u
V, v
W, w
X, x
Y, y
Z, z

H, h

HAGGARD

Here's a word that's often found in literature, from John Dryden to Thomas Hardy and Robert Louis Stevenson, to a contemporary like Don Delillo. Its meaning, "gaunt and worn in appearance, as from illness, strain, pain, exhaustion, etc.," fits perfectly in descriptions of the suffering heroes of countless novels and romances. In his recounting of prison life in *Little Dorrit* (1855), Dickens writes: "As the captive men were faded and haggard, so the iron was rusty, the stone was slimy, the wood was rotten, the air was faint, the light was dim." Just two years before, in 1853, Charlotte Brontë had written in her novel *Villette*: " . . . thin, haggard, and hollow-eyed; like a sitter-up at night."

Originally (1567) *haggard* meant "wild, untamed," and was applied to a hawk and sometimes to an owl. Shakespeare used it in *Othello*, and Ben Jonson in *The Sad Shepherd* (1637): "No Colt is so unbroken! Or hawk yet half so haggard, or unmanned!" In 1697, John Dryden, in his translation of Virgil's *Georgics*, applied the word to a wild and haunted expression in the eyes: "With haggard Eyes they stare, Lean are their Looks . . ." Afterward Dryden applied it to the harmful effect of fatigue, anxiety, terror, etc., on a person's appearance: "Staring his eyes, and haggard was his look." This led in the 1800s to the use of *haggard* in the sense of "gaunt and scraggy-looking from loss of flesh," in phrases like *a haggard look, a haggard expression, a haggard face, haggard cheeks.*

Haggard came into English from Middle French *hagard*, of uncertain origin, perhaps derived from an Old French term, *faulcon hagard* (literally) "falcon of the woods."

HAGGLING *over words*

In Shakespeare's play *Henry V* (1599), King Henry, surveying the field on which his army had battled the French, asks the Duke of Exeter about his uncle, the Duke of York:

A, *a*

B, *b*

C, *c*

D, *d*

E, *e*

F, *f*

G, *g*

H, *h*

I, *i*

J, *j*

K, *k*

L, *l*

M, *m*

N, *n*

O, *o*

P, *p*

Q, *q*

R, *r*

S, *s*

T, *t*

U, *u*

V, *v*

W, *w*

X, *x*

Y, *y*

Z, *z*

A, a

B, b

C, c

D, d

E, e

F, f

G, g

H, h

I, i

J, j

K, k

L, l

M, m

N, n

O, o

P, p

Q, q

R, r

S, s

T, t

U, u

V, v

W, w

X, x

Y, y

Z, z

> Lives he, good uncle? Thrice within this hour
> I saw him down; thrice up again and fighting;
> From helmet to the spur all blood he was.

To which Exeter replies:

> Suffolk first died: and York, all haggled over,
> Comes to him, where in gore he lay insteeped,
> And takes him by the beard; kisses the gashes
> That bloodily did spawn upon his face.

So York was "all haggled over," by which Shakespeare meant that he was hacked and mangled with irregular cuts or blows. This is an early meaning of the word *to haggle*, from the Middle English *haggen* "to cut, hew, chop," borrowed from Old Norse *hoggva* "to strike with a sharp weapon, to hack."

The current meaning of *haggle*, "to dispute, cavil, or wrangle as to terms or in settling a bargain," is first found in 1602, as a figurative sense of the earlier meaning through the notion of "hacking or chopping away" at a price, etc., in bargaining. When in 1648 Oliver Cromwell wrote in a letter, "We are so harassed and haggled out in this business," he might have envisioned being mangled in the business.

HANDSOME *is as* HANDSOME *does*

This proverb, according to the 1989 *Macmillan Dictionary of Quotations*, is one of the 479 commonest American proverbs. The saying contends that skillful or useful work beats good looks. Neither of the two senses in which *handsome* is used in the proverb, "good-looking" and "skilled at work," comes close to the word's original meaning.

Handsome was coined about 1425 with the now obsolete meaning, "easy to handle or use," as in *handsome works, handsome spears,* followed in 1530 by the extended meaning, "ready at hand, handy, convenient," as in *a handsome situation, a handsome shelter.*

A series of new meanings developed in the 1500s, namely: (1) "apt, skilled, clever," as in *a handsome speech*; (2) "of fair size or amount, considerable," as in *a handsome quantity of salmon*; (3) "ample, generous, liberal," as in *a handsome fortune.*

The prevailing current meaning, "having a fine form or figure, attractive, good-looking," is first recorded in 1590, in Spenser's *The Faerie Queene* ("a handsome stripling"), and in Shakespeare's *Othello* (1604): "This Lodovico . . . is a very handsome man."

The word is usually assumed to have been formed in English from *hand* + *-some* (as in *toothsome*), but it may have been borrowed from early modern German *handsam* or early modern Dutch *handzaam*, meaning "easy to handle or use."

See also TALL

HARLOT

Throughout its history, *harlot* has been a term of opprobrium and insult. Yet, at first it had an entirely different meaning than it has today and, unlike today, the word was applied exclusively to men.

The first appearance of *harlot* in print was in the *Ancrene Riwle* (Rules for Anchoresses), a manual of rules governing monastic life composed before 1225. The word, borrowed from Old French *herlot* (from a widespread Romance word of uncertain origin), meant "beggar, vagabond, villain, knave." In the 1300s it was variously applied to an itinerant jester or buffoon, any man of loose life, and playfully to any fellow, as in Chaucer's Prologue to *The Canterbury Tales* (about 1386):

> He [the Summoner] was a gentle harlot and kind
> A better fellow should men not find.

The first use of *harlot* in the sense of a woman, specifically "a woman of loose life, an unchaste woman, a prostitute," was in 1432–1450, in the Higden *Rolls* (official government records):

A, *a*

B, *b*

C, *c*

D, *d*

E, *e*

F, *f*

G, *g*

H, *h*

I, *i*

J, *j*

K, *k*

L, *l*

M, *m*

N, *n*

O, *o*

P, *p*

Q, *q*

R, *r*

S, *s*

T, *t*

U, *u*

V, *v*

W, *w*

X, *x*

Y, *y*

Z, *z*

A, a

B, b

C, c

D, d

E, e

F, f

G, g

H, h

I, i

J, j

K, k

L, l

M, m

N, n

O, o

P, p

Q, q

R, r

S, s

T, t

U, u

V, v

W, w

X, x

Y, y

Z, z

"The harlots of Rome were called *nonariæ*." In the 1500s, the word occurred frequently in this sense in Bible versions, where it competed with the words *whore* and *strumpet* (as in various versions of the Wycliffe Bible).

HAVOC

In the Middle Ages, the military order *havoc!* was a signal for soldiers to seize spoil, pillage, and plunder. It was used especially in the phrase *cry havoc*, meaning "to give an army the order to seize spoil," taken from Anglo-French *crier havoc*. The phrase is first found in English in the *Ordinances of War of Henry V* (1419), which warns combatants "That no man be so hardy to cry havok upon pain that he that is found beginner to die therefore."

Gradually the word passed from the military use into the general sense of devastation or destruction, and, in a weakened sense, confusion, disorder, or disarray, especially in such phrases as *to make havoc,* as in "The wicked broth . . . made havoc among those tender cells" (1868, Tennyson, *Lucretius*); *to create havoc,* as in "Several small children can create havoc in a house" (1961, *Webster's Third New International Dictionary*); *to wreak havok* as in "Nor is this feisty crew beyond wreaking havoc among themselves" (1981, *New York Times Book Review*).

As for the word's history, the Anglo-French *havoc* was apparently an altered form of Old French *havot* "plunder, devastation," used in the phrase *crier havot*, and is probably of Germanic origin.

going HAYWIRE

The informal expression *go haywire* is a well-known 20th-century Americanism that early on crossed the Atlantic and was warmly embraced by British writers like Evelyn Waugh, Margery Allingham, Ngaio Marsh, and Margaret Kennedy. The idiom, in the sense of "go out of control," was first heard in the 1920s.

A, a

B, b

C, c

D, d

E, e

F, f

G, g

H, h

I, i

J, j

K, k

L, l

M, m

N, n

O, o

P, p

Q, q

R, r

S, s

T, t

U, u

V, v

W, w

X, x

Y, y

Z, z

However, the word *haywire*'s first meaning, attested since 1905, was "poorly equipped, hastily put together, inefficient, slip-shod," used especially in the phrase *haywire outfit*, originally a contemptuous name for loggers with poor logging equipment, and later applied more broadly, as in *a haywire business, a haywire railroad,* and so on. This meaning is a reference to the actual use of haywire—light wire for binding bales of hay—for makeshift repairs.

In 1928, it was used in the phrase *go haywire* "to become mentally deranged, go crazy," in Bert Hall and John J. Niles' *One Man's War:* " . . . there was a short-legged fellow in our platoon that was going 'haywire'." In October 1929, the *New York Times* (referring to the stock market) used the phrase to mean "become defective": "When some element in the recording system becomes defective it is said to have gone haywire."

The word *haywire* by itself, meaning "out of order, awry" and also "confused, crazy," has been recorded since 1920, as in "I feel haywire all over" (1925, *American Speech*) and "A married man . . . and absolutely haywire on the subject of another woman" (1934, John O'Hara, *Appointment in Samarra*).

HECTIC

Kenneth G. Wilson, editor of *The Columbia Guide to Standard American English* (1993), describes the concept of *etymological fallacy* as "the name of a much-practiced folly that insists that what a word 'really means' is whatever it once meant long ago, perhaps even in another language." With respect to the word *hectic*, there have been some critics in the past who have been guilty of this etymological fallacy. They claimed that the meaning of this word, "characterized by feverish excitement, confusion, or haste," in such phrases as *a hectic time at school, a day of hectic activity,* was a misuse of the word. Their objection was based on the word's etymology.

A, a

B, b

C, c

D, d

E, e

F, f

G, g

H, h

I, i

J, j

K, k

L, l

M, m

N, n

O, o

P, p

Q, q

R, r

S, s

T, t

U, u

V, v

W, w

X, x

Y, y

Z, z

The original meaning of *hectic*, "of or relating to a fluctuating fever marked by flushed cheeks and a hot dry skin," first recorded in 1398, was borrowed through Old French *etique* from Late Latin *hecticus*. The word's history follows a straight line from the original meaning of a fluctuating fever to "symptomatic of the fever" (*a hectic cough, a hectic flush*), "affected with the fever, consumptive" (*a hectic girl, hectic cheeks*), and finally the figurative meaning "characterized by feverish excitement, confusion, or haste," first found in Rudyard Kipling's *Traffics and Discoveries* (1904): "Didn't I say we never met . . . without a remarkably hectic day ahead of us?"

the **HEYDAY** *of the blood*

In *A Browser's Dictionary* (1980), the poet John Ciardi gives two definitions for *heyday*: "1. The prime of one's life and vigor. *Tom Swales was a powerful man in his heyday*" and "2. The peak of popularity, as of a fashion or fad. *In the heyday of the Flapper.*" Both of these meanings date from the mid-1700s.

The earliest meaning of *heyday* is an exclamation denoting frolicsomeness, cheerfulness, surprise, wonder, etc., as in the second Duke of Buckingham's satire *The Rehearsal* (1672): "Hey day, hey day! I know not what to do, nor what to say."

This interjectional use first occurs about 1529 in the form *heyda* (and later *hoida, hoyday*), and is thought to be either an extended form of the Middle English exclamation *hei, hey* "hey," or a borrowing of German *heida, hey da* "hey there!" The change from *heida* to *heyday* in the sense of "prime of life and vigor" came from the association of the word with the common word *day*.

The meaning extended to "high spirits, frolicsomeness," found in Shakespeare: "At your age The heyday in the blood is tame, it's humble" (1603, *Hamlet*). Shakespeare's use was echoed in Tobias Smollett's picaresque novel *The Adventures of Peregrine*

Pickle (1751): "Our imperious youth . . . was now in the heyday of his blood."

HIERARCHY

According to the Peter Principle, enunciated by Laurence Peter (1969), "In a hierarchy every employee tends to rise to his level of incompetence." A hierarchy is a body of persons ranked one above the other, the lower rank being subordinate to the higher. More recently, the sociologist C. Wright Mills was quoted as saying, "In the world of celebrity, the hierarchy of publicity has replaced the hierarchy of descent and even of great wealth."

The first use of *hierarchy* was as far from the current use as earth is from heaven. The Middle English word was borrowed (through Old French) from Late Latin *ierarchia, hierarchia*, from Greek, "the power or rule of a high priest," derived from *hierárchēs* "high priest," (literally) "leader of sacred rites," from *hierós* "sacred" + *árchein* "to lead." The word's original meaning, about 1380, was "each of three divisions of angels, each division comprising three orders." This system was devised by Pseudo-Dionysius the Areopagite, a mystic and philosopher of the 5th century, who applied the term *hierarchy*, which referred to the body of Roman Catholic and Eastern Orthodox clergymen, to the body of angels in heaven.

In the 1500s, the word resumed the basic meaning of "rule or dominion in holy things; any system of priestly rule or government," as in *the ecclesiastical hierarchy.* And by 1620, *hierarchy* had come to mean "an organized body of priests or clergy in successive orders or grades." It was this meaning that was shortly after generalized to the current sense of "a body of persons or things ranked in grades or classes one above the other." According to *The Barnhart Dictionary of Etymology,* the word's sense of ranked organizations of persons or things "seems, by popular confusion of sound with *higher*, to have also been associated semantically with *higher* to explain the sense of ranks."

A, a
B, b
C, c
D, d
E, e
F, f
G, g
H, h
I, i
J, j
K, k
L, l
M, m
N, n
O, o
P, p
Q, q
R, r
S, s
T, t
U, u
V, v
W, w
X, x
Y, y
Z, z

HOBBY

The American golfer Lee Trevino likes to quip, "Golf isn't just my business. It's my hobby." A more cynical view is expressed by the humorist Fran Lebowitz: "A hobby is, of course, an abomination, as are all consuming interests and passions that do not lead directly to large, personal gain" (1978, *Metropolitan Life*).

A *hobby* was not always a favorite pastime or avocation. In 1375, when this word first appeared in print (in the forms *hoby*, *hobyn*), it denoted a pony, a small or middle-sized horse of an Irish breed. In later times, it was applied also to Welsh and Scottish breeds of small horses. In the 1500s, such a horse was often called a *hobby horse*, a name also applied to a toy consisting of a stick with a horse's head, which a child would bestride and run around with. This sense was extended in the 1600s to any favorite occupation or pursuit, as pointed out in Matthew Hale's *Contemplations* (1676): "Almost every person hath some hobby horse or other wherein he prides himself."

In the 1800s, *hobby horse* in the sense of a favorite occupation, pastime, or interest, was shortened to *hobby*, and Sir Walter Scott popularized this use in works like *The Antiquary* (1816), where he states: "I quarrel with no man's hobby," and in *Peveril of the Peak* (1823), where he writes of "the pleasure of being allowed to ride one's hobby in peace and quiet."

HODGEPODGE

Hodgepodge is a word that seems to have been made up to suggest its meaning, which is "a messy mixture of things, a jumble, a mishmash." It sounds like a typical reduplication, like *knickknack, pellmell, riffraff*, and *mishmash*, all of which were coined to suggest a jumble of unrelated things. Well, *hodgepodge* is not a frivolous reduplication, though its history is, ironically, a hodgepodge.

The word's earliest form, *hochepot*, appeared in 1292 as a term in Anglo-French law, meaning "the gathering together of properties

A, *a*

B, *b*

C, *c*

D, *d*

E, *e*

F, *f*

G, *g*

H, h

I, *i*

J, *j*

K, *k*

L, *l*

M, *m*

N, *n*

O, *o*

P, *p*

Q, *q*

R, *r*

S, *s*

T, *t*

U, *u*

V, *v*

W, *w*

X, *x*

Y, *y*

Z, *z*

to divide them equally among heirs." Early on, about 1386, Chaucer used the word in *The Canterbury Tales* in the sense of a mixture of things, perhaps alluding to the original legal meaning: "Ye have cast her words in an hochepot." The Anglo-French legal term *hochepot* was borrowed from Old French, where it meant "a stew," a compound formed from *hocher* "to shake" + *pot* "vessel, pot." About 1440, the word, spelled *hotchpot,* was used in cookery to mean "a dish containing many ingredients," as in *a hotchpot of garlic and cheese, a hotchpot of many meats.*

A major change in the word's use came in the 1500s, when its spelling (and pronunciation) was changed from *hotchpot* to *hotchpotch* to make it sound like a reduplicated word, thus reinforcing the meaning of "a confused mixture, a medley, a jumble," as in "They . . . made a mingle mangle and a hotchpotch of it . . . partly popery, partly true religion mingled together" (1549, Hugh Latimer, *Sermons*).

A further change that created the current meaning of the word occurred in the 1500s with the altering of *hotchpotch* to *hodgepodge*, as in "They have made our English tongue a gallimaufry or hodge-podge of all other speeches" (1579, E. K., editor of Spenser's *The Shepheardes Calender*).

HOMELY *and* HOMEY

Usage books, at least the good ones, warn us not to confuse *homey* and *homely*. They tell us that *homey* means "homelike," as in *a warm, homey atmosphere*, whereas *homely* means "not beautiful, plain, unattractive." This distinction is valid in the United States only. Bergen and Cornelia Evans, in their *Dictionary of Contemporary American Usage* (1957), inform us that "The English have retained the word *homely* only in its kinder connotations of domestic, familiar, kindly. . . ." The obvious question is, how did this approbative, well-meaning word for the domestic, familiar, and cozy make a 360-degree turn to become depreciative and derogatory?

When *homely* appeared in the early 1300s, it meant "belonging to the home or household, domestic," and was used in phrases like *homely trees, homely dogs*. Its meaning was soon extended to "typical of a home or domestic living; simple, everyday, commonplace," as in Chaucer's *The Summoner's Tale* (about 1386): "Then had I with you homely sufficiency / I am a man of little gluttony." The meaning was further extended to "simple, plain, unadorned" in William Caxton's 1490 translation of *Eneydos*: "Some gentlemen . . . desired me to use old and homely terms in my translations." Applied to persons, it was used in phrases like *a poor homely laboring man, a dear little homely woman*.

It was in the 1600s, from the constant use of *homely* in the sense of "plain, commonplace, simple or rough in appearance," that the meaning "not beautiful or attractive" emerged, as in Martin Fotherby's *Atheomastix* (1622): "Some parts of Man be . . . comely, some homely." In 1706, Edward Phillips's *The New World of Words* defined *homely* as "ugly, disagreeable, coarse, mean."

HORRID

Who hasn't heard the cute little poem "There was a Little Girl" and thought that it was a Mother Goose rhyme? It goes like this:

> There was a little girl
> Who had a little curl,
> Right in the middle of her forehead.
> When she was good,
> She was very good indeed,
> But when she was bad she was horrid.

A little research turned up the fact that it was actually composed by the poet Henry Wadsworth Longfellow (1807–1882) while he was taking a walk with his baby daughter in his arms.

It turns out that the first uses of *horrid* were in poetry, which may account for Longfellow's familiarity with it. Edmund

Spenser used it in 1590, John Dryden in 1697, Alexander Pope in 1717, and Thomas Gray in 1739—all, however, with a meaning of *horrid* that is completely unfamiliar to most of us. That meaning was "bristling, shaggy, rough," as in *horrid thorn, the horrid Alps, a horrid beard.* The word was borrowed from Latin *horridus* "bristling, rough, shaggy, rude," from *horrēre* "to bristle, quake, shudder," the source of *horrible* and *horror.*

A nonpoetic sense, "causing horror or aversion, dreadful, frightful, horrible," emerged in 1602 and appeared in such phrases as *a horrid murder, horrid crimes, a horrid yell.* But just like *awful, awesome, terrible,* and *horrible* lost their strong original meanings and became weak intensives (*I had an awful time. The concert was awesome. What a terrible speech! I feel horrible about the mistake.*), so *horrid* developed after 1666 a weakened, informal sense of "very bad, offensive, disagreeable," as in *a horrid shame, a horrid place, horrid stuff,* and *horrid weather.* This was of course what Longfellow meant by telling us that when the little girl was bad she was *horrid.*

HOSPITAL, HOSPICE

These twins were identical at birth, both meaning "a house for the reception and entertainment of travelers, pilgrims, and strangers; a guesthouse or inn." *Hospital* was borrowed (through Old French) from Medieval Latin *hospitale* "guesthouse, inn," from Latin *hospit-, hospes* "guest," which was also the source of *hospice* (as well as of *host, hostel,* and *hotel*).

Hospital came first, about 1300. As late as 1590, Spenser used it in *The Faerie Queene* in the sense of "a place for lodging": "They spied a goodly castle . . . Which choosing for that evening's hospital, They thither marched."

In the early 1400s, the word began to be applied to a charitable institution for the needy, such as an asylum for the poor, sick, or aged. From this use developed the word's current meaning, "an

A, a
B, b
C, c
D, d
E, e
F, f
G, g
H, h
I, i
J, j
K, k
L, l
M, m
N, n
O, o
P, p
Q, q
R, r
S, s
T, t
U, u
V, v
W, w
X, x
Y, y
Z, z

establishment for the care of the sick or wounded," first recorded in *Vicary's Anatomy* (1549) in a statement describing the objectives of St. Bartholomew Hospital in London: "For the better sustentation and comfort of the diseased and impotent persons within the said hospital."

Hospice was a late arrival, first appearing in 1818 in the sense of "a house of rest and entertainment for travelers, etc., especially one run by the monks of St. Bernard and St. Gotthard in the Alps." A description of such a house appeared in the London *Times* of December 18, 1894: "The hospice provides 20 beds, soup, bread, and coals to families, and penny dinners to sandwich-men."

The current sense of "an institution for the care of the terminally ill" is traced back to use of *hospice* in 1893 for a Dublin nursing home where destitute people who were incurably ill or dying were cared for. In 1905, the *Catholic Herald* told its readers that "The Hospice for the Dying in Cambridge Road, which is ... under the management of the Irish Sisters of Mercy, has already a few inmates." And in 1922, James Joyce wrote in *Ulysses* about "a ward for incurables" called "Our Lady's Hospice for the dying." It was in the 1960s and 1970s that the term became self-explanatory.

HUCKSTER

The Hucksters was a highly publicized film produced by MGM in 1947 from a best-selling novel by Frederic Wakeman. The *hucksters* of the title refers contemptuously to certain unscrupulous radio advertisement executives who would go to any length to land an account. While the novel and film popularized the term *huckster*, the only new thing about their use of the term was its application to radio advertising agents.

The original use of the word was not disparaging. First recorded around 1200, *huckster* was a neutral term meaning "a retailer of small goods, as in a shop, booth, or stall; a peddler, minor trader, or traveling salesman." *Huckster* has been traced to Middle Dutch *hokester* "peddler," from *hoken* "to peddle," related to English *hawk* "to peddle (wares)." This meaning remained in some use until the late 1800s, as in this passage from a December 1889 article in *The Spectator*: "From the great shops in Regent Street and Bond Street to the smallest huxters' [sic] in the slums, there are Christmas presents in the windows."

Huckster, used in the derogatory sense of "any person willing to profit in a petty way from his services, a mercenary," is seen in such examples as the haggling and petty peddler in the story *The Goblin and the Huckster* (1853) by Hans Christian Andersen, or the character in Mary Elizabeth Braddon's novel *Charlotte's Inheritance* (1868) who protests, "I am no huckster, to sell my daughter to the best bidder."

The change from a neutral to a derogatory use of the word was most likely due to a gradual mistrust and disrepute into which peddlers, especially itinerant ones, fell over the centuries because of their petty haggling.

HUMOR

"Analyzing humor," wrote E. B. White, "is like dissecting a frog. Few people are interested and the frog dies of it." This is just one of the hundreds of comments made about humor by writers, from Mark Twain to Groucho Marx, most of them not particularly humorous. What's interesting to linguists is that no writer ever defines the word *humor*. Writers just assume that everybody knows what is meant by *a sense of humor, good humor, bad humor.* But the original meaning could not be further from the current one.

In 1340, when *humor* entered the language, it meant any moisture or fluid, such as sweat, blood, or the sap of plants. From about 1380 onward, *humor* often referred to one of the four

A, a
B, b
C, c
D, d
E, e
F, f
G, g
H, h
I, i
J, j
K, k
L, l
M, m
N, n
O, o
P, p
Q, q
R, r
S, s
T, t
U, u
V, v
W, w
X, x
Y, y
Z, z

A, *a*

B, *b*

C, *c*

D, *d*

E, *e*

F, *f*

G, *g*

H, h

I, *i*

J, *j*

K, *k*

L, *l*

M, *m*

N, *n*

O, *o*

P, *p*

Q, *q*

R, *r*

S, *s*

T, *t*

U, *u*

V, *v*

W, *w*

X, *x*

Y, *y*

Z, *z*

chief fluids of the body (blood, phlegm, yellow bile or choler, and black bile or melancholy) that, according to medieval physiology, determined a person's health, mood, and disposition. From the belief in these "humors" arose around 1475 the use of this word to mean "a state of mind or feeling; mood, temper, disposition," for example, as in "Was ever woman in this humor wooed . . . Was ever woman in this humor won" (1597, Shakespeare, *Richard III*).

Ben Jonson used the word in the titles of two plays, *Every Man out of his Humour* (1599) and *Every Man in his Humour* (1601), in which he used it in the sense of "a particular inclination, a mood, fancy, whim or caprice." The meaning "an odd, jocular, or amusing quality" is found in the 1700s, in examples such as "Humour . . . in its perfection is allowed to be much preferable to wit" (1728, Jonathan Swift, *The Intelligencer*), and "That moderating and restraining balance-wheel which we call a sense of humor" (1887, John Russell Lowell, *Democracy*).

Humor was borrowed (through Old French) from Latin *hūmōrem, ūmōrem* "moisture, fluid." The word's original meaning was retained in a few modern physiological terms, such as the *aqueous humor,* which is the semi-fluid substance in front of the iris of the eye, and the *vitreous humor,* which fills the space between the iris and the retina.

HUNCH

The commonest meaning of *hunch* is "an intuitive feeling that something will happen, a presentiment or premonition." The writer William Saroyan distrusted this feeling. "More often than not," he wrote, "one is mistaken in one's hunches." The psychologist Dr. Joyce Brothers trusted it. She wrote, "Hunches are usually based on facts filed away just below the conscious level."

This meaning of *hunch* is recorded since 1904 as an extended sense of the earlier meaning (1849), "a hint, tip, suggestion," as in Zane Grey's *Wanderer of the Wasteland*: "So, son, if you're askin' me for a hunch, let me tell you, drink little a' gamble light and fight shy of the females!"

Hunch meaning "a hint, tip, or suggestion" was a figurative use of the word's original meaning, "a push, thrust, shove," which appeared in 1630. The word was derived from the verb *to hunch* "to push, thrust, shove," first recorded in 1581. This verb was perhaps the first element in *hunchbacked* (1589), but its origin is unknown.

HUSSY

Hester Prynne, the young woman in Nathaniel Hawthorne's novel, *The Scarlet Letter* (1850), is called a *hussy* by the Puritan women of the 17th-century New England town where she has been branded with a scarlet letter "A" for adulteress. One of the women, complaining about the lenient punishment given Hester, says: "If the hussy stood up for judgment before us five, . . . would she come off with such a sentence as the worshipful magistrates have awarded? Marry, I trow not."

The earliest use of *hussy* was neutral and sometimes approbative. In 1530, when it first appeared in print, it meant "the mistress of a household" and sometimes "a thrifty woman," as in Daniel Defoe's *Colonel Jack*: "Her being so good a Hussy of what money I had left her." *Hussy* was a contraction of Middle English *husewif,* an alteration of *housewif* "housewife," which in Middle English was the female equivalent of *husbonde, housebonde* "master of the house."

The derogatory use arose in the 1600s in some rural areas, where *hussy* became a mere equivalent of *woman*, and then successively "a strong country woman," "a woman of the lower classes," and "a woman of light or low character."

A, a

B, b

C, c

D, d

E, e

F, f

G, g

H, h

I, i

J, j

K, k

L, l

M, m

N, n

O, o

P, p

Q, q

R, r

S, s

T, t

U, u

V, v

W, w

X, x

Y, y

Z, z

The meaning "an ill-behaved or mischievous girl, a jade or minx," is also first seen in the 1600s, as in "Such another hussy as this was dame Alice Pierce, a concubine to our Edward III" (1647, John Trapp, *Commentary on Matthew*), and less harshly, "A more . . . impudent huzzy [sic], is not to be found in the United States" (1795, George Washington, *Writings*).

HUSTLE

No dance was more popular in the 1970s than "the hustle," a mambolike partner dance performed in discos and popularized by the movie *Saturday Night Fever*. The name of the dance is curious because it harks back to the word's earliest meaning, "a shaking together" (1715). The anachronism applies as well to the verb *to hustle* "to dance the hustle," since the earliest meaning of the verb was "to shake to and fro" (1684), as confirmed in Samuel Johnson's *Dictionary of the English Language* (1755): "*To Hustle*, to shake together in confusion."

Those of us old enough to have seen a couple hustling on the dance floor might consider Dr. Johnson's definition downright prophetic. The meaning "to shake to and fro" (1684) was borrowed from the Dutch *husselen, hutselen* "to shake, toss." That early meaning developed by the 1750s into "to push roughly, shove, jostle," as in "I was hussled [sic] by those rebellious rapscallions" (1751, Tobias Smollett, *The Adventures of Peregrine Pickle*), though Dr. Johnson barely missed recording it. An extended meaning, "to push one's way actively, to hurry or bustle," appeared in 1821, followed in 1840 in American English by the informal sense of "to obtain or produce in a pushy, rough, or illegal manner," which became the common and current meaning of the word, as in Sinclair Lewis's *Bethel Merriday* (1940): "When you grow up . . . you try to squirm into prison, or get a nice job hustling hash."

I, i

A, a
B, b
C, c
D, d
E, e
F, f
G, g
H, h
I, i
J, j
K, k
L, l
M, m
N, n
O, o
P, p
Q, q
R, r
S, s
T, t
U, u
V, v
W, w
X, x
Y, y
Z, z

IDEOLOGY

The ending *-logy,* in words like *biology, geology, psychology,* and *mythology,* means "the science or study of." The word *ideology* should therefore mean "the science or study of ideas." And that is what it meant in 1796, when it came into English from French *idéologie.* The word was coined by Count Destutt de Tracy (1754–1836), a French philosopher, to distinguish the study of the origin and nature of ideas from ancient metaphysics.

The new word was used disparagingly by the emperor Napoleon as unpractical or visionary speculation, mere theorizing, as reported by John Adams in 1813: "Napoleon has lately invented a word, which perfectly expressed my opinion . . . He calls the project ideology."

The word went out of use in these senses (except historically) by the end of the 1800s. It was revived around 1909 (through the influence of German *Ideologie*) with the now current meaning of "a set of ideas, doctrines, or beliefs, usually relating to politics or society, regarded as justifying actions." Two things stood out about this use: the word's form didn't match the sense, since *-logy* means "science or study of," *not* "a set of," and it took the plural form *ideologies.* In short, the word was a misnomer. Nevertheless, the new meaning became a great success.

The French avant-garde composer Pierre Schaeffer (1910–1995) used *ideology* broadly to deplore its effects: "We seem to be afflicted by ideologies—often, entirely incompatible ones. Thus, the ideology of scientific rigour and at the same time, the ideology of chance; ideologies of power, technology, inspiration, facility—technology with which to replace inspiration."

ILL

This little word with a long history meant originally (before 1200) "evil, wicked, depraved, perverse, etc." from Old Norse *illr* "bad, wicked, harmful." From this meaning several new ones developed. The meaning "causing pain or discomfort, offensive, painful, disagreeable" is recorded since about 1220 in such phrases as *an ill death, ill dreams, ill weather*; that of "wretched, unfortunate, disastrous" occurs around 1250 in phrases like *an ill fate, an ill moment*, and is still found in the old proverb *It's an ill wind that blows nobody good.*

The general sense of "not good, bad, poor, unsatisfactory" occurs before 1300, and is found in Shakespeare's *Romeo and Juliet*: "'Tis an ill cook that cannot lick his own fingers." The word was also used in the sense of "improper," especially in the phrase *ill manners*.

The prevailing modern sense, "out of health, sick, indisposed, not well" first appeared around 1460, in the early religious drama *Towneley Mysteries*: "Therefor full sore am I and ill." Shakespeare used it in *Much Ado About Nothing* (1600): "By my troth I am exceeding ill." The term *ill health* (often hyphenated) for a bad or unsound state of health is recorded since 1698, in a letter by John Locke: "As for writing, my ill-health gives me little heart or opportunity for it."

IMBECILE

A joke in Ambrose Bierce's *Fantastic Fables* (1899), goes like this:

> A judge said to a convicted assassin:
>
> "Prisoner at the bar, have you anything to say why the death-sentence should not be passed upon you?"
>
> "Will what I say make any difference?" asked the convicted assassin.
>
> "I do not see how it can," the judge answered, reflectively. "No, it will not."

A, *a*
B, *b*
C, *c*
D, *d*
E, *e*
F, *f*
G, *g*
H, *h*
I, *i*
J, *j*
K, *k*
L, *l*
M, *m*
N, *n*
O, *o*
P, *p*
Q, *q*
R, *r*
S, *s*
T, *t*
U, *u*
V, *v*
W, *w*
X, *x*
Y, *y*
Z, *z*

A, a

B, b

C, c

D, d

E, e

F, f

G, g

H, h

I, i

J, j

K, k

L, l

M, m

N, n

O, o

P, p

Q, q

R, r

S, s

T, t

U, u

V, v

W, w

X, x

Y, y

Z, z

> "Then," said the doomed one, "I should just like
> to remark that you are the most unspeakable
> old imbecile in seven States and the District of
> Columbia."

While *imbecile* is currently used as a noun, it was originally an adjective, and when it came into English around 1550, it did not concern feeble-mindedness or mental retardation. It was a neutral word, meaning "physically weak or impotent," borrowed from the Old French *imbécille* "weak, feeble" (from Latin *imbēcillus*). In 1730, Nathan Bailey defined it as "Weak, Feeble" in his *Dictionary*, and it was used in this sense by Shelley in *Queen Mab* (1813): "His stunted stature and imbecile frame."

The current sense of "feeble-minded, stupid, idiotic," is first found in 1804, and was used explicitly by Thomas De Quincey in 1846: "But he had the misfortune to be 'imbecile' . . . in fact, he was partially an idiot." The noun, meaning "one who is imbecile, a feeble-minded person," is found about the same time, and widely used after that as a term of insult and reproach, as in H. Bulwer-Lytton's *Alice* (1838): "These haughty imbeciles shall fall in the trap they set for us."

IMPERTINENT

We call an impudent, presumptuous, insolent person "impertinent." One might wonder why the meaning of this word is not simply "not pertinent, not pertaining (to); not to the point, irrelevant." As a usage note on a Web site points out, "Only snobs and very old-fashioned people use 'impertinent' correctly; most people would be well advised to forget it and use "irrelevant" instead to mean the opposite of 'pertinent'."

Indeed, *impertinent* made its debut around 1380 with the meaning "not pertinent, unconnected, irrelevant," and was used in this sense until the 1800s. It's found in Chaucer around 1386 in *The Canterbury Tales* ("Truly as to my judgment one thinketh it a thing impertinent"), and Shakespeare used it in *The Tempest* (before 1616): "I'll bring thee to the present business Which now's upon us: without the which, this Story were most impertinent."

The sense of "not pertinent, irrelevant" was extended to "not appropriate, incongruous, unsuitable," in phrases like *impertinent medicines, the impertinent costs of funerals.* By 1706 it was used loosely to mean "absurd, silly," especially when applied to persons, as in "The Ladies whom you visit, think a wise Man the most impertinent Creature living" (1711, Sir Richard Steele, in *The Spectator*).

From these extended uses developed the current sense of "impudent, presumptuous, insolent or saucy in speech or behavior," which is first attested in a letter in which members of a church council are disparaged for "their impertinent boldness and impudence by all men." In 1825, Jane Austen applied it to a suitor in the novel *Lady Susan*: "I like him on the whole very well; he is clever and has a good deal to say, but he is sometimes impertinent and troublesome."

INANE

Inane is an important word, much used throughout literature by writers such as Mark Twain, Charles Dickens, Rudyard Kipling, Joseph Conrad, Jack London, Somerset Maugham, and many others. And if a U.S. senator like Orrin Hatch uses it, you have to stand up, click your heels, and lend an ear as he intones oratorically: "Michael Moore is free to denounce every manifestation of American foreign policy, is he not? And we are upholding his right to do so, as ridiculous and inane and asinine as his comments are."

Originally (1662) *inane* was a serious term meaning "empty, void," referring to the "formless void" of infinite space. (*Inane* was borrowed from Latin *inānis* "empty, useless.") It was

A, a
B, b
C, c
D, d
E, e
F, f
G, g
H, h
I, i
J, j
K, k
L, l
M, m
N, n
O, o
P, p
Q, q
R, r
S, s
T, t
U, u
V, v
W, w
X, x
Y, y
Z, z

A, a
B, b
C, c
D, d
E, e
F, f
G, g
H, h
I, i
J, j
K, k
L, l
M, m
N, n
O, o
P, p
Q, q
R, r
S, s
T, t
U, u
V, v
W, w
X, x
Y, y
Z, z

frequently used as a noun, meaning "infinite space," as in John Locke's *Essay Concerning Human Understanding* (1690): "The capacious mind of man . . . makes excursions into the incomprehensible Inane."

The meaning then extended from "empty" to "empty-headed." *Inane* now means "void of sense, senseless, silly, stupid, empty-headed," first used by the poet Shelley in his drama *The Cenci* (1819): "Some inane and vacant smile." In 1880, Mark Twain wrote in *A Tramp Abroad*: "It [Baden-Baden] is an inane town, filled with sham, and petty fraud, and snobbery, but the baths are good."

INSULT, EXULT

When *to insult* came into the language, in the late 1500s, it meant "to boast, brag, triumph, especially in an insolent or scornful way," as in "The Dutch do mightily insult of their victory, and they have great reason" (1666, Samuel Pepys, *Diary*).

The meaning of *exult* is interchangeable here. Indeed, the poet Algernon Charles Swinburne used them as synonyms in his *Poems and Ballads* (1865): "As plague in a poisonous city / Insults and exults on her dead."

The two words owed their resemblance to the fact that both were borrowed from closely related Latin words, *insultāre* "to leap at or on" and *exultāre* "to leap out." Both verbs came into English at the same time and were therefore quickly differentiated. *To exult* meant "to leap for joy, rejoice, be elated," while *to insult* meant "to leap for joy insolently or scornfully." *Exult* kept its original meaning over the centuries, while *insult* went on to develop the new meaning in use today, "to assail offensively, treat with scorn or abuse; to offend, affront," a meaning totally devoid of the idea of leaping for joy or glee that was in the original sense.

The new meaning appeared in 1620 and soon became standard. A recent editorial in the *New York Times* reported: "New laws in Iraq criminalize speech that ridicules the government ... and any journalist who 'publicly insults' the government or public officials can be subject to up to seven years in prison." As a contrast, the American poet and former Poet Laureate Robert Pinsky posted an article titled "Dissed in Verse" in the online magazine *Slate*, in which he discusses some of the best-known insulting poems in English literature. Among them is an epigram by the poet Paul Engle on the Duke of Alba as painted by Goya:

> This is the kind of face that sheep
> Must count at night, when they can't sleep.

strange INTERLUDE

Georges Clemenceau, the French prime minister in World War I, is said to have once declared: "I don't know whether war is an interlude during peace, or peace an interlude during war." It is an apt illustration of the chief current meaning of *interlude*, "an interval in the course of an action or event, an intervening time or space."

The oldest meaning of *interlude,* traced back to 1303, was "a light or humorous act or skit, often involving mimicry, introduced between the acts of a long mystery or morality play." *Interlude* was formed from Latin *inter-* "between" + *lūdus* "play." Such *interludes* served as comic relief to the somber, heavily religious medieval mystery plays. By the 1500s, the word was used to mean "a comedy, a farce," as in the prologue to the comedy *Ralph Roister Doister* (before 1553), where the playwright Nicolas Udall explains: "Our Comedy or Enterlude, which we intend to play, Is named Royster Doyster in deed." Since the original comic routines were performed at intervals between acts, the word *interlude* came to mean in the 1700s "an interval between the acts of a play."

A, a
B, b
C, c
D, d
E, e
F, f
G, g
H, h
I, i
J, j
K, k
L, l
M, m
N, n
O, o
P, p
Q, q
R, r
S, s
T, t
U, u
V, v
W, w
X, x
Y, y
Z, z

A, a

B, b

C, c

D, d

E, e

F, f

G, g

H, h

I, i

J, j

K, k

L, l

M, m

N, n

O, o

P, p

Q, q

R, r

S, s

T, t

U, u

V, v

W, w

X, x

Y, y

Z, z

The current meaning, first found in 1751, was transferred from this earlier theatrical meaning. This sense is often used figuratively, as in Eugene O'Neill's 1928 play *Strange Interlude* (made into a movie in 1932), where the playwright speaks of life as the strange interlude in which "we call upon past and future to bear witness that we are living."

INTERNECINE *war*

Headlines use *internecine* as if it were an everyday household word: "Internecine Shiite Killings Resume in Iraq," "Internecine Violence Grows in Gaza," "Internecine warfare Frightens Eastern Sri Lanka." The meaning of the word in these alarming headlines is "within a nation, organization, or other group, internal," and occurs in phrases like *internecine conflict, internecine struggle,* and *internecine war.* How this word came to have this particular meaning illustrates the power of the dictionary.

The word's original meaning was "characterized by great slaughter; deadly," and *internecine war* meant "a war of extermination, a war to the death." It first appeared in 1663, in Samuel Butler's satiric poem *Hudibras*: "The Egyptians worshipp'd Dogs, and for their faith made internecine war." Butler borrowed the word from Latin *internecīnus* "marked by slaughter, fought to the death, murderous," formed from *inter-* "together, each other" + *necāre* "to kill," related to Greek *nekrós* "dead body."

When Samuel Johnson wrote his *Dictionary of the English Language* (1755), he included the word *internecine*, but being unfamiliar with the meaning of the Latin word borrowed by Butler, he defined *internecine* as "endeavouring mutual destruction," thinking that the prefix *inter-* meant "between, mutual," as it did in words like *interchange* and *interpose.* The authority of Johnson's dictionary was such that no one dared question its accuracy, and so his definition became generally accepted, as in Frederic W. Farrar's *The Early Days of Christianity* (1882):

"Eight thousand Zealots, who stabbed each other in internecine massacre."

Connection of *inter-* with *internal* has further extended the word's sense to the loose meaning "within a nation or group, internal," in its current use, so that you hear about "the internecine struggle within a church" or "internecine strife in a football league."

INVEST

Historically, this word had to do with getting dressed. *To invest* meant originally (1533) "to clothe or dress (a person), especially with the garments or insignia of an office," as in *to invest princes in royal silks and velvets*. In 1564, *invest* was extended in meaning to "endow or furnish with power, privilege, etc." In 1590 it was further extended to mean "settle or secure a right or power in (a person or body)," as in "The powers invested in Congress were in effect" (1794, Samuel Williams, *The Natural and Civil History of Vermont*).

The most far-reaching change in the meaning of *invest* is recorded in letters written in the years 1613–1616 in connection with the East Indian trade. That meaning was "to use (money) in buying anything from which interest, dividends, or profit is expected, such as property, stocks, and shares," as in "Many of them even invested their property in Indian stock" (1840, Macauley, *Essays*). *Invest* was borrowed from Latin *investīre* "to clothe in, cover," formed from *in-* "in" + *vestīre* "to clothe, dress," from *vestis* "garment." A figurative meaning arose in the 1800s, as in "He has most profitably invested his time and energy in the anti-slavery cause" (1837, Harriet Martineau, *Society in America*).

See also DIVEST

A, *a*
B, *b*
C, *c*
D, *d*
E, *e*
F, *f*
G, *g*
H, *h*
⟩ I, *i*
J, *j*
K, *k*
L, *l*
M, *m*
N, *n*
O, *o*
P, *p*
Q, *q*
R, *r*
S, *s*
T, *t*
U, *u*
V, *v*
W, *w*
X, *x*
Y, *y*
Z, *z*

A, a
B, b
C, c
D, d
E, e
F, f
G, g
H, h
I, i
J, j
K, k
L, l
M, m
N, n
O, o
P, p
Q, q
R, r
S, s
T, t
U, u
V, v
W, w
X, x
Y, y
Z, z

at ISSUE

Issue is a word politicians live and swear by. A Web site (ontheissues.org) announces on its masthead "Every Political Leader on Every Issue" and lists under the headings "International Issues," "Domestic Issues," and "Economic Issues" topics that run the gamut from Abortion to Welfare & Poverty.

It might interest candidates for office to learn that the oldest meaning of *issue* on record (before 1300) was "a way out, an exit." This is how Thackeray used the word in *The Virginians* (1859): "As my Lady Castlewood . . . passed through one door of the saloon . . . my Lord Castlewood departed by another issue." The reason *issue* meant "an exit" is that the word was borrowed from Old French *issue, eissue* "a going out, an exit," from *issir, eissir* "to go out, exit," from Latin *exīre* (formed from *ex-* "out" + *īre* "to go"), the source of English *exit*.

From "an exit" the meaning "an outflowing stream, an outlet" developed in 1375, and in 1377, "any outcome or product, especially offspring, progeny," as in "Of that damsel came forth issue . . . both good and true" (about 1450, H. Lovelich, *History of the Holy Grail*).

In 1511 appeared the legal sense "the outcome of the pleadings between contending parties." From this meaning arose that of "a matter or point to be decided" about 1566, as in "There is a mighty issue at stake . . . the good or evil of the human soul" (1874, Benjamin Jowett's translation of Plato's *Dialogues*).

J, j

A, a

B, b

C, c

D, d

E, e

F, f

G, g

H, h

I, i

J, j

K, k

L, l

M, m

N, n

O, o

P, p

Q, q

R, r

S, s

T, t

U, u

V, v

W, w

X, x

Y, y

Z, z

JEOPARDY

We know that *Jeopardy!* is a TV trivia game show. But as it happens, the word *jeopardy* has long been associated with games. The first use of *jeopardy* was as a term in the game of chess—it meant any problem in the game. The earliest example of this sense is in Chaucer's *The Book of the Duchess* (around 1369), where he writes:

> Would I had once or twice . . . know the jeopardies
> That could the Greek Pythagoras, I should have
> played the bet at chess.

From this meaning arose the sense of "any uncertain or chancy position in a game or other undertaking," as in Chaucer's *Troilus and Criseyde* (around 1374): "For Troy is brought in such a jeopardy That it to save is no remedy." *Jeopardy*, the word, was borrowed from Old French *jeu parti* "divided play or game, even game" (in which the chances of winning or losing are even).

By the 1400s the meaning was generalized to "any risk, peril, or danger," as in "I think . . . that if the colonists had been defeated, our liberties would have been for a time in considerable jeopardy" (1857, Henry Thomas Buckle, *History of Civilisation in England*).

Incidentally, the title *double jeopardy!* for the second round in *Jeopardy!* was borrowed from *double jeopardy,* the legal term for the constitutional right that protects a defendant from being tried a second time for the same crime.

JINXED!

The first recorded use of *jinx* was in a comic strip published in 1908 by Harry Conway ("Bud") Fisher, an American cartoonist. The comic strip was titled *A. Mutt*, and it featured a tall, skinny character called Mr. Augustus Mutt. In the strip, the character says, "There's a jinx on me. Here's where I quit." Later he adds, "That hedge always was a jinx to me." It was also in 1908 that

Fisher added a second character to the strip, a little fellow called "Jeff," and the immensely popular "Mutt and Jeff" team was born.

According to the *Random House Historical Dictionary of American Slang* (*HDAS*), *jinx* was an alteration of the word *jynx*, meaning "a magic charm or spell," which was borrowed from Latin and Greek *iynx* "the wryneck," an Old World bird of the woodpecker family that was used in magic for the snakelike contortions of its neck and habit of hissing like a snake.

The word was apparently reintroduced as sports slang around 1905 in the sense of "a spell of bad luck." It may have been influenced by *jinks,* the plural of *jink* "quick turn, dodge," a Scottish word best known in the phrase *high jinks*, originally (1699) "a drinking frolic consisting of deciding by a throw of dice who should perform some ludicrous act, or who should empty a large bowl of liquor, a failure in either case entailing a forfeit." A loser at high jinks may have felt, well, jinxed.

JOB *description*

Dictionaries that give the earliest date of *job* usually cite the year 1627 with the definition "a piece of work, especially a piece of work done in one's occupation or profession," as used by Thomas Middleton in *The Mayor of Quinborough* (before 1627): "I cannot read, I keep a Clark to do those jobs for need." This meaning was extended by 1660 (in Samuel Pepys's *Diary*) to "a piece of work or transaction done for hire or for profit," and by 1694 to "any business, operation, or matter to be done," as in "'Tis an ugly job: but soldiers obey commands" (1879, Robert Browning, *Martin Relph*). The meaning "a paid position of employment" is first found before 1861, in Theodore Winthrop's novel *Edwin Brothertoft*: "I will find you a fat job and plenty of pickings!"

However, the *Oxford English Dictionary* traces the word back to 1557 in the clause "doing certain jobs of work" found in documents of the English law courts. The phrase *jobs of work* connects

A, a
B, b
C, c
D, d
E, e
F, f
G, g
H, h
I, i
J, j
K, k
L, l
M, m
N, n
O, o
P, p
Q, q
R, r
S, s
T, t
U, u
V, v
W, w
X, x
Y, y
Z, z

A, a

B, b

C, c

D, d

E, e

F, f

G, g

H, h

I, i

J, j

K, k

L, l

M, m

N, n

O, o

P, p

Q, q

R, r

S, s

T, t

U, u

V, v

W, w

X, x

Y, y

Z, z

the word with the earlier phrase (about 1540) *jobs of gold*, where *job* means "a piece, lump, block," and the phrases *a job of thorns* (1560) and *jobs of straw*, where *job* means "a load, especially a cart-load." These senses of *job* suggest that the word was a variant form of the earlier (1382) *gob* "a mass or lump," as in *a gob of mud, a gob of blood, a gob of gold*. The word *gob* was apparently borrowed from Old French *gobe, goube* "a lump, mass, mouthful," related to *gober* "to gulp or swallow down," of Celtic origin, akin to Old Irish *gob* "beaklike mouth" and Gaelic *gob* "beak, mouth."

JOCKEY

A *jockey* can be many things, not just the professional rider in horse races. It can be any worker or operator, as a *computer jockey, an elevator jockey, a garage jockey, a disc jockey, a video jockey*. What's distinctive about all of these is that they are retronyms, new compounds created from a word to avoid clashing with that word, in this case the word *jockey*, which is reserved for a rider in a horse race.

In its oldest use, however, a *jockey* was just a boy or kid, as in Dickens's *Dombey & Son* (1846): "'You're Dombey's jockey, an't you?' said the first man. 'I'm in Dombey's House, Mr. Clark,' returned the boy." This meaning of the word is recorded before 1529. Originally the word was a diminutive form of the name *Jock*, a Scottish and northern English variant of *Jack*, in the sense "little Jock, Jacky." Then it came to be familiarly used to refer to or address any working man or boy, as one working in stables or with horses.

In 1638 the word was applied to a horse dealer, as in "If I had a mind to sell my mule, he was acquainted with a very honest jockey who would buy her" (Tobias Smollett, *Gill Blas*). It was later used for one who rides or drives a horse in a horse-drawn carriage, a postilion, and before 1684, in John Evelyn's *Diary*, the word was specifically used for a professional rider in horse races, the main meaning today. This meaning was extended in

1915 to a driver of an automobile, truck, or other motor vehicle, in the retronyms *car jockey, Jeep jockey, truck jockey.*

a pile of JUNK

Thomas Edison, the great inventor who used whatever object he could lay his hands on to create inventions like the electric light bulb and the phonograph, once famously said, "To invent, all you need is a good imagination and a pile of junk." *Junk* figuratively means "stuff and things, belongings," as in *We have a lot of junk in the attic.* We talk of *junk food, junk mail, junk shop, junk art, junkyard, junk bonds,* and even *junk DNA* (DNA segments with no known function).

The original meaning of *junk* was nautical, "an old or inferior cable or rope," recorded since the 1300s as *jonke, junke,* which originally meant "the rush, a plant of the genus *Juncus,* whose stems are used to make chair bottoms, baskets, etc.," borrowed about 1400 from Old French *jonc, junc* "rush, reed." These old cables or ropes were not discarded but cut up in short lengths and used for making fenders to protect a ship from being scraped, gaskets to secure furled sails, and other useful things, a meaning found in Samuel Pepys's *Diary* (1666) and in *Anson's Voyage* (1748): "We had not a sufficient quantity of junk to make spun-yarn."

The nautical meaning was extended in 1842 to "any old or discarded material, especially material that can be put to some use," as in "His 'junk', however, was not devoid of ... taste and luxury ..." (1924, John Galsworthy, *The White Monkey*), and "Collecting junk for creative work is a way of life at school" (1974, *Woman* magazine).

The neutral, even approbatory, use of *junk* allowed for the coinage of such terms as *junk jewelry* (1939) "costume jewelry," *junk mail* (1954) "unsolicited circulars, advertisements, etc., sent by mail," *junk art* (1966) "three-dimensional art made from dis-

A, a

B, b

C, c

D, d

E, e

F, f

G, g

H, h

I, i

J, j

K, k

L, l

M, m

N, n

O, o

P, p

Q, q

R, r

S, s

T, t

U, u

V, v

W, w

X, x

Y, y

Z, z

carded material," and *junk food* (1973) "standardized food, especially food sold in fast-food establishments."

JUNKET

A *press junket* is a public relations or media event sponsored by a movie studio to promote a new motion picture. Among other, less publicized junkets are the business junkets taken by corporate executives at their company's expense, and the political junkets, in which government officials take trips at the government's expense. In 1985, the U.S. Secretary of State, Dean Rusk, was quoted in *Time* magazine as saying: "Give a member of Congress a junket and a mimeograph machine and he thinks he is secretary of state."

The earliest use of the word, "a basket, originally made of rushes, especially a basket for carrying fish," is a far cry from today's meaning. It is first found in 1382, in Wycliffe's translation of the Bible (Exodus 2:3: "When she might hide him no longer, she took a junket of rushes . . . and put the little child within." The word was borrowed from Old North French *jonquette* "rush basket," from Latin *juncus* "rush, reed."

Around 1460, *junket* came to mean a cream-cheese or other cream dish originally made in a rush basket or served on a rush mat. This meaning developed into "a banquet or feast," as in Richard Vines's *Treatise on the Lord's Supper* (before 1655): "With this junkets and feasts they joined the celebration of the Lord's Supper."

Today's meaning of *junket*, defined in dictionaries as "a pleasure trip or outing, often involving expensive meals and accommodations," is traced back to the 1800s, in uses such as Fanny Burney's *The Wanderer* (1814): "I come . . . to ask the favor of your company . . . to a little junket at our farm."

K, k

A, a

B, b

C, c

D, d

E, e

F, f

G, g

H, h

I, i

J, j

K, k

L, l

M, m

N, n

O, o

P, p

Q, q

R, r

S, s

T, t

U, u

V, v

W, w

X, x

Y, y

Z, z

KID

From a most humble beginning, the word *kid* has worked its way up to become one of the most successful words in the language. *Kid* was borrowed from Old Norse *kidh* "young goat," found in Swedish and Danish *kid*, and corresponding to Middle High German *kitze* "young goat." At its introduction into English around the year 1200, *kid* simply meant "a young goat," a meaning extended in 1486 to "a young roe deer," and in 1884 to "a young antelope."

A big change occurred in 1618, when a contemptuous use of *kid* to mean "a child or young person" arose in vulgar slang in England. By the 1800s, the slang use of *kid* became an informal word for a child, so that by 1841 Lord Shaftesbury could write in his *Diary*: "Passed a few days happily with my wife and kids."

In the early 1800s *kid* also became a term of admiration for a young thief, boxer, or the like, a use defined in James Hardy Vaux's *Vocabulary of the Flash Language* (1819) as "*Kid*, . . . particularly applied to a boy who commences thief at an early age; and when by his dexterity he has become famous, he is called by his acquaintants *the kid* and so on." This use led to giving outlaws or athletes nicknames like the *Colorado Kid* and the *Sundance Kid*. This pattern led to other nicknames, such as *the Comeback Kid*, for anyone, especially a politician, who has made a surprising comeback after a defeat.

In the 1920s the word was used in addressing people informally, as in *Hello, kids, Stick around, kid, I'll tell you what I'll do, kid*. By the 1940s, popular set phrases cropped up, like *a happy-go-lucky kid, the new kid on the block, a good kid, a cute kid*, and was commonly applied to a girl or young woman, perhaps most famously in the film *Casablanca* (1942), when Rick tells Ilsa (no less than four times), "Here's looking at you, kid."

KILL

See QUELL

the whole KIT *and caboodle*

What is the origin of *kit*? The word first occurs in Middle English (1325) with the rather plain, rustic meaning of "a wooden tub, vessel, or bucket, used for holding or carrying milk, butter, fish, etc.," borrowed from Middle Dutch *kitte* "wooden container."

The original meaning was extended in the 1700s to "a traveling bag or knapsack carrying a soldier's supplies." This meaning was in turn extended in 1834 to "a collection of personal effects packed up for traveling," and in 1859 to "a collection of tools, equipment, etc., especially a collection of parts sold for a buyer to assemble," as in *a tool kit, a do-it-yourself telescope kit, a miniature-car kit.*

The earliest reference to the phrase, *the whole kit* comes from Francis Grose's *A Classical Dictionary of the Vulgar Tongue* (1785): "*Kit* . . . is also used to express the whole of different commodities; as Here, take the whole kit; i.e. take all." The poet Shelley, too, used it in his *Œdipus Tyrannus* (1821): "I'll sell you in a lump, The whole kit of them." And so did Dickens, in *Great Expectations* (1861): "A better gentleman than the whole kit on you put together."

After *the whole kit* became common in the 1800s, a similar phrase popped up: *the whole kit and caboodle,* as in "And no more schnapps, mind, until we're clear of the whole kit and caboodle" (1915, Jack London, *Jerry of the Islands*).

KNAVE *and* KNIGHT

In Old English (about 950) both of these words meant "a boy or youth," especially a boy or youth employed as a servant or at-

A, *a*
B, *b*
C, *c*
D, *d*
E, *e*
F, *f*
G, *g*
H, *h*
I, *i*
J, *j*
K, *k*
L, *l*
M, *m*
N, *n*
O, *o*
P, *p*
Q, *q*
R, *r*
S, *s*
T, *t*
U, *u*
V, *v*
W, *w*
X, *x*
Y, *y*
Z, *z*

A, a
B, b
C, c
D, d
E, e
F, f
G, g
H, h
I, i
J, j
K, k
L, l
M, m
N, n
O, o
P, p
Q, q
R, r
S, s
T, t
U, u
V, v
W, w
X, x
Y, y
Z, z

tendant. Middle English *knave* developed from Old English *cnafa* "boy" (corresponding to German *Knabe*) and Middle English *knight* developed from Old English *cniht* "boy," (earlier) "young slave" (corresponding to German *Knecht* "serf, slave"). But in early Middle English the two words began to diverge in meaning as the fortunes of the two boys changed drastically.

Around 1100, *knave* came to mean "a domestic servant of low condition." The pejoration continued into the 1200s, when *knave* came by extension to mean "any man of low or ignoble character," and later "a man given to dishonorable or deceitful ways, a crafty rogue," as in "The common practice is to accuse a man of being either a fool or a knave" (1800, Duke of Wellington).

In contrast to the knave, the knight became idealized, as "a military servant or follower (of a king or other person of rank)" exemplified in Pope's *The Rape of the Lock* (1712): "So Ladies in Romance assist their Knight, Present the spear, and arm him for the Fight." In the British feudal system, *knight* became a title of honor conferred on one who had worked his way up to a high rank in the military profession.

The distinction between a knave and a knight was carried over to games: in card games, the lowest card in a suit, the jack, was named in 1568 a *knave*; while around 1440 one of the important pieces in chess was named a *knight*. The irony in the degradation of *knave* and the glorification of *knight* is that historically the basic meaning of *knave* was the neutral "boy," whereas the basic meaning of *knight* was a servant or slave, and only in Old English did it mean a boy or youth.

L, l

A, a

B, b

C, c

D, d

E, e

F, f

G, g

H, h

I, i

J, j

K, k

L, l

M, m

N, n

O, o

P, p

Q, q

R, r

S, s

T, t

U, u

V, v

W, w

X, x

Y, y

Z, z

LARVA

The original meaning of *larva* in English was not the zoological one we learned in high school. When we think of a *larva* (plural *larvae*), we picture the wormlike caterpillar of a butterfly or moth, the nymph of a dragonfly, or the grub of other insects. It was the Swedish naturalist Carolus Linnaeus (1707–1778), who first applied the word *larva* to the early immature form of insects before metamorphosis. The word in this sense was first recorded in English in 1768, over a hundred years after it came into the language with an entirely different meaning.

The original meaning of *larva* was "a disembodied spirit, a ghost or specter," and was first used by an English clergyman, Richard Baxter, in a discourse on infant baptism titled *Plain Scripture Proof* (1691): "I live almost perpetually in my bed or chair or pulpit . . . such a *larva* I am that here am called up." He borrowed the word from Latin *lārva*, meaning "a ghost or specter, a mask," which was related to *lār* (plural *larēs*), a benevolent spirit of the dead.

Linnaeus in the 1700s, looking for a word for the form of an immature insect that masks or disguises the adult form, seized upon the Latin word for "mask" and used it in his classification of insects and other animals.

LATITUDE *and* LONGITUDE

This pair of words, essential in the physical sciences, came into English from the pen of a great literary figure, the author of *The Canterbury Tales*, Geoffrey Chaucer (1340–1400). In 1391, Chaucer presented the son of a friend of his with an astrolabe, an instrument used for calculating the daily positions of the sun and other stars. In order to explain its uses, Chaucer wrote *The Treatise on the Astrolabe*, which is considered today the oldest technical manual in English. In the treatise, Chaucer uses *latitude* to mean "extent from side to side, breadth, width," and *longitude*, "extent from end to end, length, height."

Beyond these early meanings, the two words developed in different directions. Starting with Bacon's *Of the Advancement of Learning* (1605), *latitude* has been used figuratively to mean "freedom from narrow restraints or limitations, permitted or tolerated range of action," as in "There is much greater latitude for comic than tragic artifices" (1711, Joseph Addison, in *The Spectator*). The word was also used in the sense of "extent, range, scope" by Bacon in 1605: "It is a thing of great use well to define, what, and of what latitude those points are."

On the other hand, since 1607 *longitude* has had only a short-lived figurative sense of "long continuance," as in *the longitude or brevity of a disease, the longitude of their labors*. Its main use has been technical, as in geography meaning "the angular distance east or west on the earth's surface," as opposed to *latitude* "the angular distance north or south on the earth's surface."

Both words were borrowed from Latin. *Latitude* came from Latin *lātitūdo* "breadth, width," from *lātus* "broad, wide." *Longitude* came from Latin *longitūdo*, from *longus* "long," related to English *long*.

LAUNCH

You can *launch* a rocket or spacecraft, a ship or balloon, an assault or offensive, an enterprise or business, a new product or a career—in fact, you can *launch* anything when you mean "to start or send off on a course," usually with a big splash. Yet none of these uses existed when the verb *launch* sprang into English sometime before 1300.

Launch was borrowed from Old North French *lancher, lanchier* "to hurl, throw," from Late Latin *lanceāre* "to wield a lance, pierce with a lance." It first appeared in the long medieval romance poem *Kyng Alisaunder*, about the life of Alexander the Great, and was used in the sense of "to rush, leap, plunge, vault": "He gone in the water [to] launch: Up he came in that other side."

A, *a*
B, *b*
C, *c*
D, *d*
E, *e*
F, *f*
G, *g*
H, *h*
I, *i*
J, *j*
K, *k*
L, *l*
M, *m*
N, *n*
O, *o*
P, *p*
Q, *q*
R, *r*
S, *s*
T, *t*
U, *u*
V, *v*
W, *w*
X, *x*
Y, *y*
Z, *z*

A, a

B, b

C, c

D, d

E, e

F, f

G, g

H, h

I, i

J, j

K, k

L, l

M, m

N, n

O, o

P, p

Q, q

R, r

S, s

T, t

U, u

V, v

W, w

X, x

Y, y

Z, z

The extended meaning "to hurl, shoot, discharge" appeared about 1489 in a translation from the French by William Caxton: "Launching and casting to him spears and darts." This meaning was extended in the early 1600s to the wider sense of "to send off, start on a course, release," as in "On 19 Sept. 1783 . . . they launched a sheep, a cock and a duck in the air, enclosed in a basket suspended beneath the balloon" (1959, *Chambers's Encyclopaedia*).

The figurative meanings "to start (someone) in a business or on a career; to begin a project, action, etc." came into use in 1602, as in "It was agreed that . . . as soon as I should be fairly launched in business we would be married" (Washington Irving, *Wolfert's Roost*). A second figurative meaning "to enter boldly into some action; rush or burst into something" appeared in 1608, and has been used in many contexts, such as "He then launched himself lovingly into his work" (1872, Mark Twain, *Roughing It*).

The military sense, "to mount (an assault or offensive)," is recorded since 1916, as in "Were it not for this program, our intelligence community believes that al Qaeda and its allies succeeded in launching another attack against the American homeland" (George W. Bush, Sept. 2006 press conference).

LECTURE

A *lecture* is a planned talk given before an audience on a given subject, the kind Ralph Waldo Emerson dismissed in his *Poems* (1847): "I can spare the college-bell, And the learned lecture well." A lecturer, as cynically defined in Ambrose Bierce's *The Devil's Dictionary* (1911) is "One with his hand in your pocket, his tongue in your ear and his faith in your patience."

The earliest meaning of *lecture*, attested in 1398, was "the act of reading," borrowed through Old French *lecture* from Medieval Latin *lectura* "a reading," from Latin *lect-, legere* "to read." This meaning is found in literary works of the early 1900s, as in

A, a

B, b

C, c

D, d

E, e

F, f

G, g

H, h

I, i

J, j

K, k

L, l

M, m

N, n

O, o

P, p

Q, q

R, r

S, s

T, t

U, u

V, v

W, w

X, x

Y, y

Z, z

Joseph Conrad's *Nostromo* (1904): "In about a year he had evolved from the lecture of the letters a definite conviction," and in James Joyce's *Ulysses* (1922): "What fractures of phrases did the lecture of those four whole words evoke?"

The current meaning of *lecture* is first found in print in 1536, in the *Acts of Henry VIII*: "To read one open and public lecture in every of the said Universities in any such Science or tongue...." This meaning of *lecture* derived from the fact that such discourses were *read*, never delivered impromptu or from memory.

The phrase *to read a lecture*, meaning "to deliver a speech of reproof or reprimand," occurs first in Shakespeare's *As You Like It* (1600), where Rosalind, disguised as a boy, tells Orlando: "I have heard him [her uncle] read many lectures against it, and I thank God I am not a woman, to be touched with so many giddy offences as he has generally taxed their whole sex withal." The verb *to lecture*, meaning "to admonish, reprimand," appeared in 1706.

LENIENT

In the 1650s a health-conscious person could ask the neighborhood druggist for a lenient emollient to soothe an aching back. The noun *emollient*, meaning a softening agent, appeared in 1656; the adjective *lenient,* meaning "soothing, relaxing, softening," appeared in 1652. So there you had two new modish words, both borrowed from French, which in combination spelled an advance in medicine.

Lenient in the sense of "soothing, softening" is first found in a 1652 treatise by a Dr. John French, titled *The Yorkshire Spaw*, in which he writes: "Taking ... a little Cassia, or some such lenient medicament." In 1672, the word was used as a soothing or softening agent in Richard Wiseman's *Treatment of Wounds*: "I ... cleansed the wound, and drest him up with lenients." *Lenient* was borrowed from Latin *lēnient-, lēniens* "soothing," from *lēnis* "soft, mild."

A, a

B, b

C, c

D, d

E, e

F, f

G, g

H, h

I, i

J, j

K, k

L, l

M, m

N, n

O, o

P, p

Q, q

R, r

S, s

T, t

U, u

V, v

W, w

X, x

Y, y

Z, z

The extended meaning "gentle, mild, tolerant," applied to persons or their actions or dispositions, is first attested in 1787, in G. Winter's *A New and Compendious System of Husbandry*: "The lenient laws of this happy isle do not compel men to get or save." Jane Austen used the word in this sense in her epistolary novel *Lady Susan* (1805): "I am afraid I have often been too indulgent . . . ; you must urge the necessity of reproof if you see me too lenient." And Dickens used it in this sense in *The Mystery of Edwin Drood* (1870): "We have so much reason to be very lenient to each other." This is, of course, the current meaning of the word.

LEWD *e-mails*

The U.S. Code of law reads in part: "Every obscene, lewd, lascivious, indecent, filthy or vile article, matter, thing, device, or substance [is] declared to be nonmailable matter and shall not be conveyed in the mails or delivered from any post office or by any letter carrier." If you think that every possible descriptive term for salacious material is listed in this sentence, think again. Inexplicably, the list omits *lecherous, lustful, bawdy, libidinous, licentious, prurient, wanton,* and, yes, *salacious.* Among all the synonyms, however, none is more often used than the four-letter word *lewd.*

Lewd is defined in *Random House Webster's College Dictionary* as "1. inclined to, characterized by, or inciting to lust or lechery; lascivious. 2. obscene or indecent, as language; salacious." But in the year 890 in King Alfred's translation of Bede's *Ecclesiastical History*, the first meaning of lewd (or *lǽwede* at the time) was "not in holy orders, not clerical, lay." Chaucer, in the Prologue to *The Canterbury Tales* (about 1396) used the word in this sense:

> "For if a priest be foul, on whom we trust,
> No wonder is a lewed man to rust."

Since a lay person was regarded as uneducated, by 1220 *lewd* had come to mean "unlettered, untaught," and was often used in contrasting phrases like *learned and lewd, the lewd and learned,* meaning everybody. This led in the 1300s to a rapid degradation in the word's meaning:

1. "ignorant, ill-bred, unskillful," as in Thomas Hoccleve's *Regiment of Princes* (before 1420): "I am as lewd and dull as is an ass."

2. "belonging to the lower classes; common, low, vulgar," as in William Patten's *The Expedition into Scotland* (1548): "A few lewd soldiers ran rashly out of array without standard or captain."

3. (of persons or their actions) "bad, vile, evil, wicked," as in Milton's *Paradise Lost* (1667): "So . . . into his Church lewd hirelings climb."

Lewd has since deteriorated further in meaning, being synonymous with *obscene, indecent, salacious,* and probably some of the other words listed (or omitted) in the U.S. Code of law.

dangerous LIAISONS

Dangerous Liaisons is the name of a 1988 film based on a famous French novel, *Les Liaisons dangereuses,* written by Pierre Choderlos de Laclos (1741–1803) and published in 1782. It's a story of illicit sexual relationships between members of the nobility before the French Revolution. At the time the movie premiered, *liaison* was already well established in English as a stylish French-origin word for a secret or illicit sexual affair.

The curious thing about this French loanword is that its debut in English was in the realm of cookery. *Liaison* came into English with the meaning "a binding agent or thickening for sauces, consisting mainly of egg yolks, or the process of thickening them."

A, a
B, b
C, c
D, d
E, e
F, f
G, g
H, h
I, i
J, j
K, k
L, l
M, m
N, n
O, o
P, p
Q, q
R, r
S, s
T, t
U, u
V, v
W, w
X, x
Y, y
Z, z

The first to use the term was a British nobleman, Sir Kenelm Digby, in a cookery notebook titled *The Closet Opened*, which was published posthumously in 1669. The word was borrowed from French *liaison* "a binding," from Latin *ligātiōn-, ligātiō*, from *ligāre* "to bind, tie." Cookbooks picked up the term and have used it ever since, as in *Cooking at Home* (1999), by Julia Child and Jacques Pepin, which tells the reader how to use "eggs as a liaison for sauces and as the puffing power for soufflés."

Several other technical uses of *liaison* appeared in the 1800s, the most common one being the military or other official sense of "a close connection or cooperation between two units, branches, allies, etc." There are *diplomatic liaisons, legislative liaisons, Forest Service liaisons,* and *liaison librarians,* none of them being, as far as we know, in the least dangerous.

LIBEL *suits*

An October 4, 2006, news article in the online magazine *Ars Technica*, under the heading "Bloggers face an increase in libel suits," warned its readers that "What you say on your blog or in an online forum could get you sued for libel. . . . The lawsuits so far run the gamut from bloggers being sued over public gossip about intimate events, to warning others not to date certain people, to unauthorized photos posted on MySpace, to religious criticism, and more."

The earliest meaning of *libel* (1297) was, "any formal document or written statement," (also) "a short treatise or writing," as in the Wycliffe Bible (Numbers 5:23): "And the priest shall write in a libel these cursed things." *Libel* was borrowed from Old French *libel, libelle*, from Latin *libellus* "little book," diminutive of *liber* "book."

The legal meaning evolved from the fact that, in the Middle Ages (1340), *libel* was a term in English civil and church law meaning "a plaintiff's written declaration of charges in a civil or criminal case." Since plaintiffs often brought charges that at

134

A, *a*

B, *b*

C, *c*

D, *d*

E, *e*

F, *f*

G, *g*

H, *h*

I, *i*

J, *j*

K, *k*

L, *l*

M, *m*

N, *n*

O, *o*

P, *p*

Q, *q*

R, *r*

S, *s*

T, *t*

U, *u*

V, *v*

W, *w*

X, *x*

Y, *y*

Z, *z*

trial proved to be false or defamatory, *libel* came to mean any false or defamatory accusation. This meaning was extended in 1521 to "a leaflet or pamphlet that publicly assails the character of a person," and by 1631, *libel* was broadly used in law to mean "any published statement damaging a person's reputation, or the act or crime of publishing such a statement."

LIBERTINE

Similar to the definitions of *lewd, liaison,* and *libel,* the pristine meaning of *libertine* has, over time, given way to a negative one. It exemplifies the process of degradation, or pejoration, of meaning that has infected words more often than the opposite process of upgrading, or amelioration.

Libertine is first found in Middle English (1382) in the sense of a member of the class of freedmen, or emancipated slaves, in the ancient Roman empire. The word was borrowed from Latin *lībertīnus* (literally) "one made free," from *lībertus* "made free," from *līber* "free." The word might have remained without any blemish had it not been influenced in the 1500s by the French *Libertines,* a deprecatory name given to the opponents of the French Protestant Reformer John Calvin in Geneva. By 1563, *libertine* was applied in English to any sectarian who questioned church doctrine, and later was applied to any freethinker, i.e., one who held free or loose opinions about religion.

From there it was another step downward to the current meaning of "a man who disregards moral laws, especially in relation to the female sex; one who leads a dissolute, licentious life." This meaning is found in 1593 and was used by Shakespeare in *Hamlet* (1604), where Ophelia rebukes her brother Laertes for advising her to remain virtuous and chaste while he, "like a puff'd and reckless libertine Himself the primrose path of dalliance treads."

The word *libertine* has been especially used to describe a literary genre of the 1700s that was marked by an interest in erotic

A, a

B, b

C, c

D, d

E, e

F, f

G, g

H, h

I, i

J, j

K, k

L, l

M, m

N, n

O, o

P, p

Q, q

R, r

S, s

T, t

U, u

V, v

W, w

X, x

Y, y

Z, z

tendencies and situations. Authors who wrote in this genre included Pierre Choderlos de Laclos, the Marquis de Sade, and Denis Diderot.

in LIMBO

A climactic scene in James Branch Cabell's fantasy novel *Jurgen, a Comedy of Justice* (1919) occurs when the hero, King Jurgen, is put on trial as an unworthy and obsolete illusion. "Now a court was held by the Philistines to decide whether or not King Jurgen should be relegated to limbo."

Since 1642 *limbo* has been used to mean "a condition of neglect or oblivion for people or things cast aside as outdated, outworn, or useless." An 1828 poem by Thomas Moore, titled "The Limbo of Lost Reputations," places in limbo

> "The hopes of youth, the resolves of age,
> The vow of the lover, the dream of the sage,
> The promises great men strew about them . . ."

Limbo has also come to mean "a state, place, or period of transition," as in this headline in the *New York Times* of October 18, 2006: "Sudanese Soldiers Flee War to Find a Limbo in Chad."

These meanings of *limbo* were extended from an earlier (1590) sense of "prison, confinement, incarceration," as in Thomas Carlyle's *Past and Present*: "Monks . . . must not speak too loud, under penalty of . . . limbo, and bread and water."

All of these were figurative senses of the word's earliest meaning, "a region supposed to exist on the border of hell as the abode of good persons who died before Christ's coming and of unbaptized infants," found in Middle English in the 1300s. The word *limbo* was borrowed from Latin, in phrases like *in limbo* "on the edge" and *e limbo* "outside the edge," from *limbus* "edge, border, fringe."

no LITTER*ing*

Litter is unlawfully scattered rubbish, and *to litter* in public is illegal, a danger to the environment. The *New York Herald-Tribune* reported in February of 1947 that subway litterbugs had paid $107,000 in fines in 1946.

The word *litter* didn't always mean such nasty stuff. Originally (before 1300) the word meant simply "a bed," and was borrowed through Old French *litiere* from Latin *lectus* "bed." By around 1430, this meaning was extended to "a bedding, especially one made of straw and rushes," as in "As pillows been to chambers agreeable So is hard straw litter for the stable" (John Lydgate, *Horse, Goose, and Sheep*). The *kitty litter* used today developed from this meaning.

Since animals gave birth on a litter of straw or other material, the meaning "a number of young brought forth on a litter at birth" appeared in 1486, as in *a litter of whelps, the largest cub in the litter.*

It was Jonathan Swift in the 1700s who extended the meaning of a bedding of straw, rushes, etc., to mean "fragments and leavings lying about, odds and ends, rubbish," in "Strephon . . . took a strict survey of all the litter as it lay" (1730, Swift, *Lady's Dressing-Room*). He also used the verb *to litter* (which had been used since 1398 in the sense of "provide an animal with a litter of straw") to mean "to cover with odds and ends, scatter about in disorder," in "They found the room with volumes littered round" (1726, Swift, *Cadenus and Vanessa*).

LOUSY

This word is strikingly used in the opening sentence of J. D. Salinger's famous novel of teenage alienation, *Catcher in the Rye* (1951): "If you really want to hear about it, the first thing you'll probably want to know is where I was born, and what my lousy childhood was like. . . ."

A, *a*
B, *b*
C, *c*
D, *d*
E, *e*
F, *f*
G, *g*
H, *h*
I, *i*
J, *j*
K, *k*
L, *l*
M, *m*
N, *n*
O, *o*
P, *p*
Q, *q*
R, *r*
S, *s*
T, *t*
U, *u*
V, *v*
W, *w*
X, *x*
Y, *y*
Z, *z*

A, a

B, b

C, c

D, d

E, e

F, f

G, g

H, h

I, i

J, j

K, k

L, l

M, m

N, n

O, o

P, p

Q, q

R, r

S, s

T, t

U, u

V, v

W, w

X, x

Y, y

Z, z

Lousy, meaning "very bad, wretched, miserable," is first recorded in 1807, in J. R. Shaw's *Autobiography*: "In as . . . lousy a situation as ever I remember to have been in." But this use was preceded in the 1500s by "dirty, filthy, vile, contemptible," as a general term of abuse, as in Shakespeare's *Henry V*: "What an arrant, rascally, beggarly, lousy knave it is!"

These were all figurative uses of the word's earliest meaning, "full of lice, infected with lice," found in 1377 and used until the late 1600s, as in Isaac Walton's *The Compleat Angler* (1653): "If I catch a Trout in one Meadow, he shall be white and faint, and very like to be lousy."

According to *The Barnhart Dictionary of Etymology*, "The figurative use of *lousy* is not an exclusive innovation in English; it is found in German *lausig*, French *pouilleux*, Spanish *piojoso*, etc."

LUDICROUS

Samuel Johnson, in his 1781 biography of Alexander Pope, makes the categorical statement that "The *Rape of the Lock* . . . is universally allowed to be the most attractive of all ludicrous compositions." By *ludicrous* Johnson meant to praise the poem, not to bury it; he meant that the poem was playful and witty, intended in jest. This happened to be the word's original meaning when it first appeared, in 1619, in Thomas Gataker's sermon on chance and luck, *The Nature and Use of Lots*. In this sermon, Gataker refers to four events, divine, diabolical, political, and "ludicrous, for sport and pastime." The word was borrowed from Latin *lūdicrus*, from *lūdicrum* "playful performance, stage play," from *lūdere* "to play."

The word's favorable meaning continued into the late 1700s, with the sense of "given to jesting, frivolous, humorous," as in Bishop J. Butler's *Analogy of Religion* (1736): "Men may indulge a ludicrous turn so far as to lose all sense of conduct and prudence in worldly affairs."

By a twist in point of view, the favorable meaning was turned on its head in the early 1800s with a decidedly pejorative meaning, which is the only sense today: "causing or deserving laughter; laughably absurd; ridiculous," as in Shelley's *Queen Mab* (1813): "How ludicrous the priest's dogmatic roar." In 1858, Oliver Wendell Holmes, in *The Autocrat of the Breakfast-table*, gave his blessing to the new usage: "The ludicrous has its place in the universe."

LUNCHEON *and* LUNCH

The 19th-century French Impressionist painters were famous for their luncheons. Two of the greatest paintings of the period were Édouard Manet's *The Luncheon on the Grass* (painted in 1862–1863), which shocked the art world by showing a female nude picnicking on the grass with two fully dressed men, and Pierre-Auguste Renoir's *Luncheon of the Boating Party* (1880–1881), which showed a group of Renoir's closest friends having a light midday meal on a boat.

Luncheon didn't always mean a meal. The word appeared in 1580 with the meaning "a thick piece, a hunk," but was early on used in reference to food, as in *a luncheon of bread, a luncheon of cheese, a luncheon of bacon*. According to the *OED*, it was related in some way to the North English dialectal word *lunch*, also meaning "a thick piece or hunk," which may have been an alteration of *lump* on the analogy of *hump/hunch* and *bump/bunch*.

It was in 1706 that *luncheon* first appeared with the meaning "a light meal eaten around noon," most likely as an alteration of an older and similar-sounding (and now obsolete) word, *nuncheon*, meaning "a noon meal." This word developed from Middle English (1342) *nonschench*, formed from *none* "noon" + *schench* "beverage, drink."

A, *a*
B, *b*
C, *c*
D, *d*
E, *e*
F, *f*
G, *g*
H, *h*
I, *i*
J, *j*
K, *k*
L, *l*
M, *m*
N, *n*
O, *o*
P, *p*
Q, *q*
R, *r*
S, *s*
T, *t*
U, *u*
V, *v*
W, *w*
X, *x*
Y, *y*
Z, *z*

A, a
B, b
C, c
D, d
E, e
F, f
G, g
H, h
I, i
J, j
K, k
L, l
M, m
N, n
O, o
P, p
Q, q
R, r
S, s
T, t
U, u
V, v
W, w
X, x
Y, y
Z, z

In 1829, *luncheon* was shortened to *lunch*, creating the distinction between the longer midday meal and the short, quick one most people favor.

LUXURY

"I love luxury," declared the legendary French designer Coco Chanel. "But luxury lies not in richness and ornateness but in the absence of vulgarity." Dictionaries define the word as "anything choice or costly that gratifies the appetites or tastes, whether food, dress, furniture, jewelry, or appliance of any kind." Think of luxury shops, luxury cruises, luxury hotels, and the so-called luxury trade. In 1899 Mark Twain declared: "We are . . . the most luxury-loving people on the earth."

Yet this meaning of *luxury* was a latecomer in English, first used in the 1600s. The poet Milton used it in the sense of "indulgence in what is choice or costly" in *Paradise Lost* (1667): "All now was turned to jollity and game, To luxury and riot, feast and dance."

The word's original meaning, first recorded in 1340, was "indulgence in vice, lewdness, lasciviousness, lechery," as in Chaucer's *Canterbury Tales* (about 1386): "O foul lust of luxury." *Luxury* was borrowed from Old French *luxurie* "lasciviousness, lust," from Latin *luxuria*, from *luxus* "excess, abundance, sumptuous enjoyment."

Curiously enough, the pejorative meaning of "indulgence in vice, lewdness" was retained in the French, Spanish, and Italian words developed from *luxuria*, while English usage redeemed *luxury* from vice and converted it into something virtuous.

M, m

A, a
B, b
C, c
D, d
E, e
F, f
G, g
H, h
I, i
J, j
K, k
L, l
M, m
N, n
O, o
P, p
Q, q
R, r
S, s
T, t
U, u
V, v
W, w
X, x
Y, y
Z, z

You've got MAIL

When in the Douay Bible (I Kings 9:7) Saul says to his servant, "What shall we carry to the man of God? The bread is spent in our males," he didn't mean that the bread was gone among the men. The word *male* was the way *mail* was spelled in Middle English, and the word's meaning was "a bag or pack." So what Saul meant was "The bread is gone from our bags."

So how did *mail* get to mean "letters, packages, etc. sent from one place to another"? From about 1275, when *male* came into English, it was a common word for a bag, suitcase, or other piece of luggage. The word was borrowed in Middle English from Old French *male* "bag, wallet." In the mid-1600s, a bag or packet of letters sent by post was called a *mail of letters*. In 1684, such bags or packets were called *mails* for short, and by the 1700s postal matter in general was called *the mail*. Finally, in the 1800s, *mail* came to mean "the system of collecting or delivering letters and parcels," and "the government body responsible for this," as in "Why didn't he send his poems by mail?" (1888, *The American Humorist*).

The term *electronic mail* appeared in 1970, was shortened to *e-mail* in 1982, and followed a year later by *snail mail*, a somewhat derogatory term for regular post-office mail. While *mail* is dominant in North America and Australia, Britain favors *post* for both the system and the material carried. However, the distinction is not maintained in historically fixed phrases such as *post office* and *parcel post*.

MAYHEM

In the vocabulary of sports writers, the word *mayhem* is a favorite, since scenes of violence are endemic to spectator sports. "Golf alone," wrote the journalist Colman McCarthy in a 1993 piece in the *Washington Post*, "despite huge purses, has remained immune to the violence and vulgarity that have turned other sports into spectacles of sanctioned mayhem."

A, a

B, b

C, c

D, d

E, e

F, f

G, g

H, h

I, i

J, j

K, k

L, l

M, m

N, n

O, o

P, p

Q, q

R, r

S, s

T, t

U, u

V, v

W, w

X, x

Y, y

Z, z

The history of *mayhem* is an example of generalization, having developed its current meaning of "rowdy disorder, confusion" from a specific meaning in criminal law. *Mayhem* first appeared in late Middle English (1447) in the sense of "the crime of intentionally crippling or disabling a person, as by blinding him or cutting off a limb." The word was borrowed from Anglo-French *maihem,* from Old French *mahaigne* "physical injury," from *mahaignier* "to maim, injure," the source of English *maim.*

William Blackstone, in his *Commentaries on the Laws of England* (1765), defined *mayhem* as "the violently depriving another of the use of such of his members, as may render him less able in fighting." In the 1800s, the legal meaning was broadened in popular American usage to "any violent behavior, especially physical assault," and further generalized in the 1970s to the current meaning of "rowdy disorder, confusion, chaos," a meaning that has found its way to Britain, as in "If they had gone into the centre it would have been mayhem. The people in the town centre were up for a fight because they had been drinking all day" (May 27, 2001, BBC News).

no **MEAN** *streak*

We've all heard of mixed metaphors, like *That's a whole new ball of worms* (mixing *a whole new ball game* with *to open a can of worms*), but mixed idioms are a rare breed. One appeared in a 1994 *Washington Post* headline, "Ripken's Two Grand: No Mean Streak," extolling the baseball player Cal Ripken, Jr., on his achieving his 2,000th consecutive game. The headline cleverly blended the idiom *no mean* (denoting something admirable or noteworthy, as in *no mean scholar*) with the idiom *mean streak* "a vicious or cruel trait or tendency." The mix was particularly apt, since Ripken's uninterrupted run of games was widely known as "the streak."

The expressions *no mean* and *mean streak* suggest the variety of uses to which *mean* has been put in its long history. This

A, a
B, b
C, c
D, d
E, e
F, f
G, g
H, h
I, i
J, j
K, k
L, l
M, m
N, n
O, o
P, p
Q, q
R, r
S, s
T, t
U, u
V, v
W, w
X, x
Y, y
Z, z

adjective began life before 1200 in the form *mene*, meaning "common to two or more persons or things, have in common, held jointly," often used in the phrases *in mean* "in common" and *to go mean* "to act as partners, to share," as in *They would go mean at plowing*. *Mene* developed from Old English *gemæne* "common, shared," a word descended from the Indo-European root that also produced Latin *commūnis*, the source of English *common*.

Then, before 1325, the word's meaning was extended from "common" to "ordinary, inferior in rank or ability," and further extended in the 1500s to "unimportant, insignificant." In the 1800s, new meanings were introduced in the United States, among them, "(of a horse) vicious, hard to control, violent," which passed into "(of a person) unkind, vicious, cruel," as in "Put that whip down. How very mean of you to whip poor old Tortoise!" (1872, George Eliot, *Middlemarch*).

MEASLY

The use of *measly* is perfectly illustrated in an episode in the TV cartoon sitcom *The Simpsons*, in which Homer Simpson, after smashing open his son Bart's piggy bank, cries out, "Oh no! What have I done? . . . and for what? A few measly cents, not even enough to buy one beer. Wait a minute, lemme count and make sure . . . not even close."

Measly is a carping, grudging, faultfinding word used to disparage and devalue what kindly spirits would accept with open hearts. It's defined in dictionaries as "contemptibly small, insultingly low, paltry," and used in such phrases as *a measly tip, a measly salary, a measly pension, a measly two-week's vacation*. This meaning is first found in British English in 1847, transferred from the earlier literal meaning (1696), "of or like measles; caused by measles," as in *a measly rash, measly lesions*.

So how did the meaning "contemptibly small, paltry" derive from "of or like measles"? The original meaning of *measles* was not the highly contagious disease (rubeola) that used to affect children, but a disease of swine (cysticercosis) caused by a larval tapeworm that infected pork. The infected pork were called *measly*, as in "If you find little kernels in the fat of pork . . . 'tis measly, and dangerous to be eaten" (1747, H. Glasse, *The Art of Cookery*). The figurative meaning of *measly*, "contemptibly small," derived from the *measly* little kernels of larvae.

MEAT

In Old English, the word *meat* (spelled *mete*) mainly meant "food, especially solid food," found as late as 1844, in Henry Stephens's *Book of the Farm*: "Meat is then set down . . . on a flat plate, consisting of crumbled bread and oatmeal." The proverb *One man's meat is another man's poison*, recorded since the 1570s, intended to contrast food and poison, not animal flesh and poison. The Old English word *mete* came from the same Germanic source as Old Frisian *mete*, Old Saxon *meti, mat,* Old High German *maz,* Old Icelandic *matr,* and Gothic *mats,* all meaning "food."

Other meanings of *meat* in Old English were "an article of food, a dish," and, more generally, "a meal or feast, especially dinner," found in the King James Version of the Bible (1611): "For whether is greater, he that sitteth at meat, or he that serveth?" (Luke 22:27).

Since the main kind of food or dish at a dinner consisted of the flesh of animals, the word *meat* came to mean "animal flesh other than fish and sometimes poultry." This is, of course, the word's present-day meaning, with regional variations, as J. K. Paulding observed in *Westward Ho!* (1832): "Nothing is called meat in these parts but salt pork and beef."

A, a
B, b
C, c
D, d
E, e
F, f
G, g
H, h
I, i
J, j
K, k
L, l
M, m
N, n
O, o
P, p
Q, q
R, r
S, s
T, t
U, u
V, v
W, w
X, x
Y, y
Z, z

A, a

B, b

C, c

D, d

E, e

F, f

G, g

H, h

I, i

J, j

K, k

L, l

M, m

N, n

O, o

P, p

Q, q

R, r

S, s

T, t

U, u

V, v

W, w

X, x

Y, y

Z, z

MEMENTO

The word *memento* means "an object kept as a reminder of an event, person, etc.; a keepsake or souvenir." This meaning is first found in 1768, in Cuthbert Shaw's *Monody*: "Where'er I turn my eyes, Some sad memento of my loss appears."

Memento was borrowed from Latin *memento* "remember," derived ultimately from the Indo-European base of Latin *mēns, mentis* "mind," the source of English *mental*. Its first use was in Middle English, before 1400, and referred to any of several passages in the Bible or Christian liturgy whose Latin text begins with the word *Memento*. Specifically, it denotes either of two such prayers in the canon of the Mass that commemorate, respectively, the living and the dead. The latter is described in the magazine *Catholic Culture* (November 2, 2006): "Daily in a special Memento . . . at which the priest remembers all those who have fallen asleep in the Lord, the priest implores God to grant them a place of happiness, light and peace."

In 1580, the meaning was extended to "a reminder, warning, or hint, as of future events or conduct," especially one that alludes to mortality or death. It echoed the Latin phrase *memento mori*, literally, "remember (that you must) die," and meaning "a reminder or warning of the inevitability of death, especially a skull or other symbolic object," as in Shakespeare's *Henry IV* (1598): "I make as good use of it as many a man doth of a death's-head, or a *memento mori*."

MERE

Some words develop meaning from one definition to the next, while others develop multiple definitions at the same time and battle it out until one definition reigns supreme. A good example of this is the word *mere*.

The word's original meaning (before 1390) was "pure, undiluted, unadulterated," borrowed from a Late Latin form of Latin *merus* "pure, undiluted, unmixed." Then, around 1400, the definition extended to "nothing less than, nothing short of, absolute," in such sentences as "I ... became in a little time a mere pastry-cook in the bargain" (1719, Daniel Defoe, *Robinson Crusoe*). This definition lasted until the 1800s.

However, around 1500 another meaning spun off from the first, which gave the word a negative connotation: "nothing more than, barely or only (what is specified)," as in "Even when a mere child I began my travels" (1819, Washington Irving, *Sketch Book*). This definition was viable into the 1800s as well.

This clash in meanings, lasting some 300 years, must have caused plenty of confusion, eliciting such exchanges as "Can you imagine his gall calling me a mere scholar?" "But he meant that you're an absolute scholar!" "No, I'm sure he meant I'm barely a scholar!" In the early 1800s the less favorable meaning won out, and this is the meaning that is prevalent today.

MESS

When we warn a child at play, "Please try not to make a mess!" we owe our use of *mess* to the great poet Alexander Pope. It was he who wrote, in his *Prologue to the Satires* (1768),

> If one [hog] ... Has what the frugal, dirty soil affords,
> From him the next receives it, thick or thin,
> As pure a Mess almost as it came in.

Originally, in Middle English (about 1300), a *mess* meant "a portion or serving of food," as in *a mess of cabbage, a mess of eggs*. *Mess* was borrowed from Old French *mes* "portion of food," from Late Latin *missus* "course at a meal." By the 1500s, the word denoted a quantity (of meat, fruit, condiment, etc.) sufficient for a dish, as in "Goodwife Keech ... coming in to borrow a mess of vinegar" (1600, Shakespeare, *Henry IV*). In the 1700s, *mess* came to mean "food for an animal," and from there developed by the early 1800s such meanings as "an unappetizing or

A, a
B, b
C, c
D, d
E, e
F, f
G, g
H, h
I, i
J, j
K, k
L, l
M, m
N, n
O, o
P, p
Q, q
R, r
S, s
T, t
U, u
V, v
W, w
X, x
Y, y
Z, z

A, a

B, b

C, c

D, d

E, e

F, f

G, g

H, h

I, i

J, j

K, k

L, l

M, m

N, n

O, o

P, p

Q, q

R, r

S, s

T, t

U, u

V, v

W, w

X, x

Y, y

Z, z

disgusting dish or concoction, a sloppy mixture of any kind, a hodgepodge," and figuratively, "a dirty or untidy condition of things or of a place."

Another meaning, "a company of people eating together," appeared before 1450 as an extension of the idea of a meal or dish shared by a group of students, workers, etc. This meaning came to be applied in the 1500s especially to a group in a military unit or a ship's company who ate their meals together, and later, to the place where meals were taken by such a group, as in *the officers' mess, the seamen's mess.*

METICULOUS

The meaning of *meticulous*, "very careful, scrupulous, precise," is illustrated by an article in the *Library of Congress Information Bulletin* (April 2004) titled "The Measure of a Meticulous Man," which begins: "Harry A. Blackmun was a meticulous note taker while considering more than 800 cases that came before the U.S. Supreme Court during his 24 years on the bench as an associate justice."

This meaning appeared in 1827 as an extension of the word's original meaning (1540), which was "fearful, timid," as in a 1679 letter by Sir Thomas Browne: "Mr. Wisse is a meticulous doubting man of a good nature." The connection is easy to see: a fearful or timid person will go overboard to avoid committing a mistake, and so will be timorously fussy and very careful in everything he does.

Because of a gap of some 140 years in the record between the original and the current meanings, the *OED* derives the original meaning of *meticulous* from Latin *metīculōsus* "fearful, timid," and the current meaning, from French *méticuleux* "overscrupulous," (originally "fearful, timid"), from Latin *metīculōsus*. The Latin word was formed from a blend of *metus* "fear" and *(per)īculōsus* "perilous."

MINISTER

A *minister* can be either a member of the clergy or a high government official. The former is a position of authority, the latter, one of power. But when the word came into English in the Middle Ages, around 1300, it designated the opposite: a servant, assistant, or subordinate, one who carried out duties as the representative of a superior.

Minister was borrowed from Old French *ministre* "servant," a learned borrowing from Latin *minister* "servant, priest's attendant, subordinate." Thus, Samuel Johnson wrote in *The Rambler* (1750): "The community, of which the magistrate is only the minister," playing on the irony of the titles, since *magistrate* meant literally "master" (from Latin *magister*) while *minister* meant literally "servant, assistant" (from Latin *minister,* from *minus* "less").

The change in meaning from "servant, assistant, subordinate" to "high officer of the church or state" developed from the position occupied by the servants of leaders, rulers, and other persons of importance. A "servant of God," for example, had to be someone great in his own right, as in "Joshua, the minister of Moses, ruled the people of Israel" (before 1475, Ralph Higden, *Polychronicon*). The ecclesiastical title *minister of the church* (literally, "servant of the church") was early in use (1340). The political title first appeared in Great Britain in 1589, frequently in such phrases as *minister of state, minister for foreign affairs, minister of justice, finance minister, prime minister.*

little MINX

These days, *minx* is not a word that you would use as an affectionate pet name. However, when the word came into being in 1542, its definition was "a pet dog." It was so used by Nicholas Udall, the headmaster of Westminster school: "When I am hungry, I am a little minx full of play, and when my belly is full, a mastiff." According to the *Oxford English Dictionary, minx* was

A, *a*

B, *b*

C, *c*

D, *d*

E, *e*

F, *f*

G, *g*

H, *h*

I, *i*

J, *j*

K, *k*

L, *l*

M, *m*

N, *n*

O, *o*

P, *p*

Q, *q*

R, *r*

S, *s*

T, *t*

U, *u*

V, *v*

W, *w*

X, *x*

Y, *y*

Z, *z*

A, a

B, b

C, c

D, d

E, e

F, f

G, g

H, h

I, i

J, j

K, k

L, l

M, m

N, n

O, o

P, p

Q, q

R, r

S, s

T, t

U, u

V, v

W, w

X, x

Y, y

Z, z

a contraction of the earlier *minikins*, used as a term of endearment, borrowed from Middle Dutch *minnekijn*, *minnekin* "sweetheart, darling."

The affectionate overtone of *minx* was then applied to humans, as in David Graham Phillips's novel *Susan Lenox* (before 1911): "Then he stopped, caught the baby up in both arms, burst out laughing. 'You little minx!' he said."

The disparaging use, meaning "a pert, boldly flirtatious young woman," first appeared in 1576. Not long after, the word's meaning was extended to "a lewd or wanton woman." Shakespeare used it in *Othello* in this sense when, speaking to Iago, Othello curses Desdemona: "Damn her, lewd minx! O, damn her!" The word also occurs in Thackeray's *Vanity Fair* (1848) with the same pejorative meaning: "Miss Clapp . . . is declared by the soured old lady to be an unbearable and impudent little minx."

MOOT *point*

The word *moot* stems from the Middle English word, *mot*, meaning "a meeting or assembly, especially one that served as a law court." Old English *mot* was shortened from *gemot* "meeting, assembly." The spelling *moot* first appeared around 1225 with the meaning "an action at law, a lawsuit."

In 1563, the meaning extended to "unresolved, undecided, open to question," and referred to legal questions or cases. In the early 1800s, the word began to be applied in law schools and courts to hypothetical points and cases that law students argued before a mock court for practice. The result was that *moot* came to mean "having no practical significance, academic."

That is how a phrase like *moot point* (or *moot question*) ended up with two meanings, one referring to actual court cases ("undecided, arguable"), the other referring to hypothetical ones ("purely academic"). These days, if you hear someone say "That's a moot point," you should know that the speaker is referring to either of the above definitions. Unless the speaker tells it like it is, the *moot point* in question remains, well, *moot.*

MORALE

An article in *Stars and Stripes* (November 29, 2006) informed readers that "Of the nearly 2,000 troops surveyed, 8 percent reported 'very high' morale; 19 percent reported 'high' morale; and 37 percent reported 'average' morale." *Morale*, meaning "the degree of confidence, enthusiasm, etc. of a person or group," has always been a major concern of military leaders. The morale of troops is a key determinant of victory in war. Similarly, the smooth operation of a factory, business, etc., depends on the morale of the workers or employees.

Morale was first recorded in 1752, with the entirely different meaning of "moral principles or behavior; the morals of a person or group," as in "The morale of our aristocracy . . . would be at a low ebb indeed if the public press didn't act as their guardian" (1874, Anthony Trollope, *Phineas Redux*). The word was borrowed from French *morale* "morality, moral behavior," from the feminine form of *moral* "ethical, moral."

The current meaning of *morale* was first recorded in 1842 in a military context. In military usage, *morale* was reinterpreted to mean not just moral behavior but a (happy, confident) mental or emotional state conducive to moral behavior. By 1866 the meaning was extended to include "the morale" of groups outside a military context as well.

MORTIFY

"Nothing angered and mortified me so much as the Queen's dwarf," wrote Jonathan Swift in *Gulliver's Travels* (1726) about his hero's adventures in Brobdingnag, the land of the giants.

A, *a*
B, *b*
C, *c*
D, *d*
E, *e*
F, *f*
G, *g*
H, *h*
I, *i*
J, *j*
K, *k*
L, *l*
M, *m*
N, *n*
O, *o*
P, *p*
Q, *q*
R, *r*
S, *s*
T, *t*
U, *u*
V, *v*
W, *w*
X, *x*
Y, *y*
Z, *z*

A, a
B, b
C, c
D, d
E, e
F, f
G, g
H, h
I, i
J, j
K, k
L, l
M, m
N, n
O, o
P, p
Q, q
R, r
S, s
T, t
U, u
V, v
W, w
X, x
Y, y
Z, z

The dwarf, "being of the lowest stature . . . (for I verily think he was not thirty feet high) became insolent at seeing a creature so much beneath him, that he would always affect to swagger and look big as he passed by me . . . and he seldom failed of a smart word or two upon my littleness." To be *mortified* means to be humiliated and embarrassed, as Captain Gulliver was by the insolence of the Queen's dwarf. This meaning of *mortify* came late into the language (1639), and Swift was among the first to use it.

The word's original meaning was "to deprive of life, put to death, kill," first found in Middle English in the Wycliffe Bible (before 1382). Middle English *mortifien* was borrowed from Old French *mortifier* "to cause to die," from Late Latin *mortificare*, formed from Latin *mort-, mors* "death" (+ *-ficāre* "to make, do"). "His heart was mortified within him," wrote William Caxton in *The Golden Legend* (1483), "and he was dead like a stone."

In the late 1400s, the word softened to mean "to destroy the vitality of, to wound, bruise." Today's meaning "humiliate, embarrass" is a figurative extension of this one. The only literal meaning still current, chiefly in religious contexts, is "to subdue (bodily appetites) by self-inflicted suffering," found especially in the phrase *to mortify the flesh*, as in "Mortify your flesh . . . with scourges and with thorns" (1842, Tennyson, *St. Simeon Stylites*).

The MUMMY

The original "curse of the mummy" referred to the legend surrounding the discovery of King Tut's tomb in 1923, which began when Lord Carnarvon, who funded the discovery, died suddenly from a mosquito bite shortly after the discovery. Since then, many films have been produced on the subject, beginning with *The Mummy*, produced in 1932, starring Boris Karloff.

The word *mummy* has been in English since before 1400. But its original meaning was not the bandaged body of King Tut or Im-

Ho-Tep we have come to dread on film. Its meaning was "a medicinal substance prepared from the bones or tissues of embalmed or otherwise preserved corpses." The word *mummy* was borrowed in Middle English from Medieval Latin *mumia*, *mummia* "bituminous substance (from embalmed corpses)," which was borrowed from Arabic *mūmiyā* "bituminous substance used medicinally." The word came in the Middle Ages into most European languages by way of the school of medicine in Salerno, Italy.

By 1615, though, the meaning of *mummy* was transferred from the extract taken from embalmed bodies to the bodies themselves, and travelers wrote regularly about Egyptian mummies and Peruvian mummies. Which led to King Tut, Boris Karloff, and the famous curse.

N, *n*

NAUGHTY, NAUGHTY

Naught is a somewhat bookish and quaint word that means "nothing," used primarily in idiomatic expressions like *come to naught*, as in *All her efforts came to naught*. It's a very old word, derived from Old English *nōwiht* "no thing." From this word the adjective *naughty* developed in the Middle Ages (about 1400) with the meaning "having naught, owning nothing, needy, poor." But this plain meaning was not to last.

In the 1500s *naughty* took a nasty turn in meaning, namely, "worth nothing, unworthy, bad, wicked," which evolved into "immoral, promiscuous."

Shakespeare used it in the sense of "morally bad, wicked, evil," as in "So shines a good deed in a naughty world" (1596, *The Merchant of Venice*). In later centuries this meaning weakened and began to be used ironically, as in "I am a woman as well as yourself . . . and if I have been a little naughty, I am not the first" (1742, Henry Fielding, *Joseph Andrews*). From this weakened use came the meaning "mischievous, badly behaved, disobedient," used especially of a child: "This is your last ride, till papa comes back. I'll not trust you over the threshold again, you naughty, naughty girl" (1847, Charlotte Brontë, *Wuthering Heights*).

NEAT *and* NET

These two words were twins separated at birth. Both were borrowed from Middle French *net* "clear, clean, pure," and started off with the same meaning, "finely made, clean, clear, trim, elegant." In the 1400s, *neat* (spelled *nete*) was applied to such diverse things as a jewel, a cottage, a city, a garden, and even a coffin. A century later its meaning was extended to "clear, to the point, pithy," as in *a neat explanation*, "habitually clean and tidy," and "kept in good order, trim, tidy," as in *neat quarters*.

A, *a*
B, *b*
C, *c*
D, *d*
E, *e*
F, *f*
G, *g*
H, *h*
I, *i*
J, *j*
K, *k*
L, *l*
M, *m*
N, *n*
O, *o*
P, *p*
Q, *q*
R, *r*
S, *s*
T, *t*
U, *u*
V, *v*
W, *w*
X, *x*
Y, *y*
Z, *z*

A, a

B, b

C, c

D, d

E, e

F, f

G, g

H, h

I, i

J, j

K, k

L, l

M, m

N, n

O, o

P, p

Q, q

R, r

S, s

T, t

U, u

V, v

W, w

X, x

Y, y

Z, z

In the meantime, *net* underwent a major change. Its original meaning, "clean, clear, trim, etc.," became obsolete, apparently overwhelmed by the wide use of *neat* in that sense. And so, seizing upon an implication of its basic meaning of "clean, free from impurities," it assumed in the 1400s the specialized meaning of "free and clear from deduction (of taxes, interest, etc.), remaining after all the necessary deductions," as in *net profits, net assets, net income.*

This specialized use was in turn generalized in the 1800s to "remaining after everything has been taken into account, final, conclusive," as in *the net result, net effect, net product.* Thus, the meaning of *net* went full circle, from the general to the specific and back to the general.

The source of *neat* and *net*, Middle French *net* "clear," came from Latin *nitidus* "bright, shining," from *nitēre* "to shine." The word is unrelated to *net* "open fabric or mesh for catching fish, butterflies, etc.," which is found in Old English and all other Germanic languages.

NEWFANGLED, *oldfangled?*

The word *newfangled* has intrigued language buffs since the Middle Ages, as no one seemed able to figure out the origin or meaning of *-fangled.* If something new is *newfangled*, then why isn't something old "oldfangled"? And what on earth is "fangled" anyway?

Newfangled was derived from an earlier word, *newfangle* (originally spelled *newfangel*), recorded before 1300 with the meaning "fond of novelty or new things." *Newfangel* was formed from *new* and *-fangel*, a form taken to be an Old English adjective probably meaning "inclined to catch," from the root of Old English *fang, feng* "a seizing or catching," the source of English *fang* (*see* FANG). It thus appears that the basic meaning of *newfangled* is "inclined to catch that which is new."

The word first appeared in print around 1495, and meant "overly fond of novelty or new things, too eager to take up new fashions or ideas," as in " . . . all the French curiosities and trinkets, of which our people are so new-fangled" (1670, Andrew Marvell, *Works*). As this meaning became rare, it was replaced in the mid-1500s by the current meaning, "overly new or recent, objectionably novel or modern," as in *newfangled fashions, newfangled contrivances*. "I can cheer my dogs on the prey . . . without using the newfangled jargon of curee, arbor, nombles, and all the babble of the fabulous Sir Tristrem" (1819, Sir Walter Scott, *Ivanhoe*).

NICE

The word *nice* is a classic example of amelioration, in which a word's meaning is improved and upgraded. This is a rare occurrence, compared with the opposite process of pejoration, or downgrading.

The meaning of *nice* when it first appeared in Middle English (about 1300) was "(of persons or their actions) foolish, silly, simple; ignorant, senseless, absurd." The word was borrowed from Old French *nice* "foolish, ignorant," from Latin *nescius* "ignorant," formed from *ne-* "not" + *scīre* "to know" (the source of English *science*).

A number of other disparaging meanings of *nice* occurred in Middle English, among them "wanton, dissolute" (about 1387), "timorous, cowardly" (before 1393), "fastidious, fussy" (about 1400), all apparently extended from the original. A shift away from disparagement began in the 1500s, with such meanings as "requiring or involving great precision or accuracy" (before 1522), as in *a nice experiment*; "not obvious, demanding close consideration" (before 1522), as in *a nice point, a nice distinction.*

A century later the word's meaning was further refined to "(of food or drink) dainty, choice, tasty" (1709), as in *a nice cup*

A, a
B, b
C, c
D, d
E, e
F, f
G, g
H, h
I, i
J, j
K, k
L, l
M, m
N, n
O, o
P, p
Q, q
R, r
S, s
T, t
U, u
V, v
W, w
X, x
Y, y
Z, z

A, a

B, b

C, c

D, d

E, e

F, f

G, g

H, h

I, i

J, j

K, k

L, l

M, m

N, n

O, o

P, p

Q, q

R, r

S, s

T, t

U, u

V, v

W, w

X, x

Y, y

Z, z

of tea, a nice pastry; "agreeable, satisfactory" (1747), as in *a nice walk, a nice book*; "pleasant, good-natured, attractive" (1797), as in *a nice family, nice children, to look nice*. The movement toward amelioration reached its apex in the 1800s with such meanings as "kind and considerate, friendly" (1830), especially in the phrase *to be nice (to)*: *Be nice to the neighbors*; "well done or performed" (1850), as in *a nice job, nice work, a nice try.*

NIGHTMARE

In the classic horror film *A Nightmare on Elm Street*, which appeared in 1984 and had six sequels, a teenager's frightening dream of being stalked by a murderous villain turns out to be all too real.

In the Middle Ages a nightmare was not a bad dream, not even a dream, but an evil female spirit or monster that was believed to settle on a sleeping person or animal, causing in them a feeling of suffocation. That was the meaning of *nightmare* when it first appeared in Middle English (around 1300) as *nytmare, nyghtemare,* formed from Old English *niht* "night" + *mare* "incubus." *The nightmare* was sometimes identified with the fabled succubus, the evil female spirit that was supposed to descend upon sleeping men, or with its male counterpart, the incubus.

In the 1500s, *the nightmare* came to mean any feeling of suffocation or physical distress experienced during sleep, followed a century later by "a bad dream producing the sensation of suffocating." The current meaning of *a nightmare*, "any oppressive or frightening dream," is first found in 1829, in Thomas Carlyle's writings. The figurative sense of "any unpleasant, distressing, or difficult experience" is first encountered in 1904 and used in James Joyce's *Ulysses* (1922): "History, Stephen said, is a nightmare from which I am trying to awake."

NONDESCRIPT

Nondescript is a word that often confuses people. Does it mean "not descriptive" and is the opposite of "descriptive"? Does it mean, "indescribable," or "too extraordinary to describe"?

Coined in 1669–1670 by the English naturalist John Ray (1628–1705), *nondescript* was originally a noun meaning a species, genus, or other class of plants or animals that has not been previously described. He also used the word as an adjective meaning "not previously described," as in *nondescript plants, a nondescript species of owl*. *Nondescript* was formed from *non-* "not" + *descript* "described" (1731), from Latin *dēscrīpt-, dēscrībere* "describe."

The noun's meaning was generalized in 1776 to "a person or thing of no particular kind, one not easily described or classified," a meaning used through the 1900s and still current, as in "Except for the common soldiers and a few nondescripts, they lived lives appropriate to 'gentlemen'" (1937, George Orwell, *The Road to Wigam Pier*).

The adjective's meaning was extended in 1785 to "not easily described or classified, lacking distinctive features," as in "There was a string of people already straggling in, whom it was not difficult to identify as the nondescript messengers, go-betweens, and errand-bearers of the place" (1857, Charles Dickens, *Little Dorrit*). This is the word's current meaning.

NOTORIOUS

This word is notorious for its unsavory associations. Since 1549, when the Book of Common Prayer referred to "Such persons as were notorious sinners," almost every use of *notorious* has had a pejorative connotation (*a notorious liar, notorious falsehoods, a notorious gossip*). Even where the connotation is intended to be favorable or neutral, the word is tainted by its unpleasant uses, as in "Shockley lost his company . . . and then got involved

A, *a*
B, *b*
C, *c*
D, *d*
E, *e*
F, *f*
G, *g*
H, *h*
I, *i*
J, *j*
K, *k*
L, *l*
M, *m*
N, *n*
O, *o*
P, *p*
Q, *q*
R, *r*
S, *s*
T, *t*
U, *u*
V, *v*
W, *w*
X, *x*
Y, *y*
Z, *z*

A, a
B, b
C, c
D, d
E, e
F, f
G, g
H, h
I, i
J, j
K, k
L, l
M, m
N, n
O, o
P, p
Q, q
R, r
S, s
T, t
U, u
V, v
W, w
X, x
Y, y
Z, z

in a notorious controversy over race, genetics and intelligence that destroyed his reputation" (1999, PBS TV, *Transistorized!*).

Originally the word was as neutral as *notable* and *noted*; when it first entered the language around 1495, it meant "commonly or generally known, being a matter of common knowledge," as in "My power with the managers is pretty notorious" (Richard B. Sheridan, *The Critic*). *Notorious* was borrowed from Medieval Latin *notorius* "well-known," from Latin *nōtus* "known," the source of English *notice* and *notify*.

The turning point came in the 1540s. In that decade *notorious* changed in meaning from "famous" to "infamous" when it began to be commonly applied to a sinner, criminal, etc., or to an egregious action, as in "He was charged upon oath, with having been a party in a notorious robbery, burglary, and murder" (1723, Daniel Defoe, *Colonel Jack*).

NOXIOUS
See OBNOXIOUS

NUDE *and* NAKED
No raised eyebrows, rolling eyes, or other expressions of disapproval greeted the arrival of the word *nude* into English in 1492. The word had the stodgy gravity of a judge, and was, in fact, a legal term. Applied to a statement, promise, etc., *nude* meant "not formally attested or recorded." Applied to a contract or pact, it meant "void, unenforceable." Applied to a person, a *nude executor* was not one parading around naked but simply an unpaid one. In the mid-1600s, *nude* was appropriated by naturalists, who used it in the sense of "lacking natural covering, hairless, bare," as in *nude trees, nude sheep*.

The word's first use as a noun referring to the naked human body as represented in art was in Edward Hatton's *New View of*

London (1708): "A Nude ... is a naked Figure painted or sculpted, without Drapery (or Clothing)." The corresponding adjective appeared in 1811, in *nude naiads,* and later in phrases like *nude figurines, a nude Greek goddess, a nude study of a nymph.* It was first applied in the 1880s to a model posing unclothed for a painting or sculpture, especially in the phrase *in the nude.* The meaning "carried out without clothing," as in *nude bathing,* is first found in 1884.

How does *nude* differ from *naked*? According to the *OED,* "Whereas the term *naked* is generally regarded as a neutral descriptive term, *nude* is now often used in contexts of suggestive or gratuitous display."

Nude was borrowed from Latin *nūdus* "naked, bare, simple, open," from the same Indo-European base as Old English *nacod* "naked." *Nude* came into English as a specialized term and remained specialized for the last five centuries, while *naked* continued to serve as the general or common term, both literally, as in *a naked room, naked prisoners,* and figuratively, as in *the naked truth, naked facts.*

A, a

B, b

C, c

D, d

E, e

F, f

G, g

H, h

I, i

J, j

K, k

L, l

M, m

N, n

O, o

P, p

Q, q

R, r

S, s

T, t

U, u

V, v

W, w

X, x

Y, y

Z, z

0, *0*

OBNOXIOUS

The offensive word *obnoxious* started off pretty inoffensively. In its earliest sense (in the 1570s) it meant "subject or liable (to)," as in "I am obnoxious to each carping tongue / Who says my hand a needle better fits" (1678, Anne Bradstreet). A related meaning was "subject to some authority or power," as in "Kings are . . . obnoxious to God alone" (1658, John Cleveland). These uses were consistent with the meaning of the word's source, Latin *obnoxiōsus* "subject, subordinate, liable, answerable."

The strongly pejorative meaning of *obnoxious*, "very offensive, objectionable, odious," is first recorded in 1675 and was, according to the *OED*, probably influenced by the word *noxious*. It was used in this sense by Ulysses S. Grant in 1869 in his first inaugural address as president: "I know no method to secure the repeal of bad or obnoxious laws so effective as their stringent execution." The word lost much of its sting as it got to be used loosely in the sense of "highly unpleasant or dislikeable," as in "There is probably no more obnoxious class of citizen . . . than the returning vacationist" (1922, Robert Benchley, *Welcome Home—and Shut Up!*).

The Latin *obnoxiōsus* was derived from *obnoxius* "subject or exposed to harm," from *ob-* "toward" + *noxa* "hurt, harm," the source of English *noxious*.

OBSEQUIOUS

Funeral rites are sometimes called *obsequies* (ultimately from Latin *obsequium* "dutiful service") because they dutifully comply with the wishes of the deceased person. The original meaning of *obsequious* was precisely that, "complying with the wishes of another, dutiful, obedient," as in *an obsequious son, a leader's obsequious followers*. (*Obsequious* was borrowed from Latin *obsequiōsus* "compliant, obedient.") The word is used by Shakespeare in this sense in *Hamlet*, where the king tells the Prince of Denmark that mourning for his father was commend-

A, *a*

B, *b*

C, *c*

D, *d*

E, *e*

F, *f*

G, *g*

H, *h*

I, *i*

J, *j*

K, *k*

L, *l*

M, *m*

N, *n*

O, *o*

P, *p*

Q, *q*

R, *r*

S, *s*

T, *t*

U, *u*

V, *v*

W, *w*

X, *x*

Y, *y*

Z, *z*

able, since "The survivor [is] bound In filial obligation for some term To do obsequious sorrow."

Gradually the original sense of *obsequious* shifted from the positive to the pejorative, from "compliant, obedient" (about 1475) to "servile, fawning" (1602), as in "She walked over rug after rug as an obsequious salesman displayed his wares" (2000, Frederick P. Grove, *Jane Atkinson*). Currently the word is applied only to persons who are excessively polite or fawning, or to their actions, as in *an obsequious employee given to obsequious bowing and scraping.*

OBSESS

Believers in witchcraft and the occult used to distinguish between being *obsessed* or *possessed* by an evil spirit. The earliest meaning of *obsess*, recorded in 1440, was "(of an evil spirit) to control externally, haunt or harass," as distinguished from *possess* "to control or harass internally," as in *possessed by demons.* Another early meaning of the word (1503) was "to besiege, occupy, as by an army." *Obsess* was borrowed from Latin *obsessus,* past participle of *obsidēre* "to beset, occupy."

These senses of *obsess* combined in the mid-1500s into the generalized meaning, "to harass or beset (a person or the mind), to trouble or preoccupy," used usually in the passive phrases *be obsessed by* or *be obsessed with*, as in "If a poet is anybody, he is ... somebody who is obsessed by Making" (1926, e. e. cummings). Other current phrases are *to obsess about* and *to obsess over*, as in "'Tis the season to obsess about food. Thanksgiving yams, Chanukah latkes, Christmas cookies" (Dec. 12, 2005, *Salon.com*). So, from being obsessed by ghosts and phantoms we've come, alas, to be obsessed by food.

OFFICIOUS *lies*

Officious began in the 1400s as a positive term of approval, "active or diligent in performing an office or function, dutiful, efficient." Shakespeare used the word in this sense in *Titus Andronicus* (1594): "Come, come, be every one officious, To make this banquet." Another positive meaning, first recorded in the 1560s, was "eager to serve or help, attentive, obliging, kind." Samuel Johnson, in an obituary published in 1783, described the deceased as "officious, innocent, sincere, of every friendless name the friend." *Officious* was borrowed from Latin *officiōsus* "dutiful, attentive," from *officium* "duty, service, function, office."

Sometime in the late 1500s, the positive meaning of *officious* changed to the negative one of "overly aggressive in offering help or advice; interfering, intrusive, meddlesome," as in "They that are envious towards all are more obnoxious and officious towards one" (1597, Sir Francis Bacon, *Essays*). The change may have been due to the influence of the popular phrases *officious lie, officious falsehood* (or *falsity*), that appeared in the 1570s on the model of Late Latin *mendacium officiosum*. The term meant, in the words of a 1577 translator, "An officious lie, that is, when I . . . tell an untruth for duties' sake to the end that by my lie, I may keep my neighbour harmless." An officious lie or falsehood, then, was one meant to be kind but involved interfering unduly in other people's affairs.

The word's present-day use is illustrated by a sentence from P. G. Wodehouse's novel *The Head of Kay's* (1905): "Jimmy's friends were looked upon with cold suspicion as officious meddlers."

OPTIMISM

Anyone who has read Voltaire's satiric novel *Candide, or Optimism* (in French, *Candide, ou l'Optimisme*, published in 1759) knows that by *Optimism* Voltaire meant the philosophical doctrine that this world is the best of all possible worlds. This was the popular version of a doctrine by the German philosopher Leibniz (presented in his 1710 book *Théodicée*), in which he uses *optimum* as a technical term meaning "the best or most favorable for its purpose," on the model of *maximum* and *minimum*.

A, a
B, b
C, c
D, d
E, e
F, f
G, g
H, h
I, i
J, j
K, k
L, l
M, m
N, n
O, o
P, p
Q, q
R, r
S, s
T, t
U, u
V, v
W, w
X, x
Y, y
Z, z

In *Candide*, Voltaire ridicules Leibniz's doctrine through the character of Dr. Pangloss, a teacher of "metaphysico-theologo-cosmolo-nigology," who insists, despite all evidence to the contrary, that whatever happens, happens for the best, since God chose to create this world as the best of all possible worlds. *Optimism* was borrowed from French *optimisme*, from Latin *optimum* "best."

In 1794–1796, the poets Southey and Coleridge used the uncapitalized word *optimism* in their letters to mean "the quality of being the best," as in *the beauty and optimism of Portugal*. They contrasted the word with *pessimism* in the sense of "the quality of being the worst."

The current meaning of *optimism*, "the tendency to take a favorable or hopeful view of things," is first found in 1812, in Maria Edgeworth's novel *The Absentee*. The term has been used favorably since then as in "Anne . . . wove her dreams of a possible future from the golden tissue of youth's own optimism" (1908, Lucy Maud Montgomery, *Anne of Green Gables*).

ORATION

The word *oration* is usually reserved for a great and memorable speech delivered on a solemn occasion. Famous orations include Pericles' funeral oration for the soldiers who died in the Peloponnesian war, John Hancock's March 5, 1774 oration on the Boston Massacre, and Frederick Douglass's oration in memory of Abraham Lincoln on April 14, 1876. The word *oration* is particularly fitting for such solemn occasions because its original meaning was "a prayer."

Oration appeared in English before 1335 in the sense of a short prayer said during religious services. The word came from Late Latin *ōrātiōn-, ōrātiō* "prayer," from *ōrāre* "to plead." It was the equivalent of the "collect" in the Catholic Church. The current meaning, "a formal speech or discourse, as one given at a funeral, an inaugural, etc.," is recorded since 1502, extended from the sense of a formal prayer. In an article in the *Smart Set* (May 1920) about Lincoln's Gettysburg Address, H. L. Mencken wrote: "The Gettysburg speech is at once the shortest and the most famous oration in American history. . . . It is eloquence brought to a pellucid, almost gem-like perfection."

ORDINARY

"The ordinary man," declared George Bernard Shaw in a speech in 1933, "is an Anarchist. He wants to do as he likes. He may want his neighbor to be governed, but he himself doesn't want to be governed."

For G.B.S., as for most of us, the word *ordinary* was a common, yes, ordinary word. But when it first turned up in English, before the 1400s, *ordinary* was an obscure technical term. It was borrowed from Latin *ōrdinārius*, from *ōrdin-, ōrdō* "row, rank, series," and it designated priests, judges, and the like as "having regular jurisdiction (as opposed to by special appointment)." The word appeared in such official titles as *Judge Ordinary* and (in Scotland) *Lord Ordinary*. This meaning was extended in the 1400s to "belonging to the regular order, staff, or practice," as in *ordinary ambassadors, soldiers ordinary, ordinary preachers*.

This meaning, in turn, was extended in the 1500s to the general (and often deprecatory) meaning "of the usual kind, not singular or special; commonplace, plain, typical," as in *ordinary servants, ordinary folks, ordinary language*. Samuel Johnson's *Dictionary* (1755) defined the word rather narrowly as "Ugly; not handsome: as she is an *ordinary* woman." George Bernard Shaw used it broadly in *Man and Superman* (1903): "I am well aware that the ordinary man . . . is not a philosopher."

OTTOMAN

See DIVAN

A, a
B, b
C, c
D, d
E, e
F, f
G, g
H, h
I, i
J, j
K, k
L, l
M, m
N, n
O, o
P, p
Q, q
R, r
S, s
T, t
U, u
V, v
W, w
X, x
Y, y
Z, z

P, p

PAGEANT

A pageant is an elaborate public spectacle or procession, often depicting scenes from history. This meaning of *pageant* has been known since 1805. A modern version is the *beauty pageant* (1911), a contest like the annual Miss America pageant at Atlantic City.

The word goes back to the Middle Ages. Originally, in 1403, a *pagent* meant a mystery play (one based on a Bible story), performed on a wheeled platform or wagon used as a stage. The platform or stage was also called a pageant, as described in Harold Wheeler's *Waverley Children's Dictionary* (1927–1929): "In the Middle Ages a pageant was the rough stage mounted on a cart on which the Mysteries and Miracles were played."

The figurative sense of "a display of something imagined as a procession or parade," appeared in the 1830s, as in phrases like *life's rich pageant, the pageant of history.*

The origin of *pageant* is uncertain. The early forms of the word were Anglo-French *pagin, pagent* (the final *-t* added on the model of *ancient* and other words ending in *-ent*). The words were probably borrowings from Medieval Latin *pagina*, from Latin *pāgina* "page," related to *pangere* "to fix, fasten," suggesting that the Medieval Latin word referred either to a manuscript page of a mystery play or to the stage fixed to the movable platform on which the mystery plays were performed.

PANACHE

In *Pictures and Conversations* (1975), the British novelist and essayist Elizabeth Bowen wrote: "As a novelist, I cannot occupy myself with 'characters' . . . who lack panache." By *panache* she meant "verve, flamboyance," which is what the word means today. But this meaning is very distant from the original one.

A, a
B, b
C, c
D, d
E, e
F, f
G, g
H, h
I, i
J, j
K, k
L, l
M, m
N, n
O, o
P, p
Q, q
R, r
S, s
T, t
U, u
V, v
W, w
X, x
Y, y
Z, z

A, *a*

B, *b*

C, *c*

D, *d*

E, *e*

F, *f*

G, *g*

H, *h*

I, *i*

J, *j*

K, *k*

L, *l*

M, *m*

N, *n*

O, *o*

P, *p*

Q, *q*

R, *r*

S, *s*

T, *t*

U, *u*

V, *v*

W, *w*

X, *x*

Y, *y*

Z, *z*

A *panache* meant originally a tuft or plume of feathers worn for ornament on a headdress, helmet, hat, or cap. The word was borrowed from Middle French *panache, pennache* "tuft or plume of feathers," from Late Latin *pinnāculum*, diminutive of *pinna* "feather." It has been in English since the 1550s, when it was also applied to a tassel or other ornament that looked like a tuft of feathers.

Because those who wore such decorations had an air of flamboyant confidence or swagger, in the 1890s the word acquired the figurative meaning of "dashing display, swagger, verve, flamboyance," as in the following description of Elvis Presley in W. A. Harbinson's book *The Illustrated Elvis* (1975): "[He has] a style and panache that come close to pure magic. Lithe, raunchy, the sweat pouring down his face, he now moves with the precision of an athlete, the grace of a dancer."

PANEL, PANE

These two related words graduated from the humble meaning of "a piece of cloth" to gain importance in such fields as law and construction. Before 1325, the chief meaning of *panel* was "a piece of cloth, especially a piece placed as a protective pad under a saddle." This meaning was extended around 1378 to the legal meaning of "a piece or roll of parchment on which the names of jurors are listed." Shortly thereafter, it was generalized to "a jury."

In the 1500s, *panel* was used more broadly to refer to "any listed group of people, especially a small group gathered to discuss or decide on some matter," as in *a panel of scientists, a panel of fashion experts,* which is still in use today. The legal use is also still current, as in "Said jurors, when impaneled, shall constitute a general panel for the two-week period" (*Oklahoma Statutes*, June 4, 2002).

Meanwhile, in common usage, the original meaning of "a piece of cloth" was extended around 1450 to "any piece or part serving as a division," such as a part of a wall or piece of furniture, a section of a tapestry, or a distinct part of a fence, railing, etc., as in *an automobile instrument panel, a solar panel, a door's glass panel.*

The word *pane* is not only related to *panel* but has a similar history. Before 1325, a *pane* meant "a piece of cloth, especially a part of a garment, such as the skirt of a gown." Around 1390 the word was applied to a section or side of a wall or fence, and in 1466 to "a piece or sheet of glass, especially one forming part of a window" (the chief current sense).

Panel was derived from Old French *panel, pannel*, from Late Latin *pannellus* "saddle pad, strip of cloth," from Latin *pannus* "cloth, rag." *Pane* was derived from Old French *pan* "piece of cloth, skirt, flap," from Latin *pannus* "cloth, rag."

PARAMOUR

At first *paramour* seemed destined to be a word of religious devotion. When first used as a noun, before 1325, it was as a term of endearment for Jesus or the Virgin Mary, and also, occasionally, for God. It was also used as an interjection meaning "for the love of God" when asking someone for a favor or the like.

The earliest use of this word in English was as the adverbial phrase *par amour*, meaning "with great love or desire, passionately." The phrase was borrowed from Old French *par amur, par amour* "by love, through love." Around 1375, the word passed from the spiritual to the physical, being used as a general term for a lover or for a love affair or romance. In Shakespeare's *A Midsummer Night's Dream*, there is this comic exchange between the carpenter Quince and the bellows-mender Flute:

A, *a*

B, *b*

C, *c*

D, *d*

E, *e*

F, *f*

G, *g*

H, *h*

I, *i*

J, *j*

K, *k*

L, *l*

M, *m*

N, *n*

O, *o*

P, *p*

Q, *q*

R, *r*

S, *s*

T, *t*

U, *u*

V, *v*

W, *w*

X, *x*

Y, *y*

Z, *z*

Quince: He is a very paramour for a sweet voice.

Flute: You must say "paragon." A paramour is, God bless us, a thing of naught.

The main current meaning, "an illicit lover or mistress," is first found about 1395, in Chaucer's *Canterbury Tales*: "My fourth husband was a revelour, This is to say he had a paramour."

See also PASSION

PARLOR

These days, a *parlor* has become synonymous with a public commercial establishment: *a funeral parlor, a tattoo parlor,* and (as a euphemism) *a massage parlor.*

The word's original meaning (around 1230) was a room in a monastery or convent reserved for conversation with visitors or among the residents. *Parlor* was borrowed from Old French *parleor, parleur* "room in a monastery or convent for receiving visitors, room for conversation," derived from *parler* "to speak." In the first available citation, from the *Ancrene Riwle*, a manual of rules of monastic life, *parlor* denotes a grate or window through which confessions were made or audiences held from the outside.

The word was generalized around 1384 to "a room reserved for private conversation in a house," and in 1448 to "a room reserved for entertaining guests, as in an inn or hostel." The meaning of a sitting room, drawing room, or living room developed in the late 1800s and early 1900s. Having a *parlor* in our homes is nowadays an outdated concept, but we've kept the meaning of "a place to entertain guests" through phrases such as *pizza parlor* and *beauty parlor*—locations noted for gathering in groups for social purposes.

PAROLE

The word *parole* is best known today as the conditional release of a prisoner before serving a full term, as in "The number of prisoners jailed for life who were freed on parole has fallen significantly in England and Wales" (November 6, 2006, *BBC News*).

The French word *parole* originally meant "word, speech, promise," from Late Latin *parabola* "speech, discourse," from Latin, "comparison, analogy." The earliest use of *parole* in English appeared before 1616 in the phrase *on parole*, meaning "on word of honor, by oath," as in *a prisoner on parole*. It then developed in 1659 to mean "the word of honor given by a prisoner of war to refrain from combat if released," often in the phrase *parole of honor*. In a letter written in 1882, the British statesman William E. Forster informed Lord Gladstone: "This morning we released [the Irish political leader Charles Stewart] Parnell—not for good, but on parole."

PARTY

It may be a stretch of the imagination for today's partygoers to realize that their favorite word meant originally nothing more exciting than "a part, portion, or share." *Party* was borrowed from Old French *partie* "part of a larger unit, portion, side," from *partir* "to divide, part," from Latin *partīre*, from *part-, pars* "part." Around 1300, when *party* came into use, the phrase *to divide in parties* meant "to divide into parts," and *for the most party* meant "for the most part, mostly." An extended meaning, found before 1375, was "a side, as in a dispute or battle," which developed into "any side in a formal proceeding, such as the litigants in a legal action," as in the phrase *the party of the first part* in legal documents.

From the legal use there arose the meaning "a group of people on one side in a contest, or united in a cause or policy, a faction," specifically used of a political group aiming to take part

A, a

B, b

C, c

D, d

E, e

F, f

G, g

H, h

I, i

J, j

K, k

L, l

M, m

N, n

O, o

P, p

Q, q

R, r

S, s

T, t

U, u

V, v

W, w

X, x

Y, y

Z, z

in a government, as in *the Whig party, the Labour party, the Republican party*. Another extended meaning was "a group of people engaging in a shared activity," as *a recruiting party, a hunting party, a working party*. The notion of a group of people doing things together evolved in the early 1700s to the meaning "a social gathering of people, especially at someone's house, usually involving eating and drinking, dancing, or other entertainment," as in *a dinner party, a garden party, to throw a party, He was the life of the party*.

PASSION

One of the ways a word undergoes degradation is by having its meaning pass from a sublimely religious one to one that is common or vulgar (*see* PARAMOUR). *Passion* is another example. The word was borrowed from Old French *passion*, which came from Late Latin *passiōn-, passiō* "suffering, affliction, martyrdom." Its original meaning in Middle English (around 1175) was "the sufferings of Jesus in the last days of his life until the Crucifixion." This meaning is still in use in Christian accounts and commemorations, as in the title of the 2004 film *The Passion of the Christ*.

By the 1200s, the original sense of *passion* as "suffering" was extended to "any strong or overpowering emotion," as in "Of all base passions, Fear is most accurst" (Shakespeare, *Henry VI*). The more specific meaning, "a fit or outburst of strong emotion, especially anger or rage," developed in the 1500s, especially in the phrase *to fly into a passion*.

The word was narrowed down in the late 1500s to "a strong feeling of love," and later (1648) to "strong sexual desire, lust," as in "This has been a sin of passion, not of . . . purpose" (1850, Nathaniel Hawthorne, *The Scarlet Letter*). The sense of physical desire was extended in the 1700s to "any intense liking or enthusiasm," as in *a passion for teaching*, and "an aim or goal pursued with zeal or enthusiasm."

PEDANT

Pedant is an example of a word gone from respectable to contemptuous in a relatively short time. Its first appearance is in Shakespeare's *The Taming of the Shrew* (1593), where the servant Biondello describes someone as "a merchant, or a pedant, I know not what; but . . . In gait and countenance surely like a father." In Shakespeare's use, a *pedant* meant "a teacher, tutor, or schoolmaster," a meaning he uses several times in both *The Taming of the Shrew* and *Love's Labour's Lost*. *Pedant* was borrowed from Middle French *pédant*, from Italian *pedante* "foot soldier, pedestrian" in allusion to schoolteachers constantly walking around the classroom.

As early as 1594, Christopher Marlowe used it in *Edward II* somewhat disparagingly: "I am none of these common pedants I, That cannot speak without *propterea quod* [Latin, "for the reason that, on account of"]." The decline of *pedant* may have been due to its frequent use in negative contexts, such as *a domineering pedant, a lordly pedant, a pedant's iron rule*, a contemptuous connotation thus being attached early on to the word.

As the original meaning of "teacher, tutor" faded into obsolescence, the derogatory meaning, "a person who makes an excessive show of knowledge or learning," became established and widely used, as in "O, I know he's a good fellow . . . but a hide-bound pedant for all that; an ignorant, blatant pedant" (1886, Robert Louis Stevenson, *The Strange Case of Dr. Jekyll and Mr. Hyde*).

PEEVISH

The unusual thing about the word *peevish* is that over the years it has taken on many meanings, all of them disparaging. Possibly derived (through Old French *pervers*) from Latin *perversus* "contrary, askew, perverted," originally (before 1387) *peevish* meant "perverse, wayward, uncontrollable," as in "A peevish,

A, a
B, b
C, c
D, d
E, e
F, f
G, g
H, h
I, i
J, j
K, k
L, l
M, m
N, n
O, o
P, p
Q, q
R, r
S, s
T, t
U, u
V, v
W, w
X, x
Y, y
Z, z

A, a
B, b
C, c
D, d
E, e
F, f
G, g
H, h
I, i
J, j
K, k
L, l
M, m
N, n
O, o
P, p
Q, q
R, r
S, s
T, t
U, u
V, v
W, w
X, x
Y, y
Z, z

self-willed harlotry, One that no persuasion can do good upon"
(1597, Shakespeare, *Henry IV*).

After developing several other negative meanings, which included "senseless," "mad," "harmful," and "hateful," *peevish*
settled in the 1600s into what became its current meaning,
"childishly fretful, cross, irritable, complaining," as in *a peevish,
discontented child, She's feeling a little peevish today*. The novelist John Dos Passos, reviewing a novel by e. e. cummings in
1922, exhibited a slightly peevish disposition himself when he
complained, "Why then is it that when anyone commits anything novel in the arts he should be always greeted by the same
peevish howl of pain and surprise?"

PESSIMISM
See OPTIMISM

PIETY *and* PITY

In Middle English, both of these words meant "compassion,
mercy," and the two were not entirely differentiated until the
1500s. *Pity* came first into the language, before 1250, as a borrowing from Old French *pité, pitié*, from Latin *pīetāt-, pīetās*
"dutiful conduct, piety" (in Late Latin, also "mercy, compassion"). *Piety* appeared around 1325, and Chaucer used it in the
sense of "compassion" in *Troilus and Criseyde* (around 1385):
"Some manner jealousy . . . with piety so well repressed is." This
meaning is still retained in the name *Our Lady of Piety*, referring
to the Virgin Mary holding the crucified body of Jesus on her
lap, especially as represented in the *Pietà*, Michelangelo's famous marble sculpture at St. Peter's Basilica in Rome.

Piety changed meanings around 1500 to avoid clashing with
pity. It did that by taking on an Old French meaning of "devotion to religious observances, godliness, devoutness," which had
developed from the Latin meaning of "dutiful conduct, faithful-

ness." This became the word's usual sense, as in "Simply to call these people religious . . . would convey but a faint idea of the deep hue of piety and devotion which pervades their whole conduct" (1837, Washington Irving, *The Adventures of Captain Bonneville*).

The religious meaning was extended in the mid-1500s to "devotion and faithfulness to relatives, especially to parents," as in *filial piety*, and "an instance of such devotion, a pious act or observance," as in *to carry a burden of pieties*. The latter use was extended further in the 1900s to "sanctimonious expressions of virtue or righteousness," as in *liberal and conservative pieties*.

PLUCK *and* GUTS

A popular saying attributed to President James A. Garfield is: "A pound of pluck is worth a ton of luck." By *pluck* he meant "courage, boldness, tenacity," a meaning first recorded in Francis Grose's *Classical Dictionary of the Vulgar Tongue* (1785) in the example *He wants pluck* ("He lacks courage") which Grose translates as "He is a coward."

What is the ultimate origin of *pluck*? The word first appeared as a term in wrestling and hand combat in 1440, with the meaning "a sudden sharp pull, a tug or jerk." Since the heart, lungs, or other viscera of an animal was normally removed at one pull in preparing it for cooking, it makes sense that the next meaning would be "the heart, lungs, and other viscera of an animal" (1611). Later, in the 1700s, the meaning extended to "the bowels or entrails of an animal," which in 1785 led to the figurative meaning "boldness, tenacity," a characteristic associated with strong intestines (as in "intestinal fortitude"). This meaning invites comparison with *guts*, whose meaning, "courage, boldness," was a figurative extension of the literal meaning of "intestines," except that *guts* in this sense is recorded much later, in 1893.

A, *a*

B, *b*

C, *c*

D, *d*

E, *e*

F, *f*

G, *g*

H, *h*

I, *i*

J, *j*

K, *k*

L, *l*

M, *m*

N, *n*

O, *o*

P, *p*

Q, *q*

R, *r*

S, *s*

T, *t*

U, *u*

V, *v*

W, *w*

X, *x*

Y, *y*

Z, *z*

A, a
B, b
C, c
D, d
E, e
F, f
G, g
H, h
I, i
J, j
K, k
L, l
M, m
N, n
O, o
P, p
Q, q
R, r
S, s
T, t
U, u
V, v
W, w
X, x
Y, y
Z, z

POISE

The history of the word *poise* illustrates a special type of amelioration, or elevation of senses, one in which a trivial, matter-of-fact meaning develops into a much prized one. When the word came into English in 1421, it was a technical term meaning "weight." The origin of *poise* was Middle French *pois, peis* "weight," from Latin *pēnsum*, from *pendere* "to weigh."

From its inception, *poise* went through a series of meanings involving weight until the 1600s: a specified weight (*a poise of 120 ounces*); a standard of weight (*an English poise*); a load or burden (*a great poise of duties*); heaviness (*an elephant's poise*).

A turning point occurred in 1555, when *poise* began to be used in the sense of "equality of weight, balance, equilibrium," especially in the phrase *equal poise* (replaced in 1658 by the term *equipoise*), as in "An equal poise of hope and fear does arbitrate the event" (1637, John Milton, *Comus*). This meaning was extended in the early 1700s to "balance, stability, and composure in one's carriage or bearing, especially a graceful and elegant bearing, self-possession," as in "Do I seem to have lost my solemnity, my gravity, my poise, my dignity?" (1907, Mark Twain, *A Horse's Tale*). The word thus made the transition from the prosaic "weight" to the elegiac "graceful bearing, self-possession" without losing poise.

POTPOURRI

This is a stylish word for "medley, miscellany, mixture" that carries with it a pleasant connotation. It's much used in the phrase *a potpourri of _____*, to suggest that the mixture is light and easy to take, as, for example, *a potpourri of holiday gifts, a potpourri of travel tips, a potpourri of pop art posters*. It's also used sometimes to refer to an anthology of miscellaneous writings, as in *a potpourri of the author's stories and essays*. These senses of *potpourri*, first found in the 1840s, were figurative uses of the earlier and still current meaning, "a fragrant mixture of dried flower petals and spices, kept in a container to perfume a room or house," first recorded in 1749.

The original, and now obsolete, meaning of the word appealed mainly to the sense of smell and taste. First recorded in 1611 in Randle Cotgrave's *Dictionary of the French and English Tongues*, the word meant "a dish of mixed meats cooked as a stew." The dish was also called a *hotch-potch*, a word that also came to mean a mixture of things, a hodgepodge.

Potpourri was borrowed from French *pot pourri* "dish of mixed meats," literally, "rotten pot," a loan translation of Spanish *olla podrida* "a spicy stew of mixed meats," a term that came into English in the early 1600s and remained the standard name for the dish, while the French name became obsolete.

PREDICAMENT

Predicament was an arcane term in philosophy before 1425, when it came into English. It meant any of the ten categories or classes into which Aristotle divided all things, namely, substance, quantity, quality, relation, place, time, posture, possession, action, passion. The word was borrowed from Late Latin *praedicāmentum* "category" (literally, "something asserted"), from Latin *praedicāre* "assert, declare."

In 1548 the term was generalized in meaning to "a particular class or category," used especially when two or more items are lumped together, as in *Both species belong in the same predicament.* The word was extended later (1580s) to "any condition, situation, or circumstance, any state of affairs," as in " . . . the constitutions of several of the states are in a similar predicament" (1788, Alexander Hamilton, *The Federalist Papers*).

The current meaning, "a difficult or unpleasant situation or circumstance," appeared in the early 1800s, in phrases like *a cruel*

A, *a*

B, *b*

C, *c*

D, *d*

E, *e*

F, *f*

G, *g*

H, *h*

I, *i*

J, *j*

K, *k*

L, *l*

M, *m*

N, *n*

O, *o*

P, *p*

Q, *q*

R, *r*

S, *s*

T, *t*

U, *u*

V, *v*

W, *w*

X, *x*

Y, *y*

Z, *z*

predicament, an embarrassing predicament. The silent movie star Charlie Chaplin once described the role of the little tramp he made famous: "No matter how desperate the predicament is, I am always very much in earnest about clutching my cane, straightening my derby hat and fixing my tie, even though I have just landed on my head."

PRESTIGE, PRESTIGIOUS

Writing about Napoleon in 1838, the English philosopher John Stuart Mill said: "The *prestige* with which he overawed the world is . . . the effect of stage-trick." Mill was alluding to the original meaning of *prestige*, which was "a magic trick, an illusion." The word is first recorded in 1656, in Thomas Blount's *Glossographia*, which defines *prestiges* as "deceits, impostures, delusions, cozening tricks."

Prestige was borrowed from French *prestige* "illusion, favorable impression," from Latin *praestīgia* "trick, deceit, illusion" (in Medieval Latin, also "reputation, popular esteem"), from *prestringere* "to bind tightly, to blindfold, dazzle the eyes."

In the 1820s the original meaning of *prestige* was transferred from "a magic effect or spell" to "an overawing effect or influence, glamour." Susan Sontag, in her book *On Photography* (1977) writes that photography "trades simultaneously on the prestige of art and the magic of the real."

The adjective *prestigious* underwent a parallel change. *Prestigious* came into English before 1534, over a century ahead of *prestige*, in a poem about hypocrisy by the English poet John Skelton: "Never religious, In preaching prestigious, . . . In talking seditious, In doctrine pernicious." By *prestigious* Skelton meant "using trickery, deceptive, illusory." *Prestigious* was borrowed from Latin *praestīgiōsus* "full of tricks, deceitful."

The word's current meaning, "having or showing influence or high status, held in high esteem or admiration," didn't appear until 1901 and thereafter in phrases like *a prestigious private school, a prestigious collection of modern art,* and was clearly influenced by the current meaning of *prestige.*

PRETTY

Pretty, like *nice,* was neither pretty nor nice a word when it joined the language.

It meant "canny, cunning, crafty" in Middle English (about 1405), developed from Old English *praettig* "cunning, artful," derived from *praett* "craft, trick, wile." *Pretty* was used in that sense till the 1700s, as in "There goes the prettiest Fellow in the World . . . for managing a Jury" (1712, John Arbuthnot, *History of John Bull*). A related meaning, "well-conceived, clever, artful, ingenious," developed after 1450 in phrases like *a pretty plan, a pretty stratagem.*

It was from these uses that the nicer meaning "pleasing to the senses, attractive or charming" developed by the mid-1400s. This meaning was applied to things, as in *a pretty garden, a pretty room, pretty flowers.* At the same time the word was applied to people, especially women or children, in the sense of "attractive, good-looking, especially in a delicate or diminutive way." This is the main current meaning, as in Irving Berlin's song "A pretty girl is like a melody / That haunts you day and night."

PRISTINE *condition*

One of the commonest phrases in classified ads, such as those appearing on the free online network Craigslist, is *in pristine condition,* referring to anything for sale, from a fountain pen to a used car to a house. This means the object is "in mint condition," spotless, as good as new, unused. This meaning of

A, a

B, b

C, c

D, d

E, e

F, f

G, g

H, h

I, i

J, j

K, k

L, l

M, m

N, n

O, o

P, p

Q, q

R, r

S, s

T, t

U, u

V, v

W, w

X, x

Y, y

Z, z

pristine, first occurring in American use around 1940, was roundly criticized by British writers for half a century as a distortion of the word's original (and therefore "true") meaning.

The original meaning of *pristine,* first recorded in 1534, was "of or belonging to the earliest period or state, original, primitive, primeval," as in "the pristine simplicity of our Saxon-English" (1841, Isaac D'Israeli, *Amenities of Literature*). *Pristine* was borrowed from Latin *prīstinus* "former, previous, original, ancient."

The meaning was extended in the early 1900s to "unspoiled by human contact, untouched, uncontaminated, pure." This meaning, in turn, evolved into the "spotless, unused" of classified ads. Though the 1982 *OED Supplement* pointed out that "These transferred uses . . . are regarded with disfavour by many educated speakers," its editor, R. W. Burchfield, admitted in the 1996 *New Fowler's Modern English Usage* that " . . . on the evidence before me, it is becoming increasingly difficult to find fault with many of the weakened uses." Indeed, all the uses of *pristine*, the original and the current, are now accepted in both Britain and America.

Q, q

A, a
B, b
C, c
D, d
E, e
F, f
G, g
H, h
I, i
J, j
K, k
L, l
M, m
N, n
O, o
P, p
Q, q
R, r
S, s
T, t
U, u
V, v
W, w
X, x
Y, y
Z, z

QUAINT, ACQUAINT

Despite their similar spelling, few of us would think of connecting the word *acquaint* with *quaint*. To *acquaint* means "to make known," whereas *quaint* means "charmingly strange, odd, or peculiar." But *quaint* meant originally "knowing, wise," and was borrowed from Old French *cointe* (from Latin *cognitus* "known"), even as *acquaint* was borrowed from Old French *acointer* "to make known" (from a Latin verb derived from *accognitus* "known well"). So the two words were once closely related, until *quaint* took off in a new direction.

Before 1200, *quaint* (originally spelled *cointe*) meant "knowing, wise, skilled, clever," a meaning found in Shakespeare (*a quaint orator*) and used until the 1800s in such contexts as *a quaint writer, a quaint goldsmith*. It also had the more negative senses of "cunning, crafty," as in *a quaint rogue*, and "marked by cleverness and cunning," as in *quaint deceits, quaint devices*. These two-sided, unbalanced uses of the word led in the early 1300s to such ambiguous meanings as "elegant, refined" (*quaint language*), "affected, fastidious" (*quaint expressions*), and "strange, curious" (*quaint manners*).

The outcome of these varied uses was the current meaning, "pleasingly uncommon or old-fashioned, charmingly strange, odd, or peculiar," as in Edgar Allan Poe's famous lines in *The Raven* (1845): "Once upon a midnight dreary, while I pondered, weak and weary, Over many a quaint and curious volume of forgotten lore. . . ."

QUELL *and* KILL

"Should a popular insurrection happen in one of the confederate states, the others are able to quell it." So wrote Alexander Hamilton in *The Federalist* #9 (1787), quoting the French philosopher Montesquieu. "The government suspended civil liberties . . . to quell violent protests" (February 2006, *Miami Herald*).

Not *squash*, not *crush*, not *subdue*, not *suppress*, but *quell* is the term of choice of most writers in describing the defeat of a revolt, rebellion, insurrection, riot, protest, and the like. Nobody knows why this is so, though one could argue that *quell* sounds less harsh and more neutral than its synonyms. Which is surprising, since *quell* is the deadliest of all its synonyms, at least historically.

To quell is a native English verb that originally meant "to kill (a person or animal), to strike so as to kill, destroy," found in Old English in the form *cwellan*, which is related to Middle English *cullen* "to strike down, put to death, slay," from which the modern word *kill* developed. When in the early 1200s *kill* became the favored term for "to put to death," cousin *quell* weakened its meaning to "overcome, defeat," as in *They quelled their enemies in battle.* By the 1300s, *quell* had acquired its present meaning, "to put an end to, subdue, suppress," as in *to quell a mutiny, quell the opposition, quell a quarrel.*

QUEUE

"An Englishman, even if he is alone, forms an orderly queue of one," wrote the British humorist George Mikes (1912–1987). *Queue* (pronounced as *cue)* is the standard British term for a line of people or vehicles waiting to be handled or attended to, what Americans call a *waiting line.* The word first appeared in this sense in 1837, in *The French Revolution* by Thomas Carlyle, who took it from the French word that meant "a tail." In Old French it was spelled *coue,* and was derived from Latin *cauda* "tail."

It wasn't Carlyle, though, who introduced the word into English. As early as 1592, *queue* was used in English to mean the tail of a beast, especially in reference to the tail of a lion in armorial bearings. And, in 1724, *queue* was extended in meaning to a long plait of hair hanging down the back like a tail, what we now call a pigtail.

A, a
B, b
C, c
D, d
E, e
F, f
G, g
H, h
I, i
J, j
K, k
L, l
M, m
N, n
O, o
P, p
Q, q
R, r
S, s
T, t
U, u
V, v
W, w
X, x
Y, y
Z, z

A, a

B, b

C, c

D, d

E, e

F, f

G, g

H, h

I, i

J, j

K, k

L, l

M, m

N, n

O, o

P, p

Q, q

R, r

S, s

T, t

U, u

V, v

W, w

X, x

Y, y

Z, z

In the 1960s, *queue* was adopted in computer science for a group of jobs waiting to be executed, as in "The order in which a system executes jobs on a queue depends on the priority system being used" (1996, Philip E. Margolis, *Random House Personal Computer Dictionary*).

odd QUIRK

There's something quirky about words beginning with *qui*. They often have to do with some twist of language, like *quibble, quip, quiddity,* and *quiz. Quirk* is such a word. It's of unknown origin, first appearing in 1565 (in Thomas Stapleton's *Fortress of the Faith*) in the sense of "a clever or subtle argument, a verbal trick, an evasion or subterfuge."

It was Shakespeare who extended the word's meaning in his plays. *Quirk* is found in Shakespeare's *Much Ado About Nothing* (1599), meaning "a clever or witty saying, a quip": "I may chance have some odd quirks and remnants of wit." Also occurring in Shakespeare, in *Twelfth Night* (1600), is the meaning "a peculiarity of character or behavior, an oddity or idiosyncrasy," as in *a manner full of quirks.* Finally, the word appears in Shakespeare's *All's Well That Ends Well* (1603), with the meaning "a sudden twist or turn": "I have felt so many quirks of joy and grief." *Quirk* was extended in the 1820s to "a twitch or jerk," as in *the quirk of a tail or fan,* and in the early 1900s to "a peculiarity or anomaly," as in *a quirk of fate, an unpredictable quirk of history.*

QUIZ

The history of *quiz* begins with a sort of slangy use in Franny Burney's *Early Diary* (1782): "He's a droll quiz, and I rather like him." Later sources confirm Burney's use as meaning "an odd or eccentric person, especially one whose appearance is peculiar or ridiculous," as in *a queer old quiz.* The verb *to quiz,* meaning "to make fun of, mock, or tease," followed in 1787, and "to regard with amusement, peer inquisitively at" in 1795.

It was in American English in the 1860s that *quiz* was first used as a verb meaning "to test (students) with a set of short questions," and as a noun, "a set of questions used to test students." The most likely explanation for this development was the use of *quiz* as a contraction or shortening of *inquisition, inquisitive,* and perhaps of *question.*

QUOTE, QUOTATION

In *The Quote Verifier* (2006), the quote verifier Ralph Keyes shows how the most famous quotations turn out to be misquoted, misattributed, or downright mistaken. George Washington never said, "I cannot tell a lie." It wasn't Patrick Henry who said "Give me liberty, or give me death!" And it's doubtful that George Bernard Shaw ever said that "youth is wasted on the young." Yet there's no end to books of quotations or of Web sites devoted to quotes put in the mouth of celebrities.

Many words are like quotes, in that they don't exactly reproduce their original meanings or uses. Cases in point are the words *quote* and *quotation* themselves. These words derived from a verb whose meaning had to do more with numbers in a book than with the utterances of the famous. The verb *to quote* meant originally (before 1387) "to mark (a book) with the numbers of chapters or other marginal references," borrowed from Medieval Latin *quotare* "to mark the numbers of, distinguish by numbers," from Latin *quotus* "which number," from *quot* "how many," the source of English *quota*.

Almost 200 years later (in 1548) this meaning was extended to "to copy out or repeat a passage from a book, author, etc." The word *quotation,* meaning "a passage copied out or repeated from a book, author, etc.," appeared in 1618, and the shortened form *quote* in 1885.

R, r

RACY *and* RACE

In October 2006, CBS News reported that a *racy* Republican ad about the Senate *race* had a *racial* subtext, thereby conflating three different words to make its point. The *racy* ad featured a bare-shouldered white woman winking at the Democratic candidate and whispering his name with a seductive "Call me"; it appealed to *racial* prejudices, since the candidate was a black man; and it was intended to hurt the candidate's chances in a *race* for the Senate.

Racy, meaning "improperly suggestive, risqué, provocative, erotic," as in *a racy novel, racy language, a racy ad,* appeared in 1901. It was a meaning extended from the earlier one (about 1817) of "having a distinctive vigor and pungency (said of writing, acting, etc.)," as in *a racy narrative, a racy speech, a racy style.* This meaning, in turn, was extended from the original one (1654) "having a distinctively excellent flavor; tasty and piquant," as in *a rich and racy white wine.*

The word derived from *race,* meaning "a class of wine with a distinctive flavor" (1520). This meaning of *race* was extended in 1533 to "a breed or stock of animals," as in *a race of horses,* and in the 1550s to "a group of people of common origin," as in *the human race, the Irish race.* The word was borrowed from Italian *razza* "stock, breed, line of descent," of unknown origin. The derivative *racial* appeared in 1862, and *racist* in 1932.

Race, meaning a competition or contest, is a word of different origin, borrowed in the early 1300s from a Scandinavian word related to Old English *ræs* "a running, rush." The word's meaning when it appeared was "an act of running," which evolved by 1513 to "a contest of speed" and later to "any contest or competition," as in *a congressional race.*

Postscript: The aforementioned political ad, though ingenious, was quickly scuttled.

A, *a*
B, *b*
C, *c*
D, *d*
E, *e*
F, *f*
G, *g*
H, *h*
I, *i*
J, *j*
K, *k*
L, *l*
M, *m*
N, *n*
O, *o*
P, *p*
Q, *q*
R, r
S, *s*
T, *t*
U, *u*
V, *v*
W, *w*
X, *x*
Y, *y*
Z, *z*

A, a
B, b
C, c
D, d
E, e
F, f
G, g
H, h
I, i
J, j
K, k
L, l
M, m
N, n
O, o
P, p
Q, q
R, r
S, s
T, t
U, u
V, v
W, w
X, x
Y, y
Z, z

REHEARSE, REHEARSAL

"I went home and did some rehearsing to satisfy my curiosity about whether I could play an Italian," is how Marlon Brando described his preparation for the film "The Godfather." "I put on some makeup, stuffed Kleenex in my cheeks, and worked out the characterization first in front of a mirror, then on a television monitor. . . . The people at Paramount saw the footage and liked it, and that's how I became the Godfather."

Like Brando, we associate the word *rehearse* with acting. But the earliest use of the word had no connection with plays or the theater. *Rehearse* was borrowed from Old French *rehercer, rehercier* "to rake over." In Middle English, the borrowed word was used figuratively to mean "to tell over, relate." The Middle English word *rehersen*, first recorded about 1300, meant "to describe at length, tell, relate, recount," as in *rehersen a story, rehersen an event.* Later in the 1300s the word developed the meaning "to repeat or recite something said or heard," as in *to rehearse a song or a prayer.* About 200 years passed before the word was used in the current sense of "to practice (a play, scene, part, etc.) for a formal or public performance," as in "Come, sit down, every mother's son, and rehearse your parts. Pyramus, you begin . . . and so every one according to his cue" (1600, Shakespeare, *A Midsummer Night's Dream*).

Rehearsal, derived from *rehearse* about 1395, meant originally "the telling or recounting something," as in *the rehearsal of a poem.* The current meaning of "a practice performance of a play, a piece of music, etc." appeared in 1580.

REPUGNANT

According to the American radio commentator Ian Shoales, "People on the East Coast regard people west of, say, Philadelphia as . . . slightly repugnant, alien life forms."

Shoales's use of *repugnant*, meaning "disgusting, offensive, loath-some," has been in English a relatively short time. It was first recorded in 1879, in a translation from French, and was derived from the earlier meaning (1777) of "distasteful, objectionable (to)," as in *actions repugnant to the moral sense, restrictions repugnant to one's feelings.*

The earliest use of the word, in Middle English (around 1443), didn't have the current harshly pejorative meaning. It was a neutral word, meaning simply "contrary or contradictory (to)," as in *laws repugnant to God's word.* It was also used in medieval medicine in the sense of "counteractive (to), antagonistic (to)," as in *a potion repugnant to worms.* It took several hundred years for the word to acquire its current derogatory use.

Repugnant was borrowed from Latin *repugnant-, repugnāns,* present participle of *repugnāre* "to fight back, resist, oppose."

RESOLUTE, RESOLUTION

Resolute means "decisive, determined, firm" as in *They were few, but resolute* (Percy Bysshe Shelley). *Resolution* means "decisiveness, determination, firmness," as in *My will is backed with resolution* (Shakespeare, *The Rape of Lucrece*). However, the original meanings of these words were practically the reverse of the familiar ones.

Before 1398, *resolution* meant "the process of dissolving some-thing, dissolution, decomposition, death," as in "I am even now ready to be sacrificed, and the time of my resolution is at hand" (1582, Rheims Bible, 2 Timothy 4:6). *Resolution* was borrowed from Latin *resolūtiōn-, resolūtiō* "a loosening, undoing." This meaning was extended in 1578 to "the act of breaking up or dispelling (a doubt, difficulty, etc.)," and by 1594 to "determina-tion, firmness of purpose," as in "Settl'd in his [a cherub's] face I see Sad resolution and secure" (1667, Milton, *Paradise Lost*). Before 1425, *resolute* meant "dissolved, weak," and "morally

A, a

B, b

C, c

D, d

E, e

F, f

G, g

H, h

I, i

J, j

K, k

L, l

M, m

N, n

O, o

P, p

Q, q

R, r

S, s

T, t

U, u

V, v

W, w

X, x

Y, y

Z, z

loose, dissolute." *Resolute* was borrowed from Latin *resolūtus* "undone," past participle of *resolvere* (*see* RESOLVE). By 1501 the meaning changed (probably by influence of *resolution*) to "determined, decided, firm."

RESOLVE

When in the Gettysburg Address Lincoln asked the American people "that we here highly resolve that these dead shall not have died in vain," he chose the word *resolve* because it has a stronger ring than "decide" or "agree on." "Resolve to be thyself" wrote Matthew Arnold in *Self-Dependence*. This meaning is first recorded in 1612.

Before 1398, *to resolve* meant "to dissolve, break up," as in "O that this too too solid flesh would melt, Thaw and resolve itself into a dew" (1604, Shakespeare, *Hamlet*). *Resolve* was borrowed from Latin *resolvere* "to loosen, undo," from *re-* (intensive prefix) + *solvere* "to break apart, dissolve."

This meaning was extended in 1571 to "to break up, dispel, or remove (a doubt, difficulty, etc.)," which in turn developed in 1612 into "to decide or determine (a doubtful matter), to settle (something) in one's mind," the current meaning.

RESTIVE

A *New York Times* article on September 19, 2004, describes Falluja as "the restive city west of Baghdad now under control of insurgents." Many might think that *restive* in this passage means "restless." It's a common error, already pointed out in 1883 in *Verbal Pitfalls: A Manual of 500 Words Commonly Misused* by Charles W. Bardeen.

Restive means "resisting control, unmanageable, refractory, balky," and since 1656 it has been commonly applied to horses, as in "I have seen many horses much alarmed and restive at the sight or sound of a steam engine" (1877, Anna Sewell, *Black Beauty*). That, however, was not the word's original meaning. Around 1599, when it first appeared, the word meant "inclined to rest, inactive, stationary," as in *a slow and restive temper, a sluggish and restive youth*. *Restive* was borrowed from Middle French *restif* (feminine *restive*) "standing still, motionless," ultimately from Latin *restāre* "stand back, be left, remain" (from *re-* "back" + *stāre* "to stand").

An inactive, stationary animal or person was often regarded as stubbornly standing still, resisting control, intractable, and so by around 1655 the word's meaning changed to "refusing to move or go forward, stubbornly standing still, balky" as in *a stubborn and restive animal, a restive colt*.

In the early 1900s, the word took a different turn (probably influenced by the similar-sounding *restless*) and came to be used in the sense of "restless, fidgety," as in "Such music is not for the piano, and her audience began to get restive" (1908, E. M. Forster, *A Room with a View*). This is not, however, the word's preferred meaning.

REVERIE *or* REVELRY?

Though unrelated, this twosome had once upon a time an almost identical meaning. Around 1350, *reverie* meant "wildness, boisterous partying, frolic, revelry," as in Chaucer's *The Reeve's Tale* (around 1390): "Then were there young poor scholars two . . . lusty for to play And only for their mirth and reverie." The word was borrowed from Old French *reverie* "revelry, wantonness, wildness," from *rever* "to revel, rave."

Shortly thereafter, another word came into the language with the same meaning. *Revelry*, meaning "merrymaking, boisterous partying," derived around 1410 from the verb *revel* "to make merry, take delight," which was borrowed from Old French *reveler* "to make merry, be disorderly," from Latin *rebellāre* "to

A, *a*

B, *b*

C, *c*

D, *d*

E, *e*

F, *f*

G, *g*

H, *h*

I, *i*

J, *j*

K, *k*

L, *l*

M, *m*

N, *n*

O, *o*

P, *p*

Q, *q*

R, r

S, *s*

T, *t*

U, *u*

V, *v*

W, *w*

X, *x*

Y, *y*

Z, *z*

A, a
B, b
C, c
D, d
E, e
F, f
G, g
H, h
I, i
J, j
K, k
L, l
M, m
N, n
O, o
P, p
Q, q
R, r
S, s
T, t
U, u
V, v
W, w
X, x
Y, y
Z, z

rebel, make war." *Revelry* was the stronger of the two words, and as a result retained its original meaning, while *reverie* continued to develop.

Around 1605, *reverie* referred to "a fantastic, fanciful idea or notion, a fantasy or delusion." Its present meaning of "a spell of dreamy musing, a daydream," as in *to fall into a reverie, lost in reverie*, was first encountered in 1657 and frequently found in poetry, as in "Sit in reverie and watch the changing color of the waves that break upon the idle seashore of the mind" (1855, Henry Wadsworth Longfellow, *The Song of Hiawatha*).

REVULSION

These days, *revulsion* is a term that you would probably not want to hear associated with medical procedures. However, the word's earliest meaning was, in fact, medical. *Revulsion* was borrowed from Latin *revulsiōn-, revulsiō* "a pulling or tearing away." First recorded around 1541, it meant "the act or practice of drawing away a disease, irritation, blood, etc., from one part of the body by acting on another part." Bloodletting (drawing blood from a vein) and cupping (drawing blood by applying heated cups to the skin) were popular early forms of revulsion. The more general meaning, "a drawing or being drawn back or away," is found in 1609, as in "Thrown out of employment by the revulsion of capital from other trades" (1776, Adam Smith, *The Wealth of Nations*).

The current meaning, "a sudden violent reaction, especially of disgust or loathing," is first encountered in 1816, and found in collocations like *an unnatural revulsion from baldness*, and in sentences like "We have an evolutionary revulsion from slime, our site of biologic origins" (1990, Camille Paglia, *Sexual Personae*).

ROSARY

A *rosary* is a familiar object to Roman Catholics and some other Christians. It's the string of beads fingered by the devout as they silently recite prayers, sometimes used as a religious decoration (*see the entry PRAYER* BEADS).

Around 1440, the word meant "a piece of ground for cultivating roses, a rose garden," borrowed from Latin *rosārium* "rose bed, rose garden." The next meaning, first recorded in 1547, was "a set of prayers, typically including the Apostles' Creed, the Paternoster or Lord's Prayer, the Ave Maria, and the Gloria Patri."

How did "rose garden" come to mean "set of prayers"? According to *The Barnhart Dictionary of Etymology*, the meaning "a set of prayers" probably came from Middle French *rosaire*, where the original sense of "a rose garden" apparently conveyed the idea of a "garden" of prayers, corresponding to the Medieval Latin phrase, *hortulus animae* "little garden of the soul," used as a term for a prayer book.

The final meaning of the string of beads, as in *a rosary suspended from the waist of a nun,* arose in 1598. A caption in the Scranton, Pennsylvania, *Times Tribune* of May 8, 2007, under the picture of a 95-year-old priest reads: "Monsignor Stephen Hrynuck bends under the weight of a large rosary hanging from his neck."

RUMMAGE

The word *rummage* came into English in 1526 as a nautical term meaning "the arranging or rearranging of cargo in the hold of a ship," and in 1544 as a verb meaning "to arrange or rearrange (goods) in the hold of a ship." *Rummage* was a shortened borrowing of older French *arrumage* (modern French *arrimage*) "a stowing or trimming the hold of a ship."

A, *a*
B, *b*
C, *c*
D, *d*
E, *e*
F, *f*
G, *g*
H, *h*
I, *i*
J, *j*
K, *k*
L, *l*
M, *m*
N, *n*
O, *o*
P, *p*
Q, *q*
R, *r*
S, *s*
T, *t*
U, *u*
V, *v*
W, *w*
X, *x*
Y, *y*
Z, *z*

A, *a*

B, *b*

C, *c*

D, *d*

E, *e*

F, *f*

G, *g*

H, *h*

I, *i*

J, *j*

K, *k*

L, *l*

M, *m*

N, *n*

O, *o*

P, *p*

Q, *q*

R, r

S, *s*

T, *t*

U, *u*

V, *v*

W, *w*

X, *x*

Y, *y*

Z, *z*

From the nautical use arose the generalized meaning "to search thoroughly, ransack," before 1625. This became the common use, as in "It is the nightly custom of every good mother after her children are asleep to rummage in their minds and put things straight for next morning" (1904, J. M. Barrie, *The Adventures of Peter Pan*).

The meaning "a thorough search," first occurred in 1753, but came into use mostly in the term *rummage sale*, defined in an 1858 trade dictionary as "a clearance sale of unclaimed goods at the docks, or of odds and ends left in a warehouse." The later, broader meaning is that of "a sale of miscellaneous items, especially to raise money for charity."

RUSE

A *ruse* is a clever trick or stratagem, a dodge, and it's a favorite word of sports and action–adventure writers. Here's a passage from Edgar Rice Burroughs's science-fiction novel, *At the Earth's Core* (1914): "The Sagoths were now . . . behind us, and I saw that it was hopeless for us to expect to escape other than by a ruse. . . . My ruse was successful, and the entire party of man-hunters raced headlong after me up one canyon."

Appropriately, *ruse* came into the language around 1410 as a hunting term, meaning "the doubling or turning of a hunted animal to elude the dogs, a game animal's roundabout or circuitous course." This meaning is recorded in *The Master of Game*, translated from the French by Edward of Norwich, 2nd Duke of York, who borrowed the word from Middle French *ruse,* from *ruser* "to dodge, evade, retreat." The word was extended to "any trick or stratagem of evasion" in 1581, as in "When there was no more opportunity for rapine, he out-reached the whole city by this cunning ruse" (1746, G. Turnbull, *Justin*).

S, s

A, a

B, b

C, c

D, d

E, e

F, f

G, g

H, h

I, i

J, j

K, k

L, l

M, m

N, n

O, o

P, p

Q, q

R, r

S, s

T, t

U, u

V, v

W, w

X, x

Y, y

Z, z

SAD

> "For of all sad words
> of tongue or pen,
> The saddest are these:
> 'It might have been!'"

So wrote the poet John Greenleaf Whittier in *Maud Muller* (1854), about a rustic girl's memory of a brief meeting with a wealthy judge and their momentary thoughts of love.

The word *sad*, "sorrowful, mournful, unhappy," has been a favorite since the early 1300s of poets like Chaucer, Milton, Pope, Wordsworth, Coleridge, and many others. That meaning, however, was an innovation. In Old English and early Middle English, *sad* meant "full, satiated, satisfied," the meaning found in related words outside English, such as Old High German *sat* "full, satisfied" (modern German *satt*) and Latin *satis* "enough." But among all the related languages only English carries the current meaning.

The current meaning, "sorrowful, unhappy," developed from the original "full, satisfied" in a series of intermediate meanings, among them: "solid, heavy" (about 1330), as in "For sad burdens that men take, make folks' shoulders ache" (Chaucer, *Romance of the Rose*); "settled, firm, steadfast" (about 1315), as in "In his face I see sad resolution and secure" (Milton, *Paradise Lost*); and "grave, serious" (about 1350), as in "And so, after sad deliberation, he answered the messenger" (around 1500, *The Three Kings' Sons*). The meaning "grave, serious" then led to the more negative sense of "sorrowful, unhappy."

SALIENT *point*

A *salient point* is one that stands out from the rest, a point that is prominent or conspicuous. The phrase has many near-synonyms, such as *a salient characteristic, a salient peculiarity*, and *a salient feature*, as in "Melodrama . . . is a salient feature of modern life" (1984, Stefan Kanfer, *Time*).

Salient was used originally (1646) to describe certain animals, especially frogs and fishes. The word meant "leaping, jumping," as in *salient mackerel, salient blenny. Salient* was borrowed from Latin *salient-, saliēns*, present participle of *salīre* "to leap," the source of English *sally*.

In the 1670s *salient* appeared in medical use in the phrase *salient point*, meaning the starting point of some activity. The word was extended in the mid-1800s to "standing out, prominent or conspicuous," as in *The more salient the experience, the greater its impact.* According to a report in the *Journal of the American Medical Association* (February 21, 2007), "Yearning and acceptance are the two most salient emotions individuals experience after a significant loss."

SANGUINE

"Still let us not be over-sanguine of speedy final triumph," wrote Abraham Lincoln in a letter dated August 26, 1863, in the middle of the American Civil War. By "over-sanguine" he meant "overly hopeful or confident." The word *sanguine* meant "given to hopefulness, confident of success" since the early 1500s, in reference to the medieval belief that four humors (*see the entry* HUMOR) determine whether a person's complexion and temperament will be choleric, melancholic, phlegmatic, or sanguine.

A person of *sanguine* humor was supposedly characterized by the predominance of blood in his physiology over the other three humors, as indicated by a ruddy complexion and a hopeful, confident disposition. "Of his complexion he was sanguine," so Chaucer, in the Prologue to the *Canterbury Tales* (about 1386), describes the Franklin (a landowning commoner). An earlier meaning of *sanguine* was "blood-red," found in the Wycliffe Bible (about 1382) and implied in the noun *sanguine* (1319), meaning "a cloth of blood-red color." *Sanguine* was borrowed from Old French *sanguin* (feminine *sanguine*), a learned

A, *a*

B, *b*

C, *c*

D, *d*

E, *e*

F, *f*

G, *g*

H, *h*

I, *i*

J, *j*

K, *k*

L, *l*

M, *m*

N, *n*

O, *o*

P, *p*

Q, *q*

R, *r*

S, s

T, *t*

U, *u*

V, *v*

W, *w*

X, *x*

Y, *y*

Z, *z*

A, a
B, b
C, c
D, d
E, e
F, f
G, g
H, h
I, i
J, j
K, k
L, l
M, m
N, n
O, o
P, p
Q, q
R, r
S, s
T, t
U, u
V, v
W, w
X, x
Y, y
Z, z

borrowing from Latin *sanguineus* "of or pertaining to blood," from *sanguin-, sanguis* "blood."

SATELLITE

When *satellite* was borrowed from the French in 1548, it meant essentially a bodyguard. Thomas Blount, in his English dictionary, *Glossographia* (1656), defined the word as "one retained to guard a man's person; a Yeoman of the Guard." By the 1800s, the word had come to mean, often reproachfully, "a servile or obsequious attendant to a master or employer."

In 1611, the German astronomer Johann Kepler applied the Latin word *satellites* "attendants, guards" to the secondary planets revolving around Jupiter that had been recently discovered by Galileo. In 1880, the novelist Jules Verne used the word in the novel *Begum's Fortune* to refer to an imaginary man-made device launched into an orbit around the earth. In the 1930s and 1940s, the term *satellite* became standard for any device designed to be put into terrestrial orbit, a feat achieved in 1957 with the launching of *Sputnik* by the Soviet Union.

So as not to confuse the new, human-made satellites with the astronomical ones, the retronym *artificial satellite* was coined after 1957. Since then, artificial satellites have been divided into four major types: *research satellites* (like the Hubble Space Telescope), *communications satellites* (like the Telstar and Syncom series), *weather satellites* (like the Tiros and Nimbus series), and *navigation satellites* (used by ships and aircraft).

SATURATE

The word *saturate* made its first appearance in the English-Latin dictionaries of Sir Thomas Elyot (1538) and Peter Levens (1570), where it was defined as "to satiate, satisfy." *Saturate* was used in this sense for over 200 years, as in "Cruel persons whose blood-thirsty minds nothing could saturate" (1683, *London Gazette*).

An 1816 textbook on insects, *Introduction to Entomology*, describes ants as "marching in long files . . . to any place where sugar is kept; and when they are saturated, return in the same order."

Since being satiated meant to be supplied (with food, etc.) to the full, in the 1700s *saturate* developed the extended meaning "to soak thoroughly, drench, impregnate or imbue (with)," as in "These lands of Egypt [are] saturated with moisture" (1764, Thomas Harmer, *Observations*). The word has since been widely used in both technical contexts (*saturated fats, saturated markets*) and figuratively, as in "Saturate yourself with your subject and the camera will all but take you by the hand" (1961, Margaret Bourke-White, *Portrait of Myself*).

The word was borrowed from Latin *saturāt-*, past participle stem of *saturāre* "to fill up, satiate," from *satur* "full, satiated," related to *satis* "enough," the source of English *satisfy*.

See also SAD

SCANDAL

A wave of corporate scandals swept American firms in 2002, the most notorious being the Enron accounting fraud. Scandals involving Hollywood celebrities have filled the pages of tabloids since the 1920s. Baseball fans will never forget the 1919 World Series scandal involving eight players of the Chicago White Sox (later dubbed "Black Socks").

The word *scandal*, meaning "an incident or situation that brings about public disgrace and discredit," first appeared in this sense in Shakespeare's *Henry VI* (1590), where the king, berating his uncles, cries out: "Oh, what a scandal it is to our crown, That two such noble peers as ye should jar!" This general meaning developed from the earlier (1581) religious meaning of *scandal,* "an occasion of unbelief, a moral offence," especially in the phrase

A, *a*

B, *b*

C, *c*

D, *d*

E, *e*

F, *f*

G, *g*

H, *h*

I, *i*

J, *j*

K, *k*

L, *l*

M, *m*

N, *n*

O, *o*

P, *p*

Q, *q*

R, *r*

S, s

T, *t*

U, *u*

V, *v*

W, *w*

X, *x*

Y, *y*

Z, *z*

A, *a*

B, *b*

C, *c*

D, *d*

E, *e*

F, *f*

G, *g*

H, *h*

I, *i*

J, *j*

K, *k*

L, *l*

M, *m*

N, *n*

O, *o*

P, *p*

Q, *q*

R, *r*

S, s

T, *t*

U, *u*

V, *v*

W, *w*

X, *x*

Y, *y*

Z, *z*

the scandal of the cross, meaning "the offence of the crucifixion" (translation of Late Latin *scandalum crucis*), in Galatians 5:11.

The earliest meaning of *scandal*, found repeatedly in the *Ancrene Riwle* (before 1225), is "a moral or religious lapse, a stumbling block," as in "Heresies, and Schisms, are of all others, the greatest Scandals" (1625, Bacon, *Essays*). The word was borrowed from Late Latin *scandalum* "stumbling block, temptation," related to Latin *scandere* "to climb, scale," the source of English *ascend*.

SCHEME

In its original incarnation in English, in 1553, *scheme* was a term in rhetoric meaning "a figure of speech," borrowed from Medieval Latin *schema* "shape, form, figure." During the 1600s, the word was expanded into various technical senses, including "any figure or diagram" (1612), "a map or plan" (1649), and "a table or outline" (1652).

In the early 1700s, the word's meaning broadened to "a plan or program of action, a project or undertaking," as in *a scheme to improve the language skills of students*. But this meaning took an unfavorable turn when certain ambitious enterprises proved to be underhanded or self-seeking, such as the "Mississippi Scheme," a notorious plan conceived in 1717 to colonize and exploit the Mississippi Valley that led to a frenzy of speculation, which culminated in financial ruin for many investors. The meaning of "an underhand or fraudulent plan" was reinforced by the "Ponzi scheme," an investment swindle organized by Charles Ponzi in 1919–1920. According to the *OED*, "this is now the most prominent use, and in some degree colors the other senses so far as they survive."

The verb *to scheme* "to lay schemes" (1767) has also taken on the negative coloring of the noun, now usually meaning "to devise plans with an underhand or sinister motive."

SCRUTINY

Scrutiny came into the language around 1450 as a technical term for a formal vote taken to elect a church or municipal officer by writing his name on a secret ballot. A history of the village of Headington, Oxford, relates that "On 23 May 1664 William Cornish was elected by scrutiny as one of the Mayor's eight Assistants. He stated that he had received the sacrament, took the usual oaths, and subscribed to the engagement, paying £5 and £10 for entertainment." A *scrutiny* was considered more effective than a show of hands or acclamation.

The word was borrowed from Latin *scrūtinium* "search, examination," from *scrūtārī* "to search, examine," (literally) "to rummage (through refuse)," from *scrūta* "old clothes, rags, refuse, trash." In a formal vote, searching through the pieces of paper to count the ones with the winning name was compared to searching through trash.

In 1604, the meaning of *scrutiny* was broadened to "any close search or examination, any careful investigation," as in "Whatever may first lead us to the scrutiny of natural objects, that scrutiny never fails of its reward" (1856, John Ruskin, *Modern Painters*). This is the chief current meaning, as in this headline in the May 1, 2007, issue of the *New York Times*: "Food Imports Often Escape Scrutiny."

SECRETARY

A 1931 movie starring Claudette Colbert and Herbert Marshall was titled "Secrets of a Secretary," a catchy title capitalizing on the obvious play on words of *secret* and *secretary*. It so happens that the two words are more than alliterative: actually *secretary* derives from *secret*.

Secretary was borrowed from Medieval Latin *secretarius* "clerk, scribe, confidential officer" (literally, "keeper of secrets"). The earliest meaning of *secretary*, recorded in 1387, was "a person

A, *a*

B, *b*

C, *c*

D, *d*

E, *e*

F, *f*

G, *g*

H, *h*

I, *i*

J, *j*

K, *k*

L, *l*

M, *m*

N, *n*

O, *o*

P, *p*

Q, *q*

R, *r*

S, *s*

T, *t*

U, *u*

V, *v*

W, *w*

X, *x*

Y, *y*

Z, *z*

entrusted with secrets, a confidant." In early use it was frequently applied to biblical figures, like Abraham and Moses, as being entrusted with God's secrets. The word was extended in meaning in the 1400s to an officer who assisted a king or queen in private or personal matters, and in the 1500s to a minister presiding over a government department, such as the *Secretary of State* under Queen Elizabeth. The notion of secrecy was lost after 1706, when the word took on the general meaning of "a person employed to assist with correspondence, keeping records, and other office work."

SEMINAL

The development of the microchip was described in the *New York Times* of February 11, 1985, as "a seminal event of postwar science, one of those rare developments that changes everything." This use of *seminal*, meaning "very important, highly original and influential," appeared in the mid-1800s. The philosopher John Stuart Mill described in 1838 Jeremy Bentham and Samuel Taylor Coleridge as "the two great seminal minds of England in their age."

This, the word's prevailing current meaning, developed from the figurative sense, "having the properties of seeds; containing the potential of future development," that appeared before 1640 and came to be widely used of books and other publications. In 1779, Samuel Johnson, writing about Milton's early poetry, wrote: "It is pleasant to see great works in their seminal state, pregnant with latent possibilities of excellence."

Seminal came into English in 1398 from Old French with the meaning "of or pertaining to seed or to semen," as in *seminal germination, seminal vessels, seminal power*. Old French *seminal* was borrowed from Latin *sēminālis*, from *sēmen* "seed," the source of English *semen*. The Latin word is ultimately related to English *seed*.

SEMINARY, SEMINAR

These doublets were generated from a seed. A piece of ground in which plants are raised from seed, a seed plot or plant nursery, is called in Latin a *sēminārium*, a word derived from *sēmin-*, *sēmen* "seed." In 1440 *seminary* came into English from the Latin with the meaning "a plant nursery." This meaning was extended in the 1580s to "a breeding ground for the development of learning, a place of education." In Roman Catholic usage, *seminary* has been used since 1581 to mean "a school or college for training students for the priesthood." In the 1800s, such an institution came to be called a *theological seminary*, a term used also for a school or college for training students to be ministers or rabbis.

The term *seminar* was borrowed in 1889 from German *Seminar*, which was itself a borrowing from Latin *sēminarium* "seed plot." The term was used in German universities for a group of advanced students engaged in special study or original research under the guidance of a professor. The word was extended in the 1940s in American English to "a meeting or conference for the study of a subject," as *a real-estate seminar, a seminar on global warming.*

what a SHAMBLES

"What a shambles over Iran," read the title of an article in the September 4, 2006, issue of the London *Sunday Times*. The article went on to say: "After a brief period of relative solidarity, international policy towards Iran has returned to a shambles." This meaning of *shambles*, "a scene or condition of confusion or disorder, a mess," appeared in the early 1900s, but was extended from the much earlier meaning, "a place of carnage or wholesale slaughter," as in "the Infidel-Romans . . . shall invade thee, and make thy City . . . a shambles of dead bodies" (1593, Thomas Nashe, *Christ's Tears over Jerusalem*). This meaning, in turn, was a figurative or transferred use of the meaning "a place for the sale of meat or fish, a meat or fish market," recorded before

A, a

B, b

C, c

D, d

E, e

F, f

G, g

H, h

I, i

J, j

K, k

L, l

M, m

N, n

O, o

P, p

Q, q

R, r

S, s

T, t

U, u

V, v

W, w

X, x

Y, y

Z, z

1410 in such uses as *a fish shambles, driving sheep to the shambles, a butcher's shambles.*

But the story of this word doesn't end here. In early Middle English the word was a singular *shamble*, meaning "a table or stall for the sale of meat," developed from Old English *sceamel* "a table or counter for showing goods, counting money, etc.," (originally) "a stool or footstool," ultimately derived from a Germanic adoption of Latin *scamellum* "stool," diminutive of *scammum* "bench."

a SHREWD *shrew*

Shrewd is a rare example of amelioration or improvement, in which a bad or pejorative meaning became a positive one. In Middle English (early 1300s) the word meant "wicked, evil, depraved, vile," as in "Keep ever your tongue from evil and shrewd language, & speak little & well" (1490, William Caxton, *Rule of St. Benet*). It was also often applied to weapons or wild animals in the sense of "hurtful, dangerous," as in *a shrewd arrow, shrewd mice.* For almost 200 years the word was widely applied negatively, often to qualify something in itself bad or undesirable, as in *a shrewd evil, a shrewd loss.*

In the 1500s *shrewd* passed into various weaker senses: "malicious, mischievous, naughty," as in *shrewd children, a shrewd turn*; "bad, irksome, undesirable," as in *a shrewd sign, a shrewd chance*; and finally "cunning, crafty, artful," as in *shrewd wits, serpentinely shrewd.* From the latter use the word developed by the early1600s the favorable sense of "clever, astute, sharp in practical matters," as in "His lady ... seemed a shrewd understanding woman" (before 1684, John Evelyn's Diary). The favorable meaning was also applied to clever actions, speech, etc., as in "An eminent man, who had waxed wealthy by driving shrewd bargains with the Indians" (1824, Washington Irving).

Shrewd was formed in Middle English from *shrew* "an evildoer, villain" (later, a bad-tempered woman), in allusion to a *shrew* "small, insect-eating mammal with a long, sharp snout," that was believed to be venomous, found in Old English as *scrēawa*.

SILLY

The word *silly* is a classic example of pejoration, or gradual worsening of meaning. In early Middle English (around 1200), *sely* (as the word was then spelled) meant "happy, blissful, blessed, fortunate," as it did in Old English. Old English *sǣli* "happy, blissful," developed from a Germanic base represented also by Old High German *sâlig* (modern German *selig*) "happy." This meaning lasted into the late 1400s, as in "For sely is that death ... that ... endeth pain" (around 1374, Chaucer, *Troylus and Criseyde*).

The original meaning was followed by a succession of narrower ones, including "spiritually blessed, pious, holy, good, innocent, harmless," as in "Sely innocent Daniel was cast into the lions" (1545, George Joye, *Exposition on Daniel*); "deserving pity or sympathy, helpless, pitiable," as in "These sely poor wretches be presently tormented with unfruitful labour" (1516, Thomas More, *Utopia*).

As the form (and pronunciation) *sely* changed to *silly* in the 1500s, the earlier meanings passed into increasingly less favorable senses such as "weak, feeble, insignificant," as in "When as the lofty oak is blown down, the silly reed may stand" (1621, Robert Burton, *The Anatomy of Melancholy*), and "weak in intellect, unlearned, ignorant," as in "Socrates ... found Philosophy in silly Tradesmen" (before 1633, George Herbert, *Priest to Temple*). By the late 1500s, the word's use declined to its present-day meaning of "lacking good sense, empty-headed, senseless, foolish," as in "This is the silliest stuff that ever I heard" (1595, Shakespeare, *A Midsummer Night's Dream*).

A, a

B, b

C, c

D, d

E, e

F, f

G, g

H, h

I, i

J, j

K, k

L, l

M, m

N, n

O, o

P, p

Q, q

R, r

S, s

T, t

U, u

V, v

W, w

X, x

Y, y

Z, z

SMART *as a whip*

For the first 300 years of its existence, *smart* was not a flattering word.

In both Old English and Middle English *smart* (then spelled *smeart*) meant "causing pain, sharp, cutting, severe, painful," used of a whip or rod, of blows or strokes, and sometimes of harshly critical words. *Smeart* was related to the verb *smeortan* "to be painful," which was represented in other Germanic languages by Middle Dutch *smerten* "to be painful" and Old High German *smerzan* (modern German *schmerzen*). As late as in 1600, Shakespeare used it in this sense in *Hamlet*: "How smart a lash that speech doth give my conscience."

Before the 1300s, the sense of "sharp, cutting" radiated into various extended meanings, such as "brisk or forceful," as in "He bloweth smert and loud sounds" (*Kyng Alisaunder*) and "quick, prompt, active," as in "Sampson . . . was selcuth [unusual] smert" (*Cursor Mundi*). But it was as late as 1628 that the current meaning, "quick at learning, mentally acute, clever," emerged, as in "Fimbria . . . was both a smart fellow, and a Conqueror to boot" (before 1656, James Ussher, *Annals of the World*), followed in 1656 by "sharp, pointed, witty," as in *a smart saying, a smart answer.*

In 1716 the word was first applied to clothes in the sense of "neat and trim, stylish," as in *a pair of smart boots,* and in 1719 to neatly or elegantly dressed, fashionable people, as in *smart society, the smart set.* In the 1970s, the word began to be used for electronically controlled devices, such as *smart traffic signals, smart bombs.*

SOLICIT

On April 7, 2007, the Associated Press reported from San Antonio, Texas, that "authorities have accused a 20-year-old mother of using the Internet to solicit anyone willing to abduct her son from her estranged husband." We are used to seeing or hearing the word *solicit* in such illegal or disreputable contexts.

The earliest meaning, found before 1450, was "to disturb or trouble, fill with worry, disquiet," a meaning that lasted well into the 1600s and 1700s, as in "Anxious fears solicit my weak breast" (1681, John Dryden, *The Spanish Fryar*). The word was borrowed from Middle French *soliciter* from Latin *sollicitāre* "to disturb, trouble, bother."

From the idea of disturbing or troubling arose in 1430 the meaning, "to importune, trouble, or ask persistently," used until the 1800s, as in "Had I known this before . . . I had not then so-licited your father to add to my distress" (1721, Edward Young, *The Revenge)*.

The 1500s saw the emergence of a shadier use of the word, "to tempt, entice, allure, especially for lawless or immoral purposes." The extended meaning, "(of women) to accost and importune (men) for immoral purposes," is recorded since 1710, as in "She was arrested by a constable, accused of soliciting gentlemen" (1887, *The Spectator*).

Alongside the offensive meanings, the inoffensive but some-what formal meaning, "to request or petition for something, to ask or entreat," developed in the 1500s, and used currently as in "Hanson's . . . has 700,000 e-mail addresses. 'But we use it only for news of openings and that sort of thing, not for soliciting votes,' he says" (May 11, 2007, *New York Post*).

SPECIOUS

Several writers have written in recent years articles titled *The Origin of (the) Specious*, clearly a pun on Charles Darwin's epoch-making work, *The Origin of Species*.

The pun was doubly appropriate: first, because the articles defended Darwin's theory of evolution while branding the

A, a

B, b

C, c

D, d

E, e

F, f

G, g

H, h

I, i

J, j

K, k

L, l

M, m

N, n

O, o

P, p

Q, q

R, r

S, s

T, t

U, u

V, v

W, w

X, x

Y, y

Z, z

doctrines of Creationism and Intelligent Design *specious*, i.e., seemingly plausible but actually fallacious; and second, because the word *specious* is closely related to the word *species*.

Specious didn't originally have the strongly disparaging meaning it has at present. The word was borrowed from Latin *speciōsus* "fair to the sight, beautiful in appearance," from *speciēs* "appearance, sort, type" (the source of English *species*). It started out in Middle English (before 1400) as a term of high praise and approval, meaning "pleasing to the sight, fair, beautiful, handsome," as in "That other [way] specious and fair, set about with lillies and roses" (1440, *Gesta Romanorum*).

Then, in the early 1600s, the meaning "attractive, beautiful" passed into "seemingly attractive in appearance or character but not actually so," as in "Traitorous requests . . . which he was now willing to mask with the specious pretext of justice and devotion" (1611, John Speed, *The History of Great Britain*), and "This specious reasoning is nevertheless false" (1651, Thomas Hobbes, *Leviathan*).

In the 1700s the word assumed the more strongly censorious meaning of "not genuine, insincere, false," as in "But now I have found you out, you specious hypocrite!" (1740, Samul Richardson, *Pamela*). This became the common meaning by the 1800s: "You are a specious fellow . . . and carry two faces under your hood" (1841, Charles Dickens, *Barnaby Rudge*).

SPELL, GOSPEL

A *spell* is a set of words supposed to have occult or magical powers, a charm or incantation. Spells have become an industry: there are witchcraft spells, voodoo spells, love spells, money spells, even spell kits for casting spells. *Spell* first appeared with this meaning in 1579.

But this meaning developed from a much older one, found in Old English in *Beowulf* (about 725) and in King Alfred's translations (about 888), where *spel* (as it was then spelled) meant "speech, message, story, sermon." The Old English meaning was found also in Middle English, as in *Cursor Mundi* (about 1300): "The king bade all to listen . . . And thus Jacob his spell began."

The Old English word also appeared in the compound *gōdspel* "good message," from which the word *gospel* developed in Middle English.

In the 1500s, *gospel* was commonly (and mistakenly) interpreted as "God's spell," as in a 1579 glossary of Spenser's *The Shepheardes Calender*: "And here hence I think is named the gospell, as it were God's spell or word." This interpretation led to the use of *spell* for any word or set of words having an occult or supernatural power, as in "She works by charms, by spells, . . . and such daubery as this is" (1600, Shakespeare, *The Merry Wives of Windsor*). The figurative meaning "a fascinating or enthralling charm, a magical or powerful influence," has been common since the 1600s, in such phrases as *a great speaker's spell over the audience, a novel keeping readers under its spell.*

STAMINA

Stamina, meaning "staying power, strength, endurance," is first recorded in 1726, in a letter by Jonathan Swift to the Irish dramatist Richard B. Sheridan: "I indeed think her stamina could not last much longer, when I saw she could take no nourishment." This meaning was extended figuratively in the early 1800s to "intellectual or moral vigor, capacity to persevere or endure," as in "The British Constitution has considerable stamina" (1865, *Quarterly Review*).

Stamina is first recorded in English in the mid-1600s as a plural word meaning "the native structures or basic elements from which living beings develop." The word was borrowed from Latin *stāmina* "threads," plural of *stamen* "thread, warp (of cloth), stamen (of a flower)." According to the *OED*, the original

A, a

B, b

C, c

D, d

E, e

F, f

G, g

H, h

I, i

J, j

K, k

L, l

M, m

N, n

O, o

P, p

Q, q

R, r

S, s

T, t

U, u

V, v

W, w

X, x

Y, y

Z, z

meaning of English *stamina* came partly from the Latin word, and partly from the frequent classical application of the word to the threads (*stāmina*) spun by the Fates at birth to determine how long a person will live. (In ancient mythology, the Moirae, or Fates, controlled everyone's destiny.)

The word's meaning was extended in 1701 to "natural constitution as affecting a person's length of life or resistance to disease," as in *If the stamina are not sound, the patient will succumb to disease*. It was Swift, in 1726, who first used *stamina* as a singular word and that is how the word has been generally used since, as in "Carrie Ford did absolutely nothing wrong on Forest Gunner. The only problem was that the horse's stamina ran out a bit towards the end although her [Carrie's] stamina didn't" (April 10, 2004, *BBC Sports*).

I'm STARVING!

To starve goes back to Old English *steorfan* "to die." The word and its meaning are also encountered in related Germanic languages, such as Old Frisian *sterva*, Middle Dutch and Modern Dutch *sterven*, and Old High German *sterban* (Modern German *sterben*), all meaning "to die." So how did such an all-encompassing, sturdy, everyday word change into a weak and flabby "to be very hungry" (as in *Let's eat already, I'm starving*)?

The change began in Old English, when occasionally *steorfan* was used in the narrow sense of "to die of hunger." In the 1500s, the extended sense "to cause to die of hunger" arose, as in *to starve prisoners*. (Back then, the expression *to starve to death* would have been absurd.) Today the locution "I'm starving to death" means simply "I'm very hungry." The specific meaning of "to be very hungry" was generalized in the 1900s to mean "to feel a strong need or desire," as in *a child starved for affection*.

STOUT
See TALL

STRINGENT, ASTRINGENT

One of the most famous U.S. Supreme Court opinions on the limits of free speech was that given by Justice Oliver Wendell Holmes, Jr., in 1919 in the case of *Schenk/Baer v. United States.* "The most stringent protection of free speech," wrote the jurist, "would not protect a man from falsely shouting fire in a theater and causing a panic." His wording may have been influenced by an oft-quoted aphorism of the Scottish reformer Samuel Smiles in his book *Self-Help* (1859): "No laws, however stringent, can make the idle industrious, the thriftless provident, or the drunken sober."

Stringent first bowed into the language in 1605, but with a meaning now archaic. It was borrowed from Latin *stringent-, stringēns*, the present participle of *stringere* "to bind, draw tight," and meant "astringent, constrictive, binding," referring especially to taste, as in *fruit stringent to the palate.* The current meaning of *stringent*, "strict, rigorous, severe," appeared in 1846, and has been widely used since, as in "They had devised a most stringent limitation of the royal power" (1855, Macaulay, *History of England*).

Stringent was preceded in English by *astringent* (borrowed from Latin *astringent-, astringēns*), which is first recorded in 1541. As far as taste or smell is concerned, *astringent* has won the day, being used today in the sense of "causing the mouth or nostrils to pucker up by pungency or acerbity," as in *a sweet and slightly astringent wine, a flower's astringent fragrance.*

universal SUFFRAGE

During the first two centuries of its original use (beginning around 1380), *suffrage* was exclusively a religious term meaning "prayers on behalf of another, intercessory prayers." *Suffrage* was borrowed through Old French from Medieval Latin *suffragium* "intercessory prayers," from Latin *suffrāgāri* "to show support or approval."

A, a

B, b

C, c

D, d

E, e

F, f

G, g

H, h

I, i

J, j

K, k

L, l

M, m

N, n

O, o

P, p

Q, q

R, r

S, s

T, t

U, u

V, v

W, w

X, x

Y, y

Z, z

Influenced by the basic Latin meaning of support and approval, in 1532 *suffrage* came to mean "a vote of assent or support," and in an extended sense, "a vote for or against any controversial question." After several subsidiary meanings ("approval, consent, consensus of opinion"), in 1610 the word's meaning evolved into "the collective vote of a body of persons," which led in 1789 to "the right of voting as a member of a body, state, etc.," found in the U.S. Constitution: "No state shall be deprived of its equal suffrage in the Senate." This came to be known as *universal suffrage* in 1798. The movement for *women's suffrage* began in the mid-1800s; the right to vote was granted women in the United Kingdom in 1918 and in the United States by the 20th Amendment to the Constitution in 1920.

SURROUND

It would seem at first glance that *surround,* "to go around, encircle, enclose," is made up of *sur-* "beyond" + *round.* Not so. The proof of this is that the original meaning of this word was a different one, "to overflow, inundate, flood, submerge," as in *The torrential rains surrounded the grounds.* For about 200 years, between the early 1400s and the early 1600s, *surround* meant literally "to overflow with water."

The first evidence of the current meaning is found in John Bullokar's hard-word dictionary, *English Expositor* (1616), which defined *surround* as "to compass round about." Apparently Bullokar and other users of English, influenced by the word *round,* extended the meaning of *surround* from "to overflow" to "to extend on all sides, encircle." This change in meaning came from a mistake, since the word *round* is completely unrelated to *surround.* *Round* derived from Latin *rotundus* "round, circular, rotund," while *surround* was borrowed from Middle French *soronder, souronder* "to overflow, abound," which came from Late Latin *superundāre* "to overflow" (from Latin *super-* "over" + *undāre* "to rise in waves," from *unda* "wave").

T, t

A, a

B, b

C, c

D, d

E, e

F, f

G, g

H, h

I, i

J, j

K, k

L, l

M, m

N, n

O, o

P, p

Q, q

R, r

S, s

T, t

U, u

V, v

W, w

X, x

Y, y

Z, z

TACT, CONTACT

Tact, meaning "a delicate sense of what is fitting or proper in dealing with others so as to avoid offending them," is a highly valued quality. Abraham Lincoln is quoted as having said that "Tact is the ability to describe others as they see themselves."

This meaning of *tact* was imported from French, the traditional language of diplomacy, after Voltaire had popularized it. The Scottish philosopher Dugald Stewart, in his *Outlines of Moral Philosophy* (1793), introduced *tact* in this sense: "The use made in the French tongue of the word *Tact*, to denote that delicate sense of propriety which enables a man to feel his way in the difficult intercourse of polished society."

However, *tact* had been in English earlier, since the 1600s, with the literal meaning of "touch, tactile feeling," as in "Of all the creatures, the sense of tact is most exquisite in man" (1652, Alexander Ross, *Arcana Microcosmi*). As the sense of touch is extremely delicate and sensitive by comparison to senses like those of sight or hearing, it seemed natural to extend its meaning figuratively to "delicacy and sensitiveness in one's dealing with others." Interestingly, the word *contact* "an act of touching" came into English almost at the same time as *tact*, in 1626, and was extended figuratively in 1818 to "an act of connecting or communicating," as in *to renew contact with old friends*.

Tact was borrowed through French from Latin *tāctus* "touch," from the past participle stem of *tangere* "to touch," the source of English *tangent*. *Contact* was borrowed from Latin *contāctus* "act of touching," from the past participle stem of *contingere* "to touch closely," formed from *con-* "with, together" + *tangere* "to touch."

TALENT

In the ancient world, a *talent* was a weight of gold, silver, etc., used widely as a currency. The word appeared in Old English

A, a

B, b

C, c

D, d

E, e

F, f

G, g

H, h

I, i

J, j

K, k

L, l

M, m

N, n

O, o

P, p

Q, q

R, r

S, s

T, t

U, u

V, v

W, w

X, x

Y, y

Z, z

(about 893) and in Middle English in the Wycliffe Bible (1382) in reference to the building of the Tabernacle: "And of the hundreds of talents of silver were cast the sockets of the sanctuary."

The Old English word was borrowed from Latin *talentum* "weight, money," itself a loan from Greek *tálanton* "weight, balance, sum of money." It was through the biblical parable of the talents (Matthew 25:14–30) that the word came to be widely known. In this parable, a rich man gave three of his servants talents, two of whom used the money wisely, while the third made no use of it at all. In allusion to the parable, the meaning "a person's power or ability viewed as something divinely entrusted for his use and betterment," arose around 1430, as in "They be the talents that God hath lent to man in this life: of the which He will ask most straight account" (1526, William Bonde, *Pilgrimage of Perfection*). This meaning was extended in 1602 to the current one of "a special natural ability or aptitude, an inborn skill," as in "He is chiefly to be considered in his three different talents, as . . . a critic, a satirist, and a writer of odes" (1685, John Dryden, *Sylva*).

In the 1800s, the word was transferred in meaning to "a person of talent," as in "Selfish fellows who wanted to keep young talent from the stage" (1885, J. K. Jerome, *On Stage*).

TALL, *dark, and handsome*

The word *tall* came into its meaning with an interesting caveat: it only applied to men. Originally *tall* appeared in Middle English in various highly flattering senses, such as "fair, handsome, elegant, fine" (around 1450), as in "One of the tallest young men of this parish lieth sick" (1451, *The Paston Letters*), and "strong in combat, brave, bold, valiant," as in "By Saint Mary he is a tall man . . . and do right service he can" (before 1529, John Skelton, *Magnificence*).

A, a
B, b
C, c
D, d
E, e
F, f
G, g
H, h
I, i
J, j
K, k
L, l
M, m
N, n
O, o
P, p
Q, q
R, r
S, s
T, t
U, u
V, v
W, w
X, x
Y, y
Z, z

Around 1530 *tall* took on a new meaning, "high of stature, of more than average height, long, lofty." (This can most likely be explained by the physical appearance of the men that *were* strong and valiant in combat.) The word in this sense was applied to men and to ships. By the 1600s it was also applied to women and to objects like mountains, houses, and chimneys. One way of viewing this development is that it was in line with those of other words of esteem, like *handsome* and *stout*.

Handsome changed from "easy to handle" to "of fair size" and then to "well-proportioned, good-looking" (*see* HANDSOME); *stout* developed from "proud, fierce, brave" to "strong, robust" and then to "corpulent, large." Similarly, *tall* may have changed from "brave, bold" to "high of stature" through an intermediate sense of "imposing, impressive-looking," since one of its early meanings was "fair, handsome."

The origin of *tall* is somewhat obscure. It may have developed from Old English *etæl* "swift, prompt, active," corresponding to Old High German *gizal* "quick, prompt."

tongue with a **TANG**

In Shakespeare's *The Tempest* (1612), Stephano, a drinking sailor, sings:

> But none of us cared for Kate.
> For she had a tongue with a tang,
> Would cry to a sailor, Go hang!

Before 1350, the word *tang* in Middle English meant "serpent's tongue," and also "sharp extension of a blade." It was borrowed from Old Norse *tange* "point, spit of land, pointed projection of a chisel, knife, etc."

In 1440, *tang* meant an insect's sting, which is most likely the usage that Shakespeare meant in *The Tempest*. The figurative meaning, "a sharp, penetrating taste or flavor," as in *the spicy tang of apples, the strong tang of Gorgonzola cheese*, appeared in the late 1400s, followed in 1593 by the figurative sense, "a slight touch or trace of something, a suggestion, soupçon," as in *a tang of southern dialect, the tang of wild nature*.

TARGET

According to a CNBC report in May 2007, "James Donald, president and chief executive of Starbucks told CNBC . . . that he expects to finish 2007 'right on target'." The phrase *on target*, meaning "at the goal aimed at, as forecast," developed from the use of *target* since the 1940s in the sense of "an amount of money, etc., set as an objective," as in *to achieve a minimum fundraising target of one million dollars*.

Target was borrowed from Old French *targette*, diminutive of *targe* "shield." In Middle English (around 1400) *target* was a technical term meaning "a light round shield, used especially by footmen and archers." In the mid-1700s, after shields had gone out of use, the military adopted the word *target* for a shieldlike object marked with concentric circles, set up to be aimed at in shooting practice. This meaning was extended in the late 1700s to "any object or place selected for military attack." At the same time, the word began to be used figuratively as "someone aimed at, especially a person or thing that is the object of abuse, scorn, etc.," as in *a target for popular ridicule*.

In the mid-1900s *target* came to be used informally for "an amount of money set as an objective," and later "any goal or aim to be reached," as in *a production target, a legislative target, the 26-mile target of marathon runners*.

THING

One of the oldest parliaments in the world is that of Iceland, founded in 960.

Its name, *Althing*, meant literally "general assembly," a name that would have been familiar to speakers of Old English, who also used the word *al* "all, general" and *thing* "assembly." Old English *thing* developed from a common Germanic source that included Old Frisian and Old Saxon *thing* "assembly, council lawsuit, matter, affair." In the 700s Old English *thing* had as its primary meaning "a meeting or assembly, especially a judicial assembly, a court of law, or a legislative council." It was an important word, used in many situations. It therefore evolved within a few centuries into various subsidiary meanings, among them "a matter before a law court, a legal process," then "a matter of concern, a business or affair," which led to "a doing, act, deed; an event, occurrence, incident; a fact or circumstance."

In early Middle English, *thing* was generalized further to "an object, matter, anything," as in "In the sun [are] three things sere; a body round, hot, and light, ... all at a sight" (before 1325, *Cursor Mundi*). The compounds *anything, nothing* (no thing), and *something* were formed at that time.

A similar process of generalization occurred in the Romance languages. Latin *causa*, meaning "legal process, lawsuit, cause," gave rise to French *chose* "thing" and Italian and Spanish *cosa* "thing."

THRILL

Shakespeare popularized the verb *to thrill*, using it in various contexts that expanded its meaning. He used it, among others, in *Romeo and Juliet* (1595): "a faint cold fear thrills through my veins," and in *Henry IV, Part 1* (1598): "Art thou not horribly afraid? doth not thy blood thrill at it?"

These were figurative uses meaning "to produce a quivering, exciting feeling, as of fear, awe, etc." The word's literal meaning, occurring before 1300, was "to pierce, bore, penetrate," as a sword, lance, or other weapon. The word was an altered form (by transposition of the sounds of *i* and *r*) of the earlier verb *to thirl* "to pierce, penetrate," from Old English *thyrel* "puncture, hole," from *thurh* "through." This meaning soon extended to "anything piercing, as an emotion or a sharp sound."

The current meaning, "to give a feeling of extreme pleasure or delight," as in "Mere alcohol doesn't thrill me at all" (1934, Cole Porter, *I Get a Kick Out of You*), first appeared in the late 1700s, especially in the participial form *thrilled*, as in *thrilled by the beautiful view, thrilled to have met a famous person.*

TISSUE

Mass production has degraded the meaning of *tissue.* In Middle English (before 1366), a *tissue* was a rich fabric or cloth, often interwoven with gold or silver. Chaucer used it in *Troylus and Criseyde* (around 1374) to mean a band or girdle made of rich material. *Tissue* was borrowed from Old French *tissu* "a ribbon or band of woven material," noun use of the past participle of *tître, tistre* "to weave," from Latin *text-, textere,* the source of English *text, textile,* and *texture.*

The word's meaning was extended before 1565 to "any woven fabric or stuff," which in 1711 was used figuratively as "anything like a woven fabric, a network or web (of things, usually of a bad kind)," as in *a tissue of lies, a tissue of misrepresentations.*

Around 1780 the word was reduced in meaning from cloth to paper. A *tissue paper* denoted a very thin, nearly transparent paper, mainly used for wrapping. In the 1920s the word took on its chief current meaning, "a piece of soft absorbent paper used for wiping the nose, cleaning the skin, etc., as in *facial tissue, toilet tissue, a box of tissues.*

The word's second current meaning, that of "the structure or texture of which an organism or organ is composed," as in

A, *a*
B, *b*
C, *c*
D, *d*
E, *e*
F, *f*
G, *g*
H, *h*
I, *i*
J, *j*
K, *k*
L, *l*
M, *m*
N, *n*
O, *o*
P, *p*
Q, *q*
R, *r*
S, *s*
T, *t*
U, *u*
V, *v*
W, *w*
X, *x*
Y, *y*
Z, *z*

A, a

B, b

C, c

D, d

E, e

F, f

G, g

H, h

I, i

J, j

K, k

L, l

M, m

N, n

O, o

P, p

Q, q

R, r

S, s

T, t

U, u

V, v

W, w

X, x

Y, y

Z, z

animal and plant tissue, muscle tissue, pulmonary tissue, is first recorded in 1831 as "every cellular, vascular, muscular tissue," in Thomas Carlyle's *Sartor Resartus*.

TOIL *and trouble*

> Double, double toil and trouble
> Fire burn, and caldron bubble.

This is the refrain screeched by the three witches amidst thunder and lightning in Act IV, Scene 1 of Shakespeare's *Macbeth* (1605). Everything in the refrain is clear except the word *toil*. The common meaning of this word is "hard and continuous work, exhaustive labor," but this is not the kind of evil the weird sisters had in mind. They were using *toil* in its original sense of "turmoil, contention, dispute," also "battle, strife," recorded in the 1300s. The word was borrowed through Old French *toeil* "bloody melee, trouble, confusion," from *toeillier* "to stir up, agitate, entangle," from Latin *tudiculāre,* from *tudicula* "an instrument for bruising olives," related to *tundere* "to pound, beat."

The original meaning passed into the weaker one of "a hard struggle or exertion, difficult or taxing work" in the 1590s, too late for Shakespeare to pick up and use it. But this was the meaning popularized in the 1700s, notably in such poems as Thomas Gray's *Elegy Written in a Country Church-Yard* (1751):

> Let no ambition mock their useful toil,
> Their homely joys, and destiny obscure;
> Nor Grandeur hear with a disdainful smile
> The short and simple annals of the poor.

TOILET

Because of its association with a very private activity, the word *toilet* is a prime example of the workings of euphemism, the substitution of an inoffensive or indirect term for one thought to be too blunt or offensive. Consider some of the substitutions for a compartment containing a bowl, hinged seat, and a mechanism for flushing (what was formerly called a *water closet* or *W.C.*): *bathroom, washroom, powder room, restroom, lavatory, commode, privy, ladies room, men's room, the john, the loo.*

This meaning of *toilet* is first recorded in 1895, in Funk's *Standard Dictionary of the English Language*. However, the original use of the word *toilet* wasn't even remotely connected with bathrooms. *Toilet* was borrowed from French *toilette* "a cloth or bag to put clothes in," diminutive of *toile* "cloth, net, web," from Latin *tēla* "web."

When the word came into English, in 1540–1541, it meant "a piece of cloth, bag, or case to put clothes in." This meaning was extended in the 1680s to "a cloth cover for a dressing table," then "the articles or table used in dressing," and "the process of dressing and grooming at such a table," as in *The lady spent hours at her toilet.* In the 1800s, the word came to mean "a dressing room, especially one furnished with fixtures for bathing, a bathroom." This sense developed later in the century into the word's current meaning, as in the actor Klaus Kinski's immortal remark, "Making movies is easier than cleaning toilets."

TORPEDO

The word *torpedo* was used figuratively before 1539 in the sense of "one that has a benumbing influence," as in "He used to call a pen his torpedo, whenever he grasped it, it numbed all his faculties" (1762, Oliver Goldsmith, *Life of Richard Nash*). Latin *torpēdo* literally meant "stiffness, numbness," from *torpēre* "be stiff or numb" (the source of English *torpid* "sluggish").

Since the 1500s, scientists have recognized a genus of fish named *Torpedo*. They are cigar-shaped fish that attack and kill other fish underwater by emitting deadly electric discharges.

A, a

B, b

C, c

D, d

E, e

F, f

G, g

H, h

I, i

J, j

K, k

L, l

M, m

N, n

O, o

P, p

Q, q

R, r

S, s

T, t

U, u

V, v

W, w

X, x

Y, y

Z, z

The fish's name was borrowed from the numbing effect on a body from the electric discharges.

In 1776, Captain David Bushnell, of the American Continental Army's Corps of Engineers, named his submarine mine a *torpedo* after the flat fish of the same name (which is now known as the electric ray). Captain Bushnell first tried out the invention in New York Harbor. His *torpedo* was a towed or drifting underwater mine used to defend channels and harbors; later, in the 1800s, the term was extended to a self-propelled submarine missile launched from a warship.

the grand TOUR

Tours of all kind have been fashionable since the 1600s, when the Grand Tour, a journey through western Europe by young people of means, was considered essential to their education. There have been since then *walking tours, cycling tours, bus tours, city tours, wedding tours*, and every kind of tour designed to attract *tourists*.

A *tour* in this sense means a going or traveling around from place to place, a pleasure excursion or journey. This meaning is first found in English in 1642, and was used in England especially for a short outing popularly taken in London around Hyde Park for exercise, recreation, or as a social activity.

The word goes back to the 1400s, when a *tour* meant "a turning around, a circuit," as in "They go to the mass . . . to make their tours and signs then for any devotion" (1477, William Caxton, *History of Jason*). *Tour* was borrowed from Old French *tour* "a turn, round, circuit," earlier *tourn*, from *torner, tourner* "to turn," the source of English *turn*. In the 1500s it meant "a course to turn to," and "a turn to do something, one's shift or spell," a meaning still found in *tour of duty* "a turn at a job, especially in the military," first recorded in 1800.

TOY

This word of uncertain origin burst into English in 1530 with the meaning "a thing of little or no value, a trifle," and also "a piece of fun or amusement," as in "We . . . wonder at disguisings and toys whereof we know no meaning" (1530, William Tyndale, *Works*). These were followed in 1542 by "a trifling or jesting speech or writing," as in "I never may believe these antique fables, nor these fairy toys" (1595, Shakespeare, *A Midsummer Night's Dream*). Still another meaning, "amorous sport, dallying," appeared in 1565 in the phrase *lovers' toys.*

The current sense, "an object for children to play with, a plaything," appeared before 1586 in the phrase *playing toy*, meaning "a trifle or trinket to play with." The word became common in the 1600s, and was perhaps best described in William Cowper's poem *Hope* (1781):

> Men deal with life as children with their play,
> Who first misuse, then cast their toys away.

Various theories have been proposed for the origin of the word, the most plausible being that *toy* was borrowed from Dutch *tuig*, a word with a wide variety of meanings, including "harness, rigging, tools, stuff, refuse, trash" (found also in German *Zeug* "apparatus, tools, gear, stuff, trash"), and close to the English *playing toy* in the compound *speeltuig* "play tool, plaything," found also in German *Spielzeug* "plaything, toy" and Danish *legetoi* "play tool, plaything."

TRADE

When *trade* came into English in 1300 it meant "a track or trail left by steps; footprints." *Trade* was borrowed from Middle Low German *trade* "track, course," related to Middle English *tred* "tread" and Old English *treden* "to tread." In the 1400s, the meaning of *trade* developed into "a trodden way, path, track." At the time *trade* was synonymous with the word *tread*. While

A, a

B, b

C, c

D, d

E, e

F, f

G, g

H, h

I, i

J, j

K, k

L, l

M, m

N, n

O, o

P, p

Q, q

R, r

S, s

T, t

U, u

V, v

W, w

X, x

Y, y

Z, z

the latter retained its general connection with the action of taking steps or the mark left by steps, *trade* extended its meaning in the 1500s to "a way, course, or manner of living," as in *the trade of merchandising,* and eventually to "the practice of some occupation, business, or profession."

The development of *trade* did not stop there. At first an all-encompassing word, including business and professions, in the 1600s it began to be restricted to a skilled handicraft, such as *by trade a butcher, a potter by trade,* or to the practice of buying and selling as a shopkeeper or other merchant, as in "Every man to his trade" (1732, Thomas Fuller, *Gnomologia*).

Today, *trade* means mainly "the buying and selling of goods and services, commerce," as in "International trade adds jobs to Oregon" (May 16, 2007, *Portland Business Journal*), or, as Andrew Carnegie famously put it, "Trade knows no flag."

TRAIT

Ralph Waldo Emerson, the noted 19th-century essayist and poet, was fascinated by what he considered the peculiar traits, or distinguishing characteristics, of the English people. He even wrote a book, *English Traits*, in 1856, in which he wrote: "The English race are reputed morose. . . . This trait of gloom has been fixed on them by French travellers, who . . . have spent their wit on the solemnity of their neighbors." This is a far cry from the original meaning of *trait*, which appeared in the mid-1500s in the sense of "a drawing or that which is drawn, a line, streak, or stroke," as in *the traits of a painting or a piece of writing. Trait* was borrowed from French *trait* "draft, stroke, line," from Latin *tractus* "a drawing, draft, track, course."

This meaning was extended in the 1700s to the lines or lineaments of the face, which naturally led to today's meaning of "a particular feature of character, a distinguishing quality or characteristic of a person or group," as Emerson uses it above. This usage is first found in 1752, in a letter by the English writer Horace Walpole, where he refers to "a most sensible trait of the King." It was appropriated in the early 1900s by social scientists, who have been using it in the specific sense of "a particular feature of a culture or social group," in phrases like *culture traits, trait models,* and *trait complex.*

TRANSPIRE

In *Webster's Dictionary of English Usage* (1989), discussion of this word takes up four long columns. It transpires that the use of this word in the sense of "to occur, happen" has triggered since the late 1800s a war of words that has just recently abated. Critics have disparaged this use as being pretentious and even downright wrong.

Transpire was borrowed from French *transpirer* "to breathe through, exhale," from Latin *trans-* "through" + *spīrāre* "breathe." In 1598, *transpire* was a technical term similar to *perspire* and meant "to emit or pass off in the form of a vapor or liquid," as in *to transpire moisture through the skin.* Then, in the mid-1700s, the word began to be used figuratively to mean "to escape from secrecy, leak out, become known," as in *Confidential information was allowed to transpire.* But in the late 1700s, according to the *OED*, the word was mistakenly used for "to occur, happen, take place," through a misunderstanding of such sentences as *What had transpired during his absence he did not know.* Misunderstanding or not, the usage has caught on, and is now the most common meaning of the word.

The current use of *transpire* is seen in a memorable sentence by the British mystery writer P. D. James, quoted in the London *Daily Telegraph* of April 14, 1988:

"Great literature cannot grow from a neglected or impoverished soil. Only if we actually tend or care will it transpire that every hundred years or so we might get a *Middlemarch.*"

A, a
B, b
C, c
D, d
E, e
F, f
G, g
H, h
I, i
J, j
K, k
L, l
M, m
N, n
O, o
P, p
Q, q
R, r
S, s
T, t
U, u
V, v
W, w
X, x
Y, y
Z, z

TUITION

Noah Webster, in his *American Dictionary of the English Language* (1828), illustrates the use of the word *tuition* with this sentence: "In our colleges, the tuition is from thirty to forty dollars." Today, alas, the amount would more likely be thirty thousand to forty thousand dollars.

Going back to 1436, *tuition* meant "the act of looking after or taking care of, protection, custody, care, guardianship," as in *The orphans were brought up under the tuition of a foster father.* *Tuition* was borrowed from Middle French *tuition* "guardianship," from Latin *tuitiōn-, tuitiō* "guard, protection."

As far back as 1582, the meaning of *tuition* extended to "the act or occupation of teaching a student or students, the function of a tutor," as in *The teacher was entrusted with the tuition of the children.* In 1828, Webster took *tuition* one step further to mean "the charge or fee for instruction, as at a private school or a college or university." Webster's use of *tuition* was an American English innovation, probably shortened from such phrases as *tuition fee* and *tuition money.*

U, u

A, a

B, b

C, c

D, d

E, e

F, f

G, g

H, h

I, i

J, j

K, k

L, l

M, m

N, n

O, o

P, p

Q, q

R, r

S, s

T, t

U, u

V, v

W, w

X, x

Y, y

Z, z

give or take UMBRAGE

"As a term for being offended," comments *A Dictionary of Contemporary American Usage*, "*take umbrage* is a literary term and would seem a little strange or affected in ordinary speech. Yet it is a fine phrase, suggesting one shadowed in offended pride." The last clause is a clue to the word's original meaning.

Umbrage was borrowed from Middle French *umbrage* "shadow, shade," from Latin *umbrāticum,* "of shade or shadow," from *umbra* "shade." The original meaning of *umbrage*, recorded in 1426, was "shadow, shade," used in poetry and other literary works, often specifically referring to the shade or shadow cast by trees. In *Hamlet* (1600), Shakespeare transferred the meaning to "a shadowy appearance, a faint representation," when Hamlet replies to the fashionable courtier Osric in extravagant language:

> To make true diction of him, his semblable is
> his mirror, And who else would trace him, his
> umbrage—nothing more.

Throughout the 1600s other figurative meanings developed, such as "a suspicion, a hint" and "a ground for suspicion," as in *Let's not give him the least umbrage of misconduct.* The latter sense gave rise to the meaning "annoyance, resentment, offense," which has been in English since 1620, at first in the phrase *to give umbrage (to)*, as in "The sermon ... gives great umbrage to the parliamentary party" (1842, Henry Rogers, *Essays*), and since 1683 in the phrase *to take umbrage (at)*, as in *He took umbrage at not being invited to the class reunion.*

UNCOUTH, COUTH

Uncouth is a very old word, going back to Old English *uncūth*, where it meant "unknown, uncertain, unfamiliar, strange," and was commonly applied to facts, ways, paths, lands, people, nations, etc. The word passed into Middle English mostly in the sense of "strange, uncommon, unusual," as in *an uncouth sight, uncouth dances, uncouth lands*. In the 1500s, *uncouth* took on the negative meaning of "strange in appearance or form, odd, awkward, or clumsy," as in *uncouth armor, an uncouth idol*, which subsequently (mainly in the 1700s) developed into the current meaning of "awkward, crude, and uncultured in manners, language, style, etc.," as in *uncouth gestures, uncouth words, raw and uncouth young men*.

Uncouth was formed in Old English from *un-* "not" + *cūth* "known, familiar." *Couth*, meaning "known, familiar, noted," was a standard word that became obsolete after the 1500s. However, it was revived in the late 1800s as a back-formation from *uncouth*, used mainly facetiously as the latter's antonym. It means "sophisticated, cultured, well-mannered, refined," as in the title *Crusader for Couth* for a teacher of etiquette (Dec. 21, 1981, *Time*), and *The American Kennel Club is trying to make coonhounds couth* (July 12, 2006, *The News & Observer*). These uses are meant to be amusing and not intended to be taken seriously.

UNCTUOUS

"The whale is so excessively unctuous that landsmen seem to regard the eating of him with abhorrence," wrote Herman Melville in *Moby-Dick* (1851). By *unctuous* Melville meant "greasy, oily, fatty, rich," the earliest meaning of the word, found in Middle English in the 1300s and 1400s. *Unctuous* was borrowed from Medieval Latin *unctuosus* "oily, greasy," from Latin *unctum* "ointment."

This meaning was transferred over the centuries from animals and their meat to other things having a greasy or oily nature, such as *unctuous soil, unctuous water, unctuous gas*. Since the 1700s, the word has been applied figuratively (and unfavorably) to *unctuous people*, meaning people seen as smoothly complacent, smugly ingratiating, and self-satisfied, or to their speech

A, *a*

B, *b*

C, *c*

D, *d*

E, *e*

F, *f*

G, *g*

H, *h*

I, *i*

J, *j*

K, *k*

L, *l*

M, *m*

N, *n*

O, *o*

P, *p*

Q, *q*

R, *r*

S, *s*

T, *t*

U, *u*

V, *v*

W, *w*

X, *x*

Y, *y*

Z, *z*

A, a

B, b

C, c

D, d

E, e

F, f

G, g

H, h

I, i

J, j

K, k

L, l

M, m

N, n

O, o

P, p

Q, q

R, r

S, s

T, t

U, u

V, v

W, w

X, x

Y, y

Z, z

and conduct, as in *an unctuous welcome, unctuous manners*. The novelist Mary McCarthy, in *America the Beautiful* (1961), scathingly described politicians as "for the most part, illiterate hacks whose fancy vests are spotted with gravy, and whose speeches, hypocritical, unctuous and slovenly, are spotted also with the gravy of political patronage."

UNDERTAKER

Undertaker has been so long the standard term for a person who arranges funerals that we don't recognize it as a euphemism, a mild word used to conceal a harsh one. The word was first recorded in 1698, replacing older and less refined words like *gravedigger* and *embalmer*. It wasn't coined specially for this use, however. It was merely an adaptation of a word that had been in the language since the Middle English period, with such meanings as "an assistant or helper" (1382), "one who undertakes a task or enterprise" (1540), "one who carries on business or work for another, a contractor" (1602), and "one who embarks on a business enterprise" (1615).

In the 1600s, when enterprising businessmen took charge of funerals, the meaning of *undertaker*, "one who embarks on a business enterprise," was transferred to the business of arranging funerals, as recorded in the 1698 Parish Register of the town of Chester Water, Pennsylvania: "The furnishing of funerals by a small number of men called undertakers."

Once *undertaker* acquired its new meaning, it went on to eclipse all the former meanings, demonstrating the power of euphemism. *Undertaker* was the standard term until the 1890s, when undertakers decided that it was time to replace the old euphemism with some new ones and went on to coin *funeral director* and *mortician*. Only the former survives in current use as a common euphemism for *undertaker*.

URBANE, URBAN

For close to a hundred years, from 1533 to 1623, *urbane* meant "pertaining to or characteristic of a city or town," as in *rural and urbane life*. The word was borrowed from Middle French *urbain*, or directly from Latin *urbānus*, "of or pertaining to a city or town." Originally the word's stress was, as in French, on the last syllable, but before 1634 the stress became anglicized, shifting to the first syllable. (A similar shift had occurred earlier with the variant forms *humane* and *human*, and the variants *germane* and *german*.)

When the shift to *urban* occurred, the form *urbane* assumed a new meaning: "having the characteristics of city or town people, courteous, polished, civil, refined," as in *urbane manners, urbane behavior, urbane talk*. In his 1978 book on the Kennedys, *The Brothers*, Arthur M. Schlesinger, Jr., describes John Kennedy as "urbane, objective, analytical, controlled, contained, masterful, a man of perspective." The change in meaning was strongly influenced by an extended meaning of Latin *urbānus*, "refined, polished, polite."

Of the two words, *urban* became the more important one, producing many compounds with distinctive meanings, such as *urban renewal, urban planning, urban blight, urban sprawl*, while *urbane* has remained confined to the narrow meaning it acquired in the 1600s.

URCHIN

This is a familiar word to many children, cropping up in fairy tales in phrases like *a little urchin* and *street urchins*. Tom Thumb, the diminutive hero of folktales, is often referred to as a tiny urchin. The word has a long history, having first appeared in the early 1300s as a name for a little animal with spiny hairs, later called a hedgehog. The name was borrowed from Old French *erichon, herichon* "hedgehog," from Latin *ērīcius*. The

A, a
B, b
C, c
D, d
E, e
F, f
G, g
H, h
I, i
J, j
K, k
L, l
M, m
N, n
O, o
P, p
Q, q
R, r
S, s
T, t
U, u
V, v
W, w
X, x
Y, y
Z, z

A, a

B, b

C, c

D, d

E, e

F, f

G, g

H, h

I, i

J, j

K, k

L, l

M, m

N, n

O, o

P, p

Q, q

R, r

S, s

T, t

U, u

V, v

W, w

X, x

Y, y

Z, z

term *sea urchin* for a spiny sea creature of the genus *Echinus* was first recorded in 1602.

In the 1500s, *urchin* was widely applied allusively to people who suggested a hedgehog by their appearance, such as a hunchback or a dwarf, or by their sharp wits, such as a mischievous or roguish boy or girl. The latter was generalized to "a little boy or youngster" in "Will you have this urchin, of eight weeks old? It is a babbling brat above all other" (1556, John Heywood, *The Spider and the Fly*).

After the 1600s, *urchin* was usually applied sympathetically to poorly or raggedly clothed children, as in *the little darling urchin, poor gutter urchins*, which is the current meaning, except for specialized uses. One such use is *an urchin cut* or *haircut* "a short style of haircut for women," which became popular in the 1950s, as in "Tennis player Gertrude ("Gorgeous Gussie") Moran, whose lengthy pigtails have become almost as famous as her lace panties, shocked her admirers by appearing at the London airport with a 'sort of overgrown urchin cut'" (July 17, 1950, *Time*).

UTTER, OUTER

Utter originally meant "outer," as distinguished from *inner*. In Middle English (before 1200), *the utter side of the table* or *the utter end of the cloth* meant the outer side or the outer end of those things. The word had developed from Old English *útera*, *úterra*, the comparative form of *út* "out." The use of *utter* in the sense of "outer" went on until the late 1300s, as in "For lords two beds shall be made, both utter and inner" (before 1400, *The Babees Book*).

Gradually it dawned on English speakers that this use of *utter* no longer showed a relationship to *out* and was not in harmony with its opposite, *inner,* and so around 1380 they coined the word *outer* from *out* + *-er*. That left *utter* orphaned of meaning.

So around 1412, *utter* was extended from the meaning "outer" to "utmost," specifically "to the utmost point or degree, extreme, absolute, total," as in "He had brought in . . . utter mischief and confusion" (1412, John Lydgate, *History of Troy*), and "To the . . . utter displeasure of the King" (1494, Robert Fabyan, *The New Chronicles of England*).

By the 1800s, *utter* weakened its force and began to be used as a mere intensifier, as in *utter nonsense, to make a complete and utter idiot of oneself,* or in this passage in James Joyce's *Dubliners* (1914): "*You—know—nothing.* Of course you know nothing," said Mr. Alleyne. "Tell me," he added, glancing first for approval to the lady beside him, "do you take me for a fool? Do you think me an utter fool?"

A, a
B, b
C, c
D, d
E, e
F, f
G, g
H, h
I, i
J, j
K, k
L, l
M, m
N, n
O, o
P, p
Q, q
R, r
S, s
T, t
U, u
V, v
W, w
X, x
Y, y
Z, z

V, v

VALOR

"Discretion is the better part of valor" is an old proverb that is rarely heard these days, having been replaced by the more literal, but far less literary, "Better safe than sorry." The older proverb, popularized in America by Benjamin Franklin, is traceable to Falstaff, who said (in Shakespeare's *Henry IV, Part 1*): "The better part of valor is discretion," meaning that caution and prudence are safer than rash bravery.

The word *valor,* which we define as "courage, boldness, bravery," is historically related to the word *value.* The spelling *valor* was borrowed from Old French *valour,* which took the word from Late Latin *valōr-, valor* "value, worth." In English in the 1300s, the word originally meant "worth, value," as in *a jewel of great valor, the valor of a life.* The change in meaning occurred in the 1500s, when a man's worth or value began to be measured not by his noble birth or wealth but by the boldness and courage with which he faced risk or danger. So *valor* borrowed the meaning of "courage, bravery" from the Romance languages (French *valeur,* Italian *valore,* Spanish *valor*), and after 1581 the new meaning replaced the old one, which was adequately covered anyway by the word *value.*

VENTURE

The word *venture* was an English innovation, shortened from the earlier word *aventure,* most probably because the initial *a-* of *aventure* was taken to be the article *a* and read as *a venture.* This kind of misdivision has occurred before, resulting in such words as *apron* (*a napron* read as *an apron*), *newt* (*an ewt* read as *a newt*), *nickname, umpire,* and others. *Aventure* was an early form of *adventure,* borrowed from Old French (*see* ADVENTURE).

Venture appeared before 1450, meaning "random, chance, luck," and was used especially in the phrase *at a venture* "at random, by chance," as in "And a certain man drew his bow at a

A, a

B, b

C, c

D, d

E, e

F, f

G, g

H, h

I, i

J, j

K, k

L, l

M, m

N, n

O, o

P, p

Q, q

R, r

S, s

T, t

U, u

V, v

W, w

X, x

Y, y

Z, z

venture, and smote the king of Israel" (Kings I, 22:34). In the 1500s the word was narrowed to "an action or course that depends on chance," as in *a hazardous venture, a desperate venture.* By 1584 *venture* had been further narrowed to the current meaning of "a business enterprise involving a chance of either loss or gain, a commercial speculation," used in such phrases as *venture capital, risky ventures.*

The verb *to venture* (as in "Nothing ventured, nothing gained") was also a shortened form of *aventure*, borrowed about 1430 from Old French *aventurer* "to chance, risk," derived from *aventure* "a chance happening," from Latin *adventūra* (the source of English *adventure*).

VENUE

A *New Yorker* cartoon by Ed Fisher, published on March 27, 1971, shows a trial taking place on the moon. The judge, addressing a lawyer, protests: "Not *another* change of venue, Counsellor!" A *change of venue* is a legal term meaning the moving of a trial to a new location, usually in order to find a more impartial jury.

The use of *venue* in law is first recorded in 1531, with the meaning "the place where a jury is summoned to come for the trial of a case." The word appeared originally in Middle English, in the 1300s, meaning "the act of coming, especially a coming on in order to strike," as in "The lion made a great venue, and would have him all to-rent" (1300s, *Coer de Lion*). *Venue* was borrowed from Old French *venue* "a coming," derived from *venir* "to come," from Latin *venīre*.

The legal meaning of *venue* was generalized in the 1800s to mean "the site or scene of any action or event, especially for a match or competition," as in *the venue of the annual golf tournament.* A *sports* or *sporting venue* is a stadium or other building where a competition is held: "With the 'unknown certainty' of terrorist actions and fan behavior, it is impossible to ensure a risk-free environment at America's sporting venues" (May 2005, *The Sport Journal*). This meaning was transferred in the 1960s to the theater, concerts, etc., to refer to the site or location of a performance, as in *The touring company's next venue will be in New York City's Carnegie Hall.*

VERVE

This is a word that stands firmly and uniquely on its own short legs. Since its entry into the language in 1697, no one has dared to tweak or twist it into some other word: there's no *verval, vervish, vervy, vervous,* or *vervaceous,* and surely no *verved* or *verving.* Why this is so is a mystery. If *nerve* could generate *nervous* and *nervy,* why couldn't *verve*? Perhaps the answer is that many writers have thought of *verve* as a foreign word, a stranger in our midst, not a word we may take liberties with.

Consider this: the poet John Dryden, in 1697, italicized and capitalized the word, saying, "*Verve* (as the French call it)"; Horace Walpole in 1783 italicized it, as did Lady Morgan in 1818, and the British novelist Ouida in 1863, all of which suggest that this word was thought of as a foreign term. *Verve* was, of course, borrowed from French, in which it means "fervor, spirit, animation, especially in the arts," from Old French *verve* "whim, caprice, fancy," probably ultimately from Latin *verba* "fancy words," plural of *verbum* "word."

The original meaning, "special bent or talent in writing," as in *She writes with a strong poetic verve,* became obsolete after 1780, replaced in 1803 by "intellectual vigor, great vivacity of ideas," as in "He . . . launched forth during the rest of the meal with his usual verve and fanciful extravagance of imagination" (1872, J. Morley, *Voltaire*).

A, *a*

B, *b*

C, *c*

D, *d*

E, *e*

F, *f*

G, *g*

H, *h*

I, *i*

J, *j*

K, *k*

L, *l*

M, *m*

N, *n*

O, *o*

P, *p*

Q, *q*

R, *r*

S, *s*

T, *t*

U, *u*

V, *v*

W, *w*

X, *x*

Y, *y*

Z, *z*

It wasn't until the 1880s that the word came into general English use with the meaning "energy, enthusiasm, vigor, spirit," as in *a youth full of verve and enjoyment of life, a dance staged with astonishing verve*. In a 1978 book, *Ourselves and Our Children*, Alison J. Ryerson and Wendy C. Sanford put the word to good use: "One of the final challenges for human beings is to get old with as much verve and gumption as possible. Old parents who keep on being interested in life . . . are givers of hope and affirmers of life."

VIGIL

"Vigil Strange I Kept on the Field," published by Walt Whitman in 1865, is a moving elegy for a fallen soldier and one of the best-known poems of the Civil War. In it, Whitman uses the word *vigil* twelve times to mean a "wake" (a watch by the body of a dead person before burial), emulating poets from Chaucer to Byron who had used the word in this sense.

The word's oldest and original meaning (recorded before 1225) was "the eve of a church festival or holy day, at which a devotional watch is observed," as in *the vigil of the Resurrection, the vigil of the Epiphany*. So Shakespeare used it in *Henry V* (1598): "He that outlives this day . . . shall yearly on the vigil feast his friends, and say, tomorrow is Saint Crispins." *Vigil* was borrowed from Anglo-French and Old French *vigile*, from Latin *vigilia* "a watch, watchfulness, wakefulness," from *vigil* "awake, alert." The meaning was extended to "a devotional watch, especially a nocturnal religious service," as in *to keep or hold a prayer vigil*.

The generalized meaning, "a staying awake or keeping a watch for some special reason or purpose, such as a protest or demonstration," has been current since the early 1700s in uses such as *a midnight vigil, a nocturnal vigil, a call for a peaceful three-day vigil to support striking workers*. A May 9, 2007, posting in *In-*

dymedia Ireland announced: "Womans Right to Choose Group will hold a protest vigil on Patricks Bridge on Wednesday evening at 5.15 p.m."

VIRTUAL

If you haven't seen a virtual pet, you're behind the times, since these electronic wonders have been around since the 1990s. A virtual pet is not a flesh-and-bone creature, of course, but a handheld toy with which the owner can interact as if it were a real pet, caring for it and responding to it by pushing buttons. The device is called *virtual* because it's an artificial or imaginary version of something real.

This meaning of *virtual*, "being so in essence or effect, though not formally or actually," appeared first in 1654 in a religious context, in Bishop Jeremy Taylor's *Real Presence*: "We affirm that Christ is really taken by faith, . . . they say he is taken by the mouth, and that the spiritual and the virtual taking him . . . is not sufficient." The word goes back to Middle English, its earliest meaning, which appeared in 1398, having been "possessing certain virtues or capacities," as in *virtual light, virtual heat,* and later, in 1432, "capable of producing an effect, effective, potent," as in *the sun's virtual beams, a virtual speech or sermon.*

Virtual has been used since the 1700s in other technical terms, such as *virtual focus* (in optics), *virtual displacement* (in mechanics), *virtual electrons* or *photons* (in particle physics), all meaning "being so in effect although not formally or actually so."

The word was borrowed from Medieval Latin *virtualis*, from Latin *virtūs* "moral strength, excellence, potency, manliness" (the source of English *virtue*), from *vir* "man."

A, *a*
B, *b*
C, *c*
D, *d*
E, *e*
F, *f*
G, *g*
H, *h*
I, *i*
J, *j*
K, *k*
L, *l*
M, *m*
N, *n*
O, *o*
P, *p*
Q, *q*
R, *r*
S, *s*
T, *t*
U, *u*
V, *v*
W, *w*
X, *x*
Y, *y*
Z, *z*

A, a

B, b

C, c

D, d

E, e

F, f

G, g

H, h

I, i

J, j

K, k

L, l

M, m

N, n

O, o

P, p

Q, q

R, r

S, s

T, t

U, u

V, v

W, w

X, x

Y, y

Z, z

VOCATION

An occupation is often called *a calling*, because it is a call to follow a way of life, as if one heeded a voice summoning him or her to do its bidding. This notion of a disembodied *voice* calling you (long before the telephone was invented) underlies the word.

Vocation was borrowed from Middle French, or directly from Latin *vocātiōn-, vocātiō* "a call or summons," from *vocāre* "to call," related to *vōc-, vōx* "voice." Its original meaning, in 1426, was "a call from God to follow a spiritual way of life," as in *a vocation to pastoral duty*, and later, in 1487, "the way of life to which one is called by God," as in *the priestly vocation, the vocation of a nun.*

The generalized meaning, "a person's regular occupation or profession," is first found in 1553. In Shakespeare's *Henry IV, Part 1* (1598), when Prince Henry faults him for his purse-snatching, Falstaff argues, "Why, Hal, 'tis my vocation, Hal; 'tis no sin for a man to labour in his vocation."

VOLUBLE

"The world's greatest mime, Marcel Marceau, . . . though silent onstage, is a lively and *voluble* conversationalist off-stage," wrote Donna Shor in 2007 in her society column in *Washington Life* magazine.

Voluble, meaning "fluent in speech, glib," is first recorded in 1593, in Shakespeare's *The Comedy of Errors* ("voluble and sharp discourse"). The word's original meaning had nothing to do with speech. *Voluble* was borrowed from Old French *voluble*, which inherited it from Latin *volūbilis*, from *volū-, volvēre* "to turn around, roll." The first meaning of *voluble* was "liable to change or turn around, inconstant, variable," as in "As of all voluble things there is nothing more light than renown" (1575, Geoffrey Fenton, *Golden Epistles*). This meaning was extended in 1589 to "readily revolving or rolling" (*voluble wheels, the voluble and restless earth*).

Then, in the late 1500s, Shakespeare related the word to the flow or movement of speech and it developed its current meaning, as seen in *Love's Labour's Lost* ("So sweet and voluble is his discourse"), and later (1604) in *Othello* ("a knave very voluble").

See also VOLUME

VOLUME

"Marcel Marceau speaks *volumes* with silence," ran a headline in the *Milwaukee Journal Sentinel*. The phrase *to speak volumes*, meaning "to be greatly expressive or very significant," first appeared in 1803 and was used by Shelley in 1810 in his Gothic romance *Zastrozzi*: " . . . the eyes of Zastrozzi and Matilda spoke volumes to each guilty soul."

This use of *volume* was a figurative use of the common meaning "large book, tome, especially one of a set," which appeared in 1523, and was extended from the word's original meaning, "a roll of parchment containing written matter," first recorded in 1382 in the Wycliffe Bible (Deuteronomy 17:18): "He shall describe to him a declaration of this law in a volume." *Volume* was borrowed through Old French from Latin *volūmen* "a roll, coil," from *volū-, volvere* "to turn around, roll" (the source of English *evolve, involve, revolve*).

In 1530 the word was used to refer to the size, bulk, or dimension of a book, as in *a treatise small in volume*, and was generalized after 1621 to a particular bulk, mass, size, or dimension of anything, as in "Considerable labour has been bestowed in computing the volume of lava-streams" (1830, Charles Lyell, *Principles of Geology*).

See also VOLUBLE

A, *a*
B, *b*
C, *c*
D, *d*
E, *e*
F, *f*
G, *g*
H, *h*
I, *i*
J, *j*
K, *k*
L, *l*
M, *m*
N, *n*
O, *o*
P, *p*
Q, *q*
R, *r*
S, *s*
T, *t*
U, *u*
V, *v*
W, *w*
X, *x*
Y, *y*
Z, *z*

A, a
B, b
C, c
D, d
E, e
F, f
G, g
H, h
I, i
J, j
K, k
L, l
M, m
N, n
O, o
P, p
Q, q
R, r
S, s
T, t
U, u
V, v
W, w
X, x
Y, y
Z, z

VULGAR

"Don't be vulgar," is a rebuke that a well-bred parent or spouse might utter with disgust on hearing a loved one use a profanity or blasphemy. *Vulgar* is a word whose meaning has fallen in grace over the centuries from a perfectly neutral use to one signifying "coarse, boorish." The word exemplifies pejoration or degradation of meaning.

When *vulgar* came into English, around 1391, in Chaucer's *Treatise on the Astolabe*, it was a technical term meaning "used in common or ordinary reckoning," as in *the vulgar day and night, the vulgar year. Vulgar* was borrowed from Latin *vulgāris* "of the common people, common, ordinary," from *vulgus* "the common people." Around 1430 it was generalized to mean "common, customary, ordinary," as in *the vulgar text of the Bible, the vulgar people, the vulgar view or opinion.* "To translate and reduce this said book out of French into our vulgar English" (1483, William Caxton, *Knight of the Tower*).

The notion of "common, commonplace" gradually passed into "coarsely commonplace," and by the mid-1600s it meant "lacking refinement; coarse, uncultured, ill-bred, boorish," and was applied to people and their actions, manners, etc., as in *the vulgar masses, vulgar minds, vulgar stories.* "The mean malice of the same Vulgar Scribbler, hired by the Conspirators at so much a sheet" (1678, Andrew Marvell, *The Growth of Popery*). Today the word is often synonymous with "indecent, off-color, risqué," as in "After years of profiting from some of the most vulgar shows on radio, the broadcast behemoth has suddenly turned puritanical" (May 20, 2007, *Salon.com*).

W, w

A, a

B, b

C, c

D, d

E, e

F, f

G, g

H, h

I, i

J, j

K, k

L, l

M, m

N, n

O, o

P, p

Q, q

R, r

S, s

T, t

U, u

V, v

W, w

X, x

Y, y

Z, z

WAIF *and stray*

Waifs and Strays is the title of a book of stories by O. Henry (William Sydney Porter, 1862–1910), famous for the ironic twists of plot at the end of his short stories. He probably took the title from the *Waifs and Strays' Society,* founded in England in 1881 to shelter homeless boys. The phrase *waif and stray,* meaning a poor, homeless person, especially a child, had been common since 1624, when it was used figuratively by the poet John Donne.

As far back as 1377, *waifs and strays* had been a set phrase in English common law to describe ownerless property. A *waif* meant "an ownerless or unclaimed piece of property, such as an article washed ashore." *Waif* was borrowed from Anglo-French *weyf,* "something loose or wandering."

The chief current meaning of *waif,* "a poor, homeless, or neglected child," appeared in 1785, and has since been used widely in literature, as in "Then, too, there was the mute appeal of this wee waif alone and unloved in the midst of the horrors of the savage jungle. It was this thought more than any other that had sent her mother's heart out to the innocent babe" (1914, Edgar Rice Burroughs, *The Beasts of Tarzan*).

However, the most often-quoted meaning today, which is an extension of the appearance of neglect, was born in the 1980s: "a very thin person, especially a fashion model," as in "No more waifs on the runway? Somewhat to our surprise, we're back to talking about super-skinny models again" (December 8, 2006, *Salon.com*).

WALLOP, GALLOP

Boxers have been known to *pack a wallop,* meaning "to give a powerful blow," since the early 1800s. The word *wallop,* "a heavy, resounding blow, a whack," is labeled as slang in 1823, not far behind the verb *to wallop* "to beat soundly, thrash," recorded as dialectal in 1825. Stephen Crane, in *The Red Badge of Courage* (1895) used the verb in the context of the Civil War: "He [an officer] began to blithely roar at his staff: 'We'll wallop 'im now. We'll wallop 'im now. We've got 'em sure.'"

The word *wallop* has had a long history, going back to Middle English. *Wallop* was probably borrowed from Old North French (unattested) *walope* meaning "to leap well," from a Frankish phrase related to Old Saxon *mela* "well" and *hlōpan* "to leap." Around 1350, *a wallop* meant "a horse's gallop," as in *He rode a great wallop*; around 1375, *to wallop* meant "to gallop," as in *The rider walloped homewards*. Since these actions involved quick motion, the meaning of *wallop* was extended imitatively in the mid-1500s to mean "the bubbling motion of boiling water," and *to wallop* "to boil with a noisy bubbling." These meanings were further extended in the 1700s to action involving any heavy, plunging or lurching movement, as in *to go wallop, to wallop in the dust, I walloped in the icy water of the lake*. These led eventually to the current senses of "a heavy blow" and "to beat soundly, as in "Be ready, when the 10th retire, to give the French a wallop" (1827, S. Hardman, *The Battle of Waterloo*).

Wallop and *gallop* are doublets, both meaning originally "the fastest gait of a horse" and "to ride a horse at its fastest gait."

WARP

A warped mind. A warped sense of humor. Warped values. A warped imagination. These are some of the commonest uses of the verb *warp*, meaning "to twist, distort, or pervert (the mind, sense, judgment, principles, etc.)," first occurring in 1601.

The earliest meaning of *warp* was "to throw, fling, cast," found in Middle English (about 1200) *warpen*, borrowed from Old English *weorpan* "to throw, strike, hit" related to Latin *verber* "a whip, lash, rod." Before 1225 the word took on various figurative and mostly negative meanings, such as "to drive out, expel, reject, trample underfoot," which apparently developed by the

A, a

B, b

C, c

D, d

E, e

F, f

G, g

H, h

I, i

J, j

K, k

L, l

M, m

N, n

O, o

P, p

Q, q

R, r

S, s

T, t

U, u

V, v

W, w

X, x

Y, y

Z, z

1400s into "to twist (an object) out of shape" and "to become bent or twisted by shrinkage, contraction, etc.," as in "Age will . . . warp our backs" (1593, Thomas Nashe). The latter gave rise to the current figurative meaning, first used in 1601, in Ben Jonson's *Fountains of Self-Love*: "Me thinks thy servant Hedon . . . has grown out of his garb a-late, he's warped." Here's a later example: "We have warped the word 'economy' in our English language into a meaning which it has no business whatever to bear" (1857, John Ruskin, *Political Economy*).

WEIRD *and wonderful*

We owe the weird and wonderful word *weird* to Shakespeare, who used it six times in *Macbeth* (1605): five times in the phrase *the weird Sisters* and once in *the weird Women*, all referring to the three witches who plot Macbeth's downfall. Shakespeare borrowed the phrase from its use in Middle English (about 1400) to describe the three Fates or deities of ancient mythology who determine the destiny of human beings, *weird* meaning "having the supernatural power to control a person's fate, claiming to deal with fate or destiny."

The Middle English word was originally a noun meaning "fate, destiny," and was used attributively in the phrase *the weird Sisters*. *Weird* developed from Old English *wyrd*, from a Germanic base represented also by Old Saxon *wurd*, Old High German *wurt*, and Old Norse *urdhr*, all meaning "fate."

It was the poet Shelley who, in the period 1816–1820, extended the meaning of *weird* from "having a supernatural power" to "of a mysterious or unearthly character, strange, uncanny," as in *a weird sound of stillness, weird winter nights*, and "strange or odd in appearance," as in *Mutable as shapes in the weird clouds* (1816, *Alastor*).

The alliterative expression *weird and wonderful*, meaning "marvelous in a strange way," has been in use since the 1850s, often ironically. In the opening sentence above, though, it's meant to be straightforward.

WENCH

Wench is no longer your run-of-the-mill everyday word, yet it figured prominently in literature from the early Middle Ages to the late 1800s. For many centuries, it was the common word for a female child, competing with *girl* until the two became differentiated, *wench* becoming increasingly less acceptable as the word for young girls. *Wench* was a shortened form of the early Middle English word *wenchel* "a child of either sex"; also, the meaning "a servant" developed from Old English *wencel*, a word probably related to the Old English adjective *wancol* "unsteady, insecure, wavering."

During the 1300s *wench* developed various contemptuous uses, such as "a wanton woman, a mistress," as in *a common wench* (the verb *to wench* meant "to frequent prostitutes"), and "a female servant, a maidservant," as in *a kitchen wench* (in America in the 1700s, the word was specifically applied to female slaves used as servants). In the 1600s, the word was also used as a familiar or endearing (and sometimes belittling) form of address for a wife or sweetheart, as in Shakespeare's *Henry VIII* (1613), where Queen Katharina says to Patience, her maid, "When I am dead, good wench, let me be used with honor."

WORRY *not*

Worry has produced clichés like *Why worry? I should worry? What, me worry? Not to worry, Don't worry*, and others. The word is so commonplace that we hardly think of it as meaning anything but "to be anxious, uncomfortable, ill at ease." But a little history goes a long way to correct this impression.

To begin with, in medieval England, *to worry* (or *worien*, as it was spelled then) was what we might consider today a major

A, *a*
B, *b*
C, *c*
D, *d*
E, *e*
F, *f*
G, *g*
H, *h*
I, *i*
J, *j*
K, *k*
L, *l*
M, *m*
N, *n*
O, *o*
P, *p*
Q, *q*
R, *r*
S, *s*
T, *t*
U, *u*
V, *v*
W, *w*
X, *x*
Y, *y*
Z, *z*

A, a

B, b

C, c

D, d

E, e

F, f

G, g

H, h

I, i

J, j

K, k

L, l

M, m

N, n

O, o

P, p

Q, q

R, r

S, s

T, t

U, u

V, v

W, w

X, x

Y, y

Z, z

crime. The word meant "to kill by choking, to strangle," and was used before the 1300s to describe the brutal killing of people and animals. Middle English *worien* developed from Old English *wyrgan* "to strangle, throttle." To the credit of the Anglo-Saxons, it also meant "to choke on food," and the phrases *to be worried* or *to worry oneself* meant "to devour food so greedily as to choke."

Another early meaning was "(of dogs or wolves) to kill quarry by seizing it by the throat and biting and shaking," which led in the 1500s to the figurative meaning of "to harass by rough or aggressive treatment," as in *enemies worrying and preying upon one another*, and in the 1600s to the somewhat lighter sense of "to annoy, vex, or pester," as in *to worry visitors with foolish questions*. Finally, around the 1820s, the current meaning, "to distress or agitate, to make or be anxious or ill at ease," appeared in phrases like *to fret and worry* and *don't be worried*.

Is it a coincidence that you get a strangling sensation in your chest when you're worried about something? Perhaps not.

WORSHIP

The formation of *worship* is a key to its meanings and how they developed. The word is formed of *worth* and *-ship*, and its original meaning in Old English (about 888) was "the condition of being worthy, worthiness." This meaning was extended in late Old English (about 1000) to "the respect and honor shown someone worthy," found in such phrases as *to do worship* "to pay respect or show honor," and *to have or hold in worship* "to show honor to," always referring to a person of distinction.

The religious meaning of *worship* that is current today, "reverence or veneration paid to a divinity or to God," first appeared in the early 1300s. The phrases *place of worship* and *house of worship* for a church, synagogue, etc., appeared in 1777 and 1883 respectively.

A pair of curious compounds used between 1570 and 1871 were *worship-worthy* and *worshipworth*, as in "None is worshipworth save God alone" (1882, John Payne, *The 1001 Nights*), curious, because their coiners seemed unaware that *worship* was formed of *worth* and *-ship*, and so *worshipworth* meant literally "worthinessworth."

all WRONG

When General Omar Bradley opposed expanding the Korean War, he called it "the wrong war, at the wrong place, at the wrong time, and with the wrong enemy." By *wrong* he meant "not right, improper, mistaken, bad." This meaning of *wrong*, however, was not the word's original one. The meaning that's familiar to us developed by degrees from "twisted or bent in shape, crooked, deformed," first found around 1200 in the form *wrang*, and used in such phrases as *a wrang nose, wrang trees*. Middle English *wrang* was borrowed from Old Norse *(w)rangr* "awry, crooked."

Throughout the 1200s, *wrong* always referred to some object having a distorted form or course, such as a fishhook or a twisting road. During the next century, the word was extended to actions, and used mainly in the figurative sense of "deviating from the right or proper course, perverse," as in *a wrong deed, a wrong judgment*. It was further extended in the 1400s to "not factual or true, erroneous, false," as in *a wrong assumption, wrong beliefs*, followed by "not proper or fitting, unsuitable," as in *the wrong profession, a wrong choice*.

It was through various set phrases that *wrong* developed its current meaning, "not right." Some of those phrases were: *it would be wrong to* (do something), found in the 1590s; *laugh on the wrong side of one's mouth* (1809); *barking up the wrong tree* (1833); *put one's money on the wrong horse* (1897).

A, a

B, b

C, c

D, d

E, e

F, f

G, g

H, h

I, i

J, j

K, k

L, l

M, m

N, n

O, o

P, p

Q, q

R, r

S, s

T, t

U, u

V, v

W, w

X, x

Y, y

Z, z

Y, y

YELP! YELP! YELP!

"Yelp, yelp, yelp, howl the hounds," wrote the writer R. S. Surtees in *Jorrock's Jaunts and Jollities* (1838), using *yelp* as a syllable imitating the quick, sharp bark of some dogs. At its origin, however, the word was not onomatopoeic or imitative.

In Middle English, the word *yelp* meant "a boasting, vain or ostentatious speaking," as in *all idle yelp*. The corresponding Middle English verb, *to yelp*, meant "to boast, speak vainly or ostentatiously." Both noun and verb went back with these meanings to Old Saxon *gelp* "arrogant speech," *galpōn* "to boast, cry aloud."

The change in meaning from vain boasting to the loud cry or bark of dogs, foxes, etc., developed by comparing disparagingly the utterances of boastful people to the loud noises made by animals. The change in meaning occurred chiefly in the 1500s. The word has been used figuratively since the 1700s to apply to humans in the sense of "to call or cry out sharply," as in "I have always despised the whining yelp of complaint" (Robert Burns).

YIELD

Is there a connection between the slang word *gelt* "money" (from Yiddish, from Middle High German) and the English noun *yield*? The answer is "yes." This wouldn't be apparent from the present meaning of *yield*, which is "that which is produced," as in *this year's yield of corn*. But it would be apparent from the original meaning of *yield*, which was "payment, sum of money paid."

The noun *yield* developed from Old English *yld, ield* "payment, sum of money paid as a tribute, tax, etc.," corresponding to Middle Dutch *gelt* "payment, money." This is still a meaning used today: "income produced by a financial investment, usually shown as a percentage of cost" as in *high-yield stocks and bonds*.

A, a
B, b
C, c
D, d
E, e
F, f
G, g
H, h
I, i
J, j
K, k
L, l
M, m
N, n
O, o
P, p
Q, q
R, r
S, s
T, t
U, u
V, v
W, w
X, x
Y, y
Z, z

A, a

B, b

C, c

D, d

E, e

F, f

G, g

H, h

I, i

J, j

K, k

L, l

M, m

N, n

O, o

P, p

Q, q

R, r

S, s

T, t

U, u

V, v

W, w

X, x

Y, y

Z, z

However, it took many more years for today's common meaning of *yield* to develop from its original one. *To yield* appeared in Old English as *ieldan, eldan* "to give in payment, pay, render as due" and "to give back, repay, recompense, reward," often in the phrase *God yield you,* "God reward you." This use was extended in Middle English (before 1225) to "give as a favor, grant, bestow," as in *to yield to one's wishes.* The meaning "to give way, submit, surrender," as in *to yield ground, to yield precedence,* appeared in 1297, followed by "to give or put forth, to produce," which gave rise to the noun meaning, "that which is produced, produce."

And, as we know, produce yields money.

Z, z

| A, a |
| B, b |
| C, c |
| D, d |
| E, e |
| F, f |
| G, g |
| H, h |
| I, i |
| J, j |
| K, k |
| L, l |
| M, m |
| N, n |
| O, o |
| P, p |
| Q, q |
| R, r |
| S, s |
| T, t |
| U, u |
| V, v |
| W, w |
| X, x |
| Y, y |
| Z, z |

ZANY *capers*

Zany, meaning "absurdly or ludicrously comical, clownish," has long been applied to the mad slapstick and antics of comics like the Marx Brothers and the Three Stooges. This use of the word first occurs in 1869, and was described in Judith Krantz's novel *Scruples* (1978) as "the brand of humor known as 'zany', consisting largely of sight gags and the sight of appealing people making cheerful fools of themselves."

Though the -*y* ending makes *zany* sound like an adjective similar to *crazy, silly, nutty* (with the comparative and superlative degrees *zanier* and *zaniest*), the word actually evolved from a noun that appeared in 1596 as *Zani* (the form *zany* showed up in the late 1600s). The word was borrowed from French *zani* or directly from its source, Italian *zani, zanni* "comic who attends in a ludicrous way the buffoon or clown," a dialectal form of *Gianni*, short for *Giovanni* "John."

A *zany* was a popular stock character in old Italian comedies who assisted the clown by imitating his acts in a ludicrously clumsy way. Shakespeare, Ben Jonson, and other writers used the word, as in "I protest I take these wise men . . . no better than the fools' zanies" (1599, *Twelfth Night)*. Over the centuries the word developed many disparaging new meanings, including "a clumsy assistant, a hanger-on, a bad imitator, a buffoon, a fool," as in "He was not content to be a mere zany, he aspired to rival his master as a wit" (1880, *Quarterly Review*). Used at first attributively, as in "Zany art," the noun passed into adjective use in the late1800s in phrases like *zany doings, zany humor,* and as in "He will make some of your zany squires shake in their shoes" (1869, R. D. Blackmore, *Lorna Doone*).

ZEST

"If you have zest and enthusiasm," wrote the noted self-help author Norman Vincent Peale (1898–1993), "you attract zest and enthusiasm." By *zest* he meant "keen relish or pleasure, hearty enjoyment, gusto." This meaning is first encountered in Boswell's *Life of Johnson* (1791): "If I were to reside in London, the exquisite zest with which I relished it in occasional visits might go off." Boswell's use was an extension of the earlier (1709) sense, "something that adds flavor or relish to one's enjoyment," as in "That sweet minor zest Of love, your kiss" (1819, Keats, *Lines to Fanny*).

These were all figurative uses of the original literal meaning of the word, which was "orange or lemon peel used as a flavoring," first recorded in Thomas Blount's hard-words dictionary *Glossographia* (1674). This meaning is still used, mainly by cooks and in cookbooks, a recent one being Lori Longbotham's *Lemon Zest* (2002), which contains scores of zesty lemon-based recipes.

Zest was borrowed from French *zeste* "orange or lemon peel," which earlier meant "the thick skin dividing the kernel of a walnut," of uncertain origin.

ZIP, ZILCH

"Nothing—zip, zilch, zero!" is an informal way of emphasizing nullity or nothingness. In 2000, pushing for normal trade relations with China, President Bill Clinton argued that such a move "grants no greater access to China to any part of the American economy, nothing, zip, zilch, nada, zero."

Zip is first recorded in 1900 as a dialectal word meaning "zero." But because it was preceded by some 25 years by an identically spelled word (often in reduplicated form, *zip, zip* or *zip-zip*) imitative of the sound made by a bullet or other swiftly flying object, most dictionaries declared the word imitative in origin. Possibly *zip* was an alteration of *zero*, perhaps influenced by the imitative word.

The slang word *zilch*, which has been facetiously defined as "the amount you have left after paying your taxes," first occurred in

A, a
B, b
C, c
D, d
E, e
F, f
G, g
H, h
I, i
J, j
K, k
L, l
M, m
N, n
O, o
P, p
Q, q
R, r
S, s
T, t
U, u
V, v
W, w
X, x
Y, y
Z, z

the Winter 1966 issue of the University of South Dakota's *Current Slang*, defined as "Nothing, zero." But the *OED* has bracketed references to *Mr. Zilch*, which Berrey and Van Den Bark's *American Thesaurus of Slang* (1940) describe as an "indefinite nickname," suggesting that the name *Zilch* (found as a comic name in the humor magazine *Ballyhoo* in 1931) was the source of the word.

Still, the *OED* etymologizes *zilch* as "origin uncertain." Other dictionaries conjecture as the word's origin a dubious blend of *zip* and *nil*. Again, possibly *zilch* was an alteration of *zero*, perhaps influenced by the name *Zilch*.

The bottom line, though, is that what we know of the true origin of these words is zip, zilch, zero.

Glossary of Names and Terms

ALFRED THE GREAT (about 849–899), king of the Anglo-Saxon kingdom of Wessex from 871 to 899, noted for his "Doom Book" or code of laws, and for encouraging education, scholarship, and literature.

AMELIORATION. The upgrading or elevation of a word's meaning, as when a word with a negative or derogatory sense develops a positive or favorable one. Example: a *knight* meant originally a young servant or slave, but by the process of amelioration it came to mean a person of honorable military rank.

AMERICAN ENGLISH. The English language as spoken and written in the United States.

ANCRENE RIWLE. A manual of religious rules of conduct for anchoresses, written by a priest before 1225 to three sisters. The work is an important source book of early Middle English, containing many details of everyday life.

ANGLO-FRENCH or **ANGLO-NORMAN.** The variety of French spoken by the Normans, who ruled England after its conquest by William of Normandy in 1066. It was the chief language of the English upper classes through the 1200s, used in the courts, in commerce, and in literature. Anglo-French greatly influenced Middle English in vocabulary, grammar, and pronunciation. Also called **Norman French.**

ANGLO-SAXON. 1. A member of the West Germanic peoples who occupied Great Britain in the 400s and 500s. **2.** The language of these peoples until 1066; **Old English.**

ANGLO-SAXON CHRONICLE, THE. A collection of manuscripts dealing with the history of the Anglo-Saxons from the reign of Alfred the Great to 1154.

AUTHORIZED VERSION. Another name for the **King James Bible.**

BACK-FORMATION. The formation of a new word from an existing word by removing a suffix or other element from the older word. Examples: *donate* from *donation*, *edit* from *editor*, *statistic* from *statistics*.

BACON, FRANCIS (1561–1626), English philosopher, essayist, and statesman, known for his *Essays* (1597), *The Proficience and Advancement of Learning* (1605), *Novum Organum* (1620), and *Sylva Sylvarum* (1626).

BASE. A word or other element of a prehistoric language, such as Proto-Germanic or Proto-Indo-European, reconstructed by comparing features shared by recorded languages assumed to have descended from the prehistoric language. Also called root.

BAILEY, NATHAN (DIED 1742), English lexicographer, whose *An Universal Etymological Dictionary*, published in 1721, was the first widely used dictionary of the 1700s. Bailey's work influenced Samuel Johnson's great *Dictionary of the English Language* (1755).

BEOWULF. An Old English epic poem of 3,182 lines, composed by an unknown poet between 750 and 800. The poem is untitled, but it's known by the name of its hero, Beowulf (literally, "Barley wolf"), a young Scandinavian warrior who travels from Geatland, Sweden, to Denmark to defeat the monster Grendel. Later he becomes king of Geatland. The poem is considered the greatest Old English literary work.

BLENDING. The formation of a word by combining parts of two other words, as *spork,* produced by blending *spoon* and *fork.* A word so formed is called a *blend* or *portmanteau word.* Examples of blends are *smog* (from *smoke* and *fog*), *brunch* (from *breakfast* and *lunch*), and *chortle* (from *chuckle* and *snort*).

BLOUNT, THOMAS (1618–1679), English lexicographer, author of *Glossographia* (1656), a dictionary of hard words, the first to include etymologies, illustrations, and many unusual terms in the arts and sciences.

BOOK OF COMMON PRAYER. The primary prayer book of the Church of England and the Episcopal Church of America, composed in 1549 to replace the Latin prayers with English ones as part of the Protestant Reformation. The Book was revised several times, notably in 1662. It has influenced standard English usage.

BORROW. To take a word from another language and integrate it into one's own. Such words are called *borrowings* or *loanwords.* Examples: *accustom, beauty* (from French); *balcony, opera* (from Italian); *bother, galore* (from Irish); *judo, karate* (from Japanese). A form of borrowing in which a meaning or expression is translated from a foreign language is called a *loan translation.* Examples of loan translations are *Milky Way* (from Latin *via lactea*), *Adam's apple* (from French *pomme d'Adam*), and *worldview* (from German *Weltanschauung*).

BRITISH ENGLISH. The English language as spoken and written in Great Britain.

BRYTHONIC. A subdivision of Celtic that includes Welsh, Breton (the language of Brittany), and Cornish (the language of Cornwall).

CANTERBURY TALES, THE. A classic of Middle English poetic literature, written by Geoffrey Chaucer from 1385 to about 1400. It consists of a collection of tales told by a group of pilgrims traveling from the town of Southwark to the city of Canterbury to visit the shrine of Thomas Becket, the Archbishop of Canterbury, at Canterbury Cathedral, where he was murdered in 1170. The 22 tales, told by an assortment of characters that include a knight, a miller, a cook, a lawyer, a friar, and other types living in medieval England, vary both in themes and poetic structure. The work was unfinished.

CAWDREY, ROBERT (born about 1538), English schoolteacher who produced one of the first English dictionaries, *A Table Alphabeticall,* made essentially to define hard words, and published in 1604.

CAXTON, WILLIAM (about 1415–1492), the first English printer and seller of English books. Among the many books he published were two editions of *The Canterbury Tales.*

CELTIC. A branch of the Indo-European family of languages that includes Gaulish, Brythonic, and Goidelic. Modern Irish, Gaelic, and Welsh are Celtic languages.

CHAUCER, GEOFFREY (about 1343–1400), English poet and writer of works in Middle English, notably his masterpiece, *The Canterbury Tales.*

COGNATE. Any word having a common ancestor with another word or words. Example: English *brother*, German *Bruder*, Latin *frāter*, Russian *brat'*, and Sanskrit *bhrā̊tā*, are cognates, having descended from the reconstructed Indo-European base *bhrāter-.*

COINAGE. Any word or phrase created to name or identify an idea, event, invention, etc. Acronyms, back-formations, blends, compounds, and reduplications are typical coinages.

COMBINING FORM. A bound or hyphenated form of a word, designed to combine with free words or other combining forms. Examples: *aero-, bio-, geo-, -graphy, -logy.*

COMPOUND. A word made up of two or more other words. Examples: *newspaper, eyebrow, handbag, doghouse, blue-collar, backslapping, must-see.*

CURSOR MUNDI. A Middle English religious poem composed in the 1300s, purporting to describe the course of the world since the Creation. Its many versions attest to its great popularity during the Middle Ages.

DERIVATION. The process of forming new words by adding a prefix or suffix to another word. Such words are called *derivatives.* Examples: *friendly, unreal, hopeful, drinkable.*

DIMINUTIVE. A suffix that expresses smallness, such as *-y* or *-ie* in *doggy, birdie; -ling* in *duckling* and *princeling; -ette* in *kitchenette;* and *-let* in *piglet.*

DOUAY BIBLE. A Catholic translation of the Bible from the Latin into English, published in 1582 at the English College at Douai, France. The authors were Catholic exiles from England who opposed the Protestant Reformation.

DOUBLET. One of two or more words of the same ultimate origin that have entered the language through different routes. Doublets usually diverge in meaning. Examples: *frail* and *fragile, guarantee* and *warranty, secure* and *sure, shirt* and *skirt.*

DRYDEN, JOHN (1631–1700), English poet and literary critic.

EARLY MODERN ENGLISH. The English language spoken or written between about 1500 and 1700.

ENGLISH. The West Germanic language of the people of England, developed from Old English, Middle English, and Modern English into one of the world's most extensively used languages of communication. The chief forms or dialects of English are British English and American English.

EPONYM. The name of a place, a people, an institution, invention, etc., that derives from the name of a real or fictitious person. Examples: *America* (from *Amerigo* Vespucci), *boycott* (from Charles Boycott), *guy* (from *Guy Fawkes*), *Celsius* (from Anders *Celsius*).

ETYMOLOGY. The study of the history of words; also, a word's history. An etymology is an account of a word's origin and development. A word's *etymon* is the form from which it originated. Example: The etymon of English *motor* is Latin *mōtor* "mover."

EUPHEMISM. A word or phrase used to replace one that is thought to be too harsh, coarse, unpleasant, or offensive. Examples: *bathroom* (for "toilet"), *pass away* (for "to die"), *the dickens* (for "the devil").

EXTENSION. An expansion of a word's range of meanings by changes in the breadth or scope of its use. A common extension occurs when a word with a literal or concrete meaning assumes a figurative meaning. The process is also called **transfer.**

FAERIE QUEENE, THE. An epic poem written by Edmund Spenser and published in 1596, consisting of an allegorical presentation of twelve virtues, such as temperance, chastity, and friendship, as exemplified by Arthurian knights. It was written in praise of Queen Elizabeth I and is noted for introducing the Spenserian stanza.

FIELDING, HENRY (1707–1754), English novelist, author of *The History of Tom Jones, a Foundling* (1749).

FIGURATIVE MEANING. A meaning extended from the concrete or literal to the abstract or metaphorical. Example: the figurative meaning of *gamut* "the complete series of musical notes" is "the entire range or compass of anything," as in *the gamut of human emotions.*

FLORIO, JOHN (about 1553–1625), English lexicographer and translator, author of *A World of Words,* an Italian-English dictionary, published in 1538, containing many popular Elizabethan usages. It was used by Shakespeare and other writers of the period.

FOLK ETYMOLOGY. The changing of an unfamiliar word or meaning to one that sounds more familiar, thereby altering the actual etymology. Examples: Algonquian *otchek* "a groundhog" became by folk etymology *woodchuck*; Spanish *cucaracha* became by folk etymology *cockroach.*

FRANKISH. The West Germanic language of the ancient Franks, spoken from the 4th to the 6th century in areas covering northern France, western Germany, Belgium, and the Netherlands. Frankish had a major impact on Old French.

FREQUENTATIVE. A form of a word that indicates repeated action, such as words ending in -*le* (*dribble, jiggle*) or -*er* (*chatter, flicker*), or reduplications such as *chitchat* and *booboo*.

GAELIC. The Celtic language of Scotland, also called *Scottish Gaelic*.

GAULISH. The Celtic language spoken in Gaul, the ancient Celtic region of western Europe corresponding to parts of modern Italy, France, Belgium, the Netherlands, and Germany.

GENERALIZATION. The broadening of a word's meaning, as *thing* "a meeting or assembly" becoming generalized to "any matter." It is the opposite of *specialization*.

GENEVA BIBLE. A Protestant translation of the Bible into English, published in Geneva from 1557 to 1560. It was the first English Bible to use verse numbers.

GERMANIC. A branch of the Indo-European language family, comprising the East Germanic group (Gothic, Vandalic, Burgundian), the North Germanic group (Norwegian, Danish, Swedish, Icelandic), and the West Germanic group (English, German, Dutch, Flemish).

GESTA ROMANORUM. A collection of anecdotes and tales, originally in Latin and translated into English in the 1400s.

GOIDELIC. A subdivision of Celtic that includes Gaelic, Irish, and Manx.

GOTHIC. The extinct East Germanic language of the Goths, a Germanic people who established kingdoms in Italy and Spain after the 3rd century.

GREEK. The Indo-European language of the Greek or Hellenic people, one of the earliest Indo-European languages on record, including Mycenaean Greek (about 1600–1100 b.c.e.), Ancient or Classical Greek (about 800–300 b.c.e.), Medieval Greek (about 330–1453), and Modern Greek (since 1453).

HIGH GERMAN. The group of West Germanic dialects spoken in central and southern Germany, Austria, and Switzerland. Standard literary German developed from High German.

HOCCLEVE, THOMAS (about 1370–1426), English poet and scribe, a contemporary admirer of Chaucer, the author of *The Regiment of Princes*, a long poem setting forth the "regiment" or rules of conduct for a prince.

HOLLAND, PHILEMON (1552–1637), English scholar and translator, noted for his translations of the works of the

Roman historians Livy, Pliny, and Suetonius.

IDIOM. A phrase or expression whose meaning cannot be deduced from the literal meanings of its parts. Typical idioms are *bite the bullet* ("endure an unpleasant situation"), *cheek by jowl* ("side by side"), and *a diamond in the rough* ("one whose unrefined appearance belies good character").

INDO-EUROPEAN. A family of languages that includes most of the languages of Europe and many of South and Central Asia. Its major subdivisions are Celtic, Germanic, Greek, Indo-Iranian, Italic, and Slavic.

ITALIC. A subdivision of Indo-European that includes Latin and the Romance languages.

JARGON. The language or vocabulary of a particular trade, business, or profession. In computer jargon, a *hacker* is a computer enthusiast. In law-enforcement jargon, a *perp* is a person suspected of perpetrating a crime.

JONSON, BEN (1572–1637), English playwright and poet, a friend of Shakespeare.

KING JAMES BIBLE. An English translation of the Bible, published in 1611 during the reign of King James I. Known also as the Authorized Version, it has had a profound influence on English literature.

KYNG ALISAUNDER. A long romance poem written in Middle English, probably in the 1200s, dealing with the life of Alexander the Great and considered the best medieval narration of his career.

LATE LATIN. The Latin language from about 300 to the 700s C.E.

LATE MODERN ENGLISH. The English language from about 1700 to the present.

LATIN. The Italic language of the people of ancient Latium, the region surrounding Rome, and the formal language of the Roman Republic and Empire. It is subdivided into Late Latin, Medieval Latin, and Vulgar Latin. The Romance languages descended from Vulgar Latin.

LEARNED BORROWING. A Latin word, usually an abstract or technical one, borrowed by a Romance language, as distinguished from a word descended from Vulgar Latin. Learned borrowings are voluntary and involve a minimal amount of modification in orthography and pronunciation.

LOAN TRANSLATION. *See* **borrow.**

LOANWORD. A word taken into a language from a foreign source; a borrowing.

LOW GERMAN. The group of West Germanic dialects spoken mainly in northern Germany, as distinguished from High German.

LYDGATE, JOHN (about 1370–1451), English poet, translator, and playwright, author of *Siege of Thebes* and *Fall of Princes*, considered the most prolific writer of his time.

MEDIEVAL LATIN. The Latin used in the Middle Ages, from about 700 to 1500, chiefly as the language of scholars and clergymen. Medieval Latin borrowed words freely from Greek and Germanic sources.

MIDDLE DUTCH. The Dutch language spoken or written between 1150 and 1500.

MIDDLE ENGLISH. The English language spoken or written between the Norman invasion in 1066 and the introduction of the printing press into England in the 1470s. Roughly, the period encompasses the years 1100–1500.

MIDDLE FRENCH. The French language covering the period from about 1350 to 1600.

MIDDLE HIGH GERMAN. The High German spoken or written between 1100 and 1500, preceded by Old High German and followed by Modern German. The Yiddish language developed from one or more dialects of Middle High German.

MIDDLE LOW GERMAN. The Low German spoken between 1100 and 1500. It was the lingua franca of the Hanseatic League, used widely in commerce around the North Sea and the Baltic Sea.

MILTON, JOHN (1608–1674), English poet, the author of *Paradise Lost* (1667).

MODERN ENGLISH. The English language from about 1500 to the present, comprising Early Modern and Late Modern English.

MORTE D'ARTHUR. A Middle English prose narrative of the legends of King Arthur, written by Sir Thomas Malory about 1470 and published by William Caxton.

NASHE, THOMAS (1567–1600?), an Elizabethan poet and critic, author of *An Almond for a Parrot* (1589) and the autobiographical *Have with You to Saffron-Walden* (1596).

NEOLOGISM. A newly coined or borrowed word, phrase, or meaning. The coinage *decarcerate* "to release from prison" and the loanword *sudoku* (Japanese for a number-arrangement puzzle) are recent neologisms.

NEW LATIN. The form of Latin developed after 1500, used chiefly for religious, literary, and scientific purposes.

NORMAN CONQUEST. The invasion of England by the Duke of Normandy (also known as William the Conqueror) in 1066 after the Battle of Hastings. The Conquest introduced the Norman aristocracy, culture, and language into England.

NORMAN FRENCH. Another name for **Anglo-French.**

NORMANS. The French-speaking descendants of Scandinavians (their name derived from "Norseman") who settled parts of northern Europe in the 800s, including the part of northern France that became known as Normandy.

OLD ENGLISH. The English language before 1100, also known as **Anglo-Saxon.** It was closely related to Old Frisian and was greatly influenced by Old Norse.

OLD FRENCH. The French language from about 800 to 1350. It was originally a dialect of Vulgar Latin that developed into one of the Romance languages.

OLD FRISIAN. The West Germanic language of the people of Friesland on the North sea coast. Old Frisian closely resembled Old English.

OLD HIGH GERMAN. The form of High German spoken in southern Germany and parts of Austria and Switzerland from about 500 c.e. to 1100.

OLD ICELANDIC. The dialect of Old Norse spoken in Iceland until about 1500.

OLD NORSE. The Germanic language spoken in the Scandinavian countries until about 1300, consisting chiefly of Old Icelandic and Old Norwegian.

OLD NORWEGIAN. The dialect of Old Norse spoken in Norway until about 1500.

OLD SAXON. The form of Low German spoken in northwestern Germany from the 800s to the 1100s.

PEJORATION. The downgrading or depreciation of a word's meaning, as when a word with a positive or neutral sense develops a negative or unfavorable one. Example: *Silly* meant originally "blessed, happy," but by pejoration it came to mean "foolish."

PORTMANTEAU WORD. A word formed by the process of **blending**; a blend.

PREFIX. A word element attached to the beginning of a word to change its meaning. Examples: *un-* is a prefix meaning "not," as in *untrue*; the prefix *re-* means "again," as in *reappear*.

PROTO-GERMANIC. The assumed prehistoric ancestor of Germanic, descended from Proto-Indo-European and reconstructed from shared features of recorded languages.

PROTO-INDO-EUROPEAN. The assumed prehistoric ancestor of Indo-European, presumed to have existed from about 3000 b.c.e. to about 2000 b.c.e.

REDUPLICATION. The doubling of a word or part of a word; a new word formed by such a doubling. Examples: *pooh-pooh, flip-flop, mishmash, hurdy-gurdy.*

ROMANCE. The group of modern languages that descended from Vulgar Latin, including French, Italian, Spanish, Portuguese, Romanian, Catalan, and Provençal.

ROOT. 1. The basic form of a word; the form left after all the prefixes, suffixes, and other parts have been removed from a word. 2. A reconstructed word or other element of a prehistoric language; a base.

SANSKRIT. The classical literary language of India, belonging to the Indo-Iranian branch of Indo-European. It was the ancient sacred liturgical language of the Hindus of India.

SCANDINAVIAN. The group of North Germanic languages comprising one of the three branches of Germanic and including Danish, Swedish, Norwegian, and Icelandic.

SCOTT, SIR WALTER (1771–1832), Scottish novelist and poet, author of *Ivanhoe* (1819) and *The Lady of the Lake* (1810).

SEMANTIC CHANGE. The gradual changes in meaning that many words undergo over time. Major processes of semantic change include *generalization, specialization, amelioration, pejoration*, and *extension*.

SHAKESPEARE, WILLIAM (1564–1616), English playwright and poet, regarded as the greatest and most influential writer of the English language.

SLAVIC. A branch of the Indo-European language family, consisting of East Slavic (Russian, Ukrainian, Belarusian), West Slavic (Czech, Slovak), and South Slavic (Slovenian, Croatian, Serbian).

SPECIALIZATION. The narrowing of a word's meaning, as when *computer*, originally meaning "a person who computes or calculates mathematically," became specialized as a calculating machine and later as the modern electronic and digital device. Specialization is the opposite of *generalization*.

SPENSER, EDMUND (about 1552–1599), English poet, noted for inventing the verse form known as the Spenserian stanza, used in his epic poem *The Faerie Queene.*

STEM. The part of a word that remains when inflections (grammatical parts that show gender, number, person, tense, etc.) are removed. Examples: *sing* is the stem of *singing, sang, sung*; *big* is the stem of *bigger* and *biggest.*

SUFFIX. A word element attached to the end of a word to change its meaning. Examples: *-ation, -ity, -ness* are noun suffixes; *-al, -ible, -ish* are adjective suffixes; *-ize* is a verb suffix; *-ly* is an adverb suffix.

SWIFT, JONATHAN (1667–1745), Irish satirist, author of *Gulliver's Travels* (1726).

TRANSFER. 1. Another word for extension. 2. to carry over a word's use from one area of meaning to another. Example: The meaning of *sanguine* was transferred from "blood-red, bloody" to "hopeful, confident."

TREVISA, JOHN (1342–1402), English translator, whose early bible translations influenced the King James Version.

VULGAR LATIN. The spoken form of Latin of the ancient Roman Empire, whose various dialects evolved into the Romance languages.

WELSH. The Celtic language of Wales, currently the most widely spoken Celtic language.

WYCLIFFE BIBLE. The first complete English translation of the Bible, which appeared about 1382. It was translated from the Vulgate (the Latin version authorized by the Roman Catholic Church) under the supervision of John Wycliffe (about 1320–1384), English theologian and proponent of religious reform.

Frequently Consulted Sources

ETYMOLOGY

Ayers, Donald M. English Words from Latin and Greek Elements, 2nd ed. Tucson: University of Arizona Press, 1986.

Barnhart, Robert K. The Barnhart Dictionary of Etymology. New York: H. W. Wilson, 1988.

Baxter, J. H., & Charles Johnson. Medieval Latin Word-List. London, 1934.

Bloch, Oscar, & Walther von Wartburg. Dictionnaire étymologique de la langue Française (Etymological Dictionary of the French Language), 5th ed. Paris: Presses Universitaires de France, 1968.

Bosworth, Joseph, & T. Northcote Toller. An Anglo-Saxon Dictionary. Oxford: Clarendon Press, 1898.

Brugmann, Karl. Vergleichende Grammatik der Indogermanischen Sprachen (A Comparative Grammar of the Indo-European Languages). New York: B. Westermann, 1888.

Buck, Carl D. A Dictionary of Selected Synonyms in the Principal Indo-European Languages. Chicago: University of Chicago Press, 1949; paperback, 1988.

De Vries, Jan. Altnordisches etymologisches Wörterbuch (Old Norse Etymological Dictionary). Leiden, 1961.

Hoad, T. F. The Concise Oxford Dictionary of English Etymology. Oxford: Clarendon Press, 1986.

Holthausen, Ferdinand. Altenglisches etymologisches Wörterbuch (Old English Etymological Dictionary). Heidelberg, 1963.

Kluge, Friedrich, & Alfred Götze. Etymologisches Wörterbuch der Deutschen Sprache (Etymological Dictionary of the German Language). Berlin: Walter de Gruyter, 1953.

Lewis, Robert E. Middle English Dictionary. Ann Arbor: University of Michigan Press, 2000.

Mathews, Mitford M. *A Dictionary of Americanisms on Historical Principles.* Chicago: University of Chicago Press, 1950.

Onions, C. T. *The Oxford Dictionary of English Etymology.* Oxford: Clarendon Press, 1966.

Partridge, Eric. *Origins: A Short Etymological Dictionary of Modern English.* London: Routledge & Kegan Paul, 1958.

Pokorny, Julius. *Indogermanisches etymologisches Wörterbuch* (Indo-European Etymological Dictionary). Bern, 1959.

Skeat, Walter W. *Principles of English Etymology.* Oxford: Clarendon Press, 1892—*An Etymological Dictionary of the English Language.* Oxford, 1879–1882.

Souter, Alexander. *A Glossary of Later Latin to 600 a.d.* Oxford: Oxford University Press, 1996.

Walde, Alois, & J. B. Hofmann. *Lateinisches etymologisches Wörterbuch* (Latin Etymological Dictionary). Heidelberg: C. Winter, 1982.

Weekley, Ernest. *Etymological Dictionary of Modern English.* London, 1921.

USAGE

Burchfield, Robert W. *The New Fowler's Modern English Usage.* Oxford: Oxford University Press, 1996.

Evans, Bergen, & Cornelia Evans. *A Dictionary of Contemporary American Usage.* New York: Random House, 1957.

Follett, Wilson. *Modern American Usage.* New York: Hill and Wang, 1966.

Fowler, H. W. & F. G. Fowler. *The King's English*, 3rd ed. Oxford: Clarendon Press, 1931.

Garner, Bryan A. *Garner's Modern American Usage.* Oxford: Oxford University Press, 2003.

Manser, Martin H., with Jeffrey McQuain. *Guide to Good Word Usage.* New York: World Almanac, 1989.

McQuain, Jeffrey. *Power Language.* Boston and New York: Houghton Mifflin, 1996.

Webster's Dictionary of English Usage. Springfield, MA: Merriam-Webster, 1989.

GENERAL REFERENCE

Lighter, J. E. *Random House Historical Dictionary of American Slang.* New York: Random House, 1994–1997.

McArthur, Tom. *The Oxford Companion to the English Language.* Oxford: Oxford University Press, 1992.

Mencken, H. L. *The American Language.* New York: Alfred A. Knopf, 1963.

OED Online. Oxford University Press, 2000–2007.

The Oxford English Dictionary (OED), 2nd ed. Oxford: Clarendon Press, 1989.

Pyles, Thomas, & John Algeo. *The Origins and Development of the English Language*, 3rd ed. New York: Harcourt Brace Jovanovich, 1982.

Random House Webster's College Dictionary, 2nd ed. New York: Random House, 1997.

Robertson, Stuart, & Frederic G. Cassidy. *The Development of Modern English.* Englewood Cliffs, NJ: Prentice-Hall, 1957.

About the Author

Sol Steinmetz is a well-known lexicographer and the former Editorial Director of Random House Reference. He has contributed articles to the *Encyclopedia Americana* and *The Oxford Companion to the English Language* and has been a consultant to the *Encarta World English Dictionary* and the *Oxford English Dictionary*. His books include *The Story of Yiddish in America, Youthopia USA, Meshuggenary,* and most recently, *The Life of Language: The Fascinating Ways Words are Born, Live & Die.*